A HISTORY OF PHILOSOPHY
Volume 11: Logical Positivism and Existentialism

Frederick Charles Copleston was born in 1906, read Greats at Oxford, and joined the Society of Jesus in 1930. He was appointed Professor of the History of Philosophy at Heythrop College in 1939 and was Professor of Metaphysics at the Gregorian University in Rome from 1952 to 1965. When Heythrop became part of London University in 1970, he became its first principal as well as Professor of the History of Philosophy and Dean of the Faculty of Theology of London University. He retired in 1974, when he was appointed Emeritus Professor, and died in 1994.

"We can only applaud at the end of each act and look forward to applauding again at the final curtain"
—*The Times Literary Supplement*

T0323128

By the same author and published by Bloomsbury

A HISTORY OF PHILOSOPHY

FREDERICK COPLESTON

A History of Philosophy

Volume 11

logical positivism
and existentialism

BLOOMSBURY CONTINUUM

LONDON · OXFORD · NEW YORK · NEW DELHI · SYDNEY

BLOOMSBURY CONTINUUM
Bloomsbury Publishing Plc
50 Bedford Square, London, WC1B 3DP, UK
29 Earlsfort Terrace, Dublin 2, Ireland

BLOOMSBURY, BLOOMSBURY CONTINUUM and the Diana logo are trademarks of
Bloomsbury Publishing Plc

First published in Great Britain 1956
First paperback edition 1999
This edition 2003
Reprinted 2008, 2010 (twice), 2011, 2013 (twice), 2019

A catalogue record for this book is available from the British Library

Library of Congress Cataloguing-in-Publication data has been applied for

ISBN: PB: 978 0 8264 6905 2; SET: 978 0 8264 6948 9

15

Printed and bound in Great Britain by CPI Group (UK) Ltd, Croydon CR0 4YY

To find out more about our authors and books visit www.bloomsbury.com and sign up for our newsletters

TABLE OF CONTENTS

PREFACE

A PART from the first chapter, which has been rewritten, this collection of essays is a reprinting of a volume which appeared in 1956 under the title *Contemporary Philosophy*, with the subtitle *Studies of Logical Positivism and Existentialism*. I am grateful to the publishers for having allowed me to replace the former first chapter by a new version. As it was a question of reprinting a book, not of writing a new one, I could not have expected them to consider a more extensive revision, even if I had had the time and the inclination to undertake the work. It does not follow, of course, that I have not changed or modified my ideas on various matters. But it is a common enough occurrence for authors to agree to the reprinting of material which, given sufficient time, they might wish to rewrite.

The title *Contemporary Philosophy* is, taken by itself, clearly misleading. For example, phenomenology, which has been an important and influential movement in some countries, is not treated. Nor is transcendental Thomism which has found an eminent representative in the English-speaking world in the Canadian philosopher and theologian Bernard Lonergan, author of *Insight*.[1] Moreover, apart from more or less distinct currents of thought, there are areas of contemporary philosophy which are passed over in silence or to which only passing reference is made. Such omissions should not be taken as expressing judgments of value.

Possible objections to the title of this book are to some extent met by the subtitle. For in a set of essays devoted mainly to logical positivism and existentialism the field is clearly limited. It can still be objected, however, that logical positivism is dead and that though existentialism in one form or another may have been taken up by certain theologians and represented as the

---

[1] Bernard Lonergan's second major tome, is *Method in Theology*, London, Darton, Longman & Todd, 1972

philosophy of modern man, in the philosophical world it is a spent force.

In regard to this line of objection it seems to me that a distinction is appropriate. On the one hand it is commonly and, generally speaking, rightly said that logical positivism in an explicitly and clearly defined form has passed into history, while it is also clear that for various reasons existentialism does not now enjoy the vogue in France and Germany which it once had. On the other hand, it seems obvious to me that the positivist mentality is much wider and more lasting than logical positivism in its technical presentation, and that it can be discerned in the attitudes of some philosophers who disclaim the label "logical positivist" with indignation. As for existentialism, it raises problems of importance which do not depend simply on the amount of *Angst* or *angoisse* discernible in the atmosphere.

Reflections of this sort obviously suggest the need for a fresh treatment of positivism and existentialism, in terms, that is to say, of ways of thought and of recurrent problems more than in terms of certain historical expressions of these ways of thought. Or, rather, the reflections suggest the need for a more prolonged effort to penetrate beneath more or less transitory phenomena (definite systems) to recurrent attitudes and ways of thinking. But this would be impracticable in the case of the reprinting of a collection of essays. The new first chapter includes some references to logical positivism which make my own attitude to it sufficiently clear, in regard to certain aspects that is to say. But I have not attempted to make any changes in the four chapters on existentialism (which represent lectures given to a fairly general audience at the Royal Institute of Philosophy early in 1955), though it might well be considered desirable in itself to include some reference to the use which has been made in a theological setting of Martin Heidegger's earlier philosophizing.

It has been already remarked that the title *Contemporary Philosophy* is not intended to imply any judgment of value about modern currents of thought which have been passed over in silence. Neither is it intended to imply any particular delimitation of the scope of philosophy. In the course of the first chapter I have, I hope, made it clear that I am not one of those people who dismiss logical or conceptual analysis as failing to qualify as " real " philosophy. At the same time it seems to me absurd to represent metaphysical systems and world-views as illegitimate enterprizes, at any rate, when they express personal thought and vision. Provided that we do not use the word " philosophy " in a way which is quite incompatible with the ordinary use of words, we can regard the term as covering a variety of activities and lines of reflection. An English philosopher is, of course, free to regard the writings of some of his continental colleagues as bogus philosophy; and the continental philosopher is free to look on the analytic movement in England in an analogous manner. But such judgments are obviously judgments of value; and the implied definitions of philosophy are stipulative definitions. There is clearly nothing wrong in making such judgments of value and in recommending particular interpretations of the word " philosophy", provided that one does not try to conceal what one is doing. But if we look at the matter from a purely descriptive point of view, it is obvious that the word is justifiably used to cover a great deal more than the content of a definition which is designed to exclude this or that type of philosophy. The present writer is inclined to claim that a prominent function of philosophy is the critical examination of presuppositions in various areas. But he certainly would not wish to say that this is all that philosophy is or can be.

One thing leads on to another. To study, for example, the language of morals is a perfectly legitimate activity. But the study can hardly be adequately pursued without reference to the context of a form of life, man's moral consciousness and life. And this in turn implies the need for some sort of philosophical anthropology. Narrow definitions of philosophy can be inhibiting, even if sometimes they draw attention in an indirect manner to distinctions which are worth noting.

CHAPTER I

CONTEMPORARY BRITISH PHILOSOPHY

I

EXPERIENCE suggests that in some countries the notion that most British philosophers are logical positivists is still not uncommon. Alfred North Whitehead (1861–1947) is respected as the most eminent British metaphysician since F. H. Bradley (1846–1924). But he is seen, rightly, of course, as standing apart from the main stream of thought in Great Britain. Other recent and contemporary British philosophers of note (unless perhaps someone has heard of Samuel Alexander, 1859–1938) tend to be regarded as positivists. Obviously, this is not the case where the so-called analytic movement is influential, as in Scandinavia; but it is a not uncommon impression in countries where the philosophical outlook is markedly different from that which prevails in England.

In Britain itself the accusation which is not infrequently brought against the prevaling line of philosophical thought, especially against what is sometimes described as Oxford philosophy[1] is one of triviality. Philosophers nowadays, we have been told, concern themselves " only with the different ways in which silly people can say silly things "[2]. Logical positivism was at any rate provocative, forthright, clear-cut. The logical positivists took science seriously; they had a definite programme; they knew what their presuppositions were and what they were trying to do. The linguistic philosophers, however, give themselves with delight to trivial

---

[1]When the term " Oxford philosophy " is used disparagingly, it probably means the sort of philosophizing pursued by the late J. L. Austin (1911–1960).

[2]*My Philosophical Development*, by Bertrand Russell (London, Allen and Unwin, 1959), p. 230.

themes; and if they do happen to discuss important issues, they are adept at trivializing them and turning the discussion into an academic game. Further, they appear neither to have nor to wish to have any clear idea of their assumptions or of what they are about. The old philosophers produced world-views, sometimes accompanied by ways of life. Their modern successors disclaim any intention of providing world-views or of telling people how they ought to act; but at the same time they are past masters at insinuating a certain world-view, without clearly stating it, and at recommending, in a covert manner, a generally conservative attitude. They leave everything as it is and tell us that we have no good reason for not continuing to say what we do say. For this reason the new philosophy can be acquitted of any charge of corrupting the youth. " Linguistic philosophy corrupts no one. What it does do is bore them "[3]. From a Marxist point of view, it is a thoroughly bourgeois philosophy.[4]

The statement that what is described as linguistic philosophy is boring does not seem to me a profitable subject for discussion. Some are bored by classical music, others are not. Some are bored by gossip, others delight in it. True, if all British students of philosophy were so bored by the subject as presented to them that they turned from it in disgust, it would be difficult to find sufficient suitable applicants for vacant posts in philo-sophical departments. But this does not appear to be the case. Nor, as far as I know, is there any diminution in the number of those studying philosophy. So let us disregard the boredom aspect of the situation and turn to more manageable themes.

---

[3] *Words and Things*, by Ernest Gellner (London, Gollancz, 1959), p. 218. This book is a well known and vigorous attack on " linguistic philosophy." The author attempts what might be described as a sociological unmasking of the linguistic philosophers.

[4] For a very temperate and reasoned critical examination of modern British philosophy by a Marxist philosopher see *Marxism and the Linguistic Philosophy*, by Maurice Cornforth (London, Lawrence and Wishart, 1965).

The notion that most British philosophers are logical positivists is a misconception. The modern analytic movement, which, from a negative point of point, can be considered as a reaction against British idealism, antedated logical positivism in the proper sense. It is certainly true that G. E. Moore (1873–1958) suggested that a large part of the difficulty encountered in discussing and solving philosophical problems was due to a lack of clarity and precision in the formulation of questions and to a careless lumping together of several distinct questions as though they were one question.[5] But this suggestion was not equivalent to the claim that metaphysical problems were meaningless. If I suggest that system-builders have often been too hasty and slapdash and that they have skated lightly over awkward questions, I am not necessarily a positivist. To be sure, the bent of Moore's mind was towards meticulous analysis. And as he thought that there are a number of common sense propositions the truth of which is known by all but the correct analysis of which is uncertain, he laid emphasis on analysis of meaning.[6] His own interests led him into what might be described as a phenomenology of perception. But though he gave a very powerful impetus to the analytic movement, he did not go in for dogmatic pronouncements about the nature of philosophy. He doubtless thought that careful analysis was what was needed. But when he did talk about philosophy in general, what he said followed more or less traditional lines. In any case a man who held that

---

[5]For example, Bradley maintained that Reality is spiritual. Moore did not say that Reality was not spiritual, still less that it could not be spiritual. He asked for a clarification of the question whether Reality is or is not spiritual. Must we perhaps distinguish several distinct questions, before we can carry on any profitable discussion?

[6]If we know that p is true, how can we be ignorant of the meaning of p? Moore tried, of course, to explain what he meant by analysis, but perhaps not very successfully. In any case I think that it is true to say that it is the example of his practice rather than his theory of analysis which has proved an influential factor.

"good" is a non-natural indefinable property of good things could hardly be described as a positivist.[7]

As for Bertrand Russell (1872–1970), in the course of his long life he made a number of different statements about philosophy. On occasion he identified philosophy in a strict sense with logical analysis.[8] He also made positivist-sounding statements, such as that all definite knowledge belongs to science or that whereas science is what we more or less know, philosophy is what we do not know.[9] But he never accepted the principle of verifiability as a criterion of meaning. On the contrary, he insisted that it is one of the jobs of the philosopher to keep alive interest in those " ultimate questions " which science is unable to answer[10]. He did not think that the metaphysician could answer them either. But he did not describe them as meaningless on the ground that they were not scientific questions. Further, Russell tended to look on reductive analysis[11] as a way of obtaining knowledge about the world. He expressed indeed sympathy with logical positivism. But he always believed that philosophy should keep in close touch with empirical science and that philosophical theories should be built on a scientific foundation. His sympathy with logical positivism was largely due to his conviction that logical positivists, unlike " Oxford philosophers ", take science seriously. It does not follow, however, that he accepted the positivist criteron of meaning and ruled out metaphysics as so much nonsense. When he wished to do so, he was quite ready to play the part of a metaphysician.

The case of Ludwig Wittgenstein (1889–1951), considered

---

[7]Moore wavered in this view; but it appears that at the end of his life he still held it and repudiated any concessions which he might have made.

[8]Cf. *Our Knowledge of The External World* (London, Allen and Unwin, 1914), p. 42.

[9]Cf. *Logic and Knowledge* (London, Allen and Unwin, 1956), p. 281. There are some similar remarks in Russell's *History of Western Philosophy* (London, Allen and Unwin, 946).

[10]*Unpopular Essays* (London, Allen and Unwin, 1950), p. 41.

[11]The theory of logical constructions *can* be presented as a purely linguistic theory. But as applied, say, to physical objects, it has obvious ontological implications, which indeed Russell never attempted to conceal.

as the author of the *Tractatus Logico-philosophicus*, is admittedly somewhat different. For this remarkable classic was studied by and exercised an influence on the logical positivists of the Vienna Circle. Indeed, it has been maintained that the principle of verifiability, considered as a criterion of meaning, is implicitly contained in the *Tractatus*. Wittgenstein himself, however, maintained that the logical positivists had misunderstood him. And even if he was inclined to think that nobody had understood him, it is clear that there were considerable differences between the *Tractatus* and the logical positivism of the Vienna Circle.[12] In any case Wittgenstein very soon abandoned the theory of language expounded in the *Tractatus* and developed a theory which was incompatible with logical positivism in the proper sense.

Logical positivism was brilliantly introduced into England by A. J. Ayer in his *Language, Truth and Logic*, the first edition of which was published in 1936.[13] This work may not have won many notable converts in the ranks of professional philosophers; but it certainly excited a great deal of interest and exercised a considerable influence up to the time of the second world war. Nowadays, when logical positivism has been submitted to criticism not only by opponents but also by its own adherents,[14] when its sweeping generalizations are frowned on by contemporary philosophers, and when we are accustomed to think in terms of a logical positivist " interlude " in the development of modern British thought, it is difficult to appreciate the fluttering in the dovecotes which was caused by the popularization in England of the good news from Vienna.

The fluttering in the dovecotes was caused, I think, more

---

[12]The *Tractatus* includes an ontology. Further, Wittgenstein's remarks about the "mystical" were uncongenial to the members of the Vienna Circle. As for the principle of verifiability, Wittgenstein did indeed say that to understand a proposition is to understand its truth-conditions. But we cannot discuss here the various remarks which he made or is recorded as having made about the principle.

[13]London, Gollancz. Second edition 1946.

[14]Professor Ayer himself has considerably modified his position, as can be seen from later writings, such as *Philosophical Essays* (1954), *The Concept of a Person* (1963), *The Origins of Pragmatism* (1968) and *Metaphysics and Common Sense* (1969). (These books are published by Macmillan.)

by the implications of logical positivism in the spheres of religious belief and theology than by anything else. For it was clearly impossible, from the logical point of view, to reconcile traditional Christian theism with acceptance of the principle of verifiability as presented by Rudolf Carnap in his essay on the elimination of metaphysics[15] or by A. J. Ayer in *Language, Truth and Logic*. Attempts to effect such a combination were, in my opinion, singularly unsuccessful. To be sure, it was possible for a man to accept logical positivism or logical empiricism and at the same time to profess Christianity, if he was prepared to undertake a radical revision of Christianity and to interpret credal statements relating to God as so many stories which Christians tell themselves to serve as a psychological background and support to an ethical policy. This was the line taken by Professor R. B. Braithwaite (b. 1900) in his celebrated lecture, *An Empiricist's View of the Nature of Religious Belief*.[16] Similarly, logical positivism could be combined with Christianity,, if statements about God were reinterpreted as statements about Jesus or about man. But such procedures were programmes for the " secularization " of Christianity rather than attempts to combine traditional theism with logical positivism. It was also possible to reinterpret the principle of verifiability, so that verifiability through *sense*-experience was no longer insisted on. But in this case logical empiricism in its original form was obviously abandoned.[17]

---

[15]This essay, originally published in 1932, is included, in an English translation, in *Logical Positivism*, edited by A, J, Ayer (Glencoe, Illinois, the Free Press; London, Allen and Unwin, 1959).

[16]Cambridge, Cambridge University Press, 1955. This lecture is much referred to by supporters of the " secularization " of Christianity movement. The point of calling statements about God " stories " is that, for Braithwaite, they are neither true nor false. A pragmatic function is attributed to these " stories." And they are said to be " entertained " rather than believed.

[17]If a theologican insists that statements about God are susceptible of, say, eschatological verification (through the beatific vision, for example), it does not necessarily follow that he is engaged in the futile task of trying to reconcile Christian belief with the original doctrines of the Vienna Circle. He may feel that logical positivism, in spite of its shortcomings, embodied a truth, namely that beliefs, to be significant for man, must make some difference within the field of possible human experience. This truth, he may be convinced, is separable from insistence on verifiability through *sense*-experience.

The members of the Vienna Circle were not, of course, concerned simply with attacking metaphysics. They had a positive programme, the unification of the sciences through the creation of a common language. In other words, they focused their attention on scientific language. And in so far as their criterion of meaning was based on an analysis of the scientific hypothesis, the way was open for anyone to claim that when a logical positivist described a given utterance as " literally meaningless," he was not saying substantially more than that the utterance was not a statement of empirical science. Because of their preoccupation with the language of science as a paradigm of meaningful language, the logical positivists tended to lump together other forms of language as " emotive," as possessing only expressive-evocative significance. They thus failed to do justice to the complexity of language.

Insight into the complexity of language is generally associated with the name of Ludwig Wittgenstein. This is understandable in view of the striking way in which Wittgenstein abandoned the picture-theory of the proposition expounded in the *Tractatus* and developed the theory of language-games which appears in the posthumously published *Philosophical Investigations*.[18] Besides, Wittgenstein has tended to be the object of a species of personality-cult. And though his influence on modern British thought has been considerable, it can be exaggerated. J. L. Austin, for example, formed his philosophical outlook quite independently of Wittgenstein. He did not need to be converted by a Cambridge philosopher from the " scientism " of the Vienna Circle. On the contrary, he was perfectly well aware of the complexity of language and of the narrowness of logical positivism.

The Wittgensteinian theory of language-games is, however, useful for making a point. There are a variety of games; but no one game represents the " essence of game." No one game is the game, the paradigm to which all games must conform under pain of being described as pseudo-games. No one kind of

---

[18]Oxford, Blackwell, 1953. *The Blue and Brown Books* (Oxford, Blackwell, 1958) contains notes dictated by Wittgenstein to pupils during the period 1933–5.

game is privileged, except for a specific purpose. If we want physical exercise, we choose tennis or golf rather than chess or a game of cards. But if we want to play a game after dinner before the fire, we obviously choose chess or a game of cards rather than tennis or football or golf. Analogously, while describing is one use of language, it is not the only use. Thanking, praising, cursing, praying, questioning, commanding and so on are also uses of language. And no form of language is privileged except for a specific purpose. The language of science is of obvious importance. But it does not constitute a paradigm, except for the specific purpose for which it has been developed. It would be most unenlightening to say, for example, that ethical language is " meaningless," because it will not fit the paradigm of the descriptive language of science. The ethical " language-game " has to be investigated on its own merits. And if we wish to understand the meaning of ethical terms, we have to examine their uses in the language-game where they have their native home. Similarly, if we wish to know the meaning of the word " God," we have to reflect on its use in the language of religion.[19] To say that it is meaningless, because it is not a term of empirical science, inhibits inquiry into a language-game which expresses a form of life.

The point which I have been trying to make can be stated without any specific reference to Wittgenstein. Logical positivism involved the elevation of descriptive language, and in particular of the language of science, to the rank of the paradigm or model language. And its criterion of meaning was the result of an extension or extrapolation of a certain analysis of synthetic or empirical statements, namely as predictions of possible sense experiences. If, however, a philosopher rejects this narrow concept of meaning and insists on the complexity of language and the variety of meaningful language-games or linguistic activities, he cannot properly be described as a

---

[19]The slogan associated with the later thought of Wittgenstein is " meaning is use " or " don't ask for the meaning, ask for the use." That is to say, meaning is determined by a term's function in the relevant language-game. This concept of meaning has been challenged. But whether it is adequate or not, it is not the same as the logical positivist concept of meaning.

logical positivist. He may perhaps insist that an hypothesis cannot count as a *scientific* hypothesis, unless it can in principle be empirically tested, directly or indirectly.[20] But to use the idea of empirical verifiability as an instrument for distinguishing scientific hypotheses is not the same thing as to use it as a general criterion of meaning.

3

It must be admitted, however, that those who regard most British philosophers as positivists do not necessarily intend to imply that logical positivism in the technical sense (as presented, for example, in *Language, Truth and Logic*) is the prevailing British philosophy. They may be thinking, for instance, of therapeutic positivism and also of what might be described as linguistic positivism. Or they may mean simply that British philosophers seem to them to be hostile to metaphysics, or that metaphysics is commonly mistrusted and discounted by British philosophers. In this case, of course, they will not be shaken in their general impression of British philosophy simply by having it pointed out to them that not even the author of *Language, Truth and Logic* would speak in quite the same way nowadays. And they may regard the transition from the *Tractatus* to the *Philosophical Investigations* as a substitution of one form of positivism for another.

Wittgenstein, it is true, did not hesitate to make dogmatic pronouncements about the nature and function of philosophy. In the *Tractatus* he maintained that there are no philosophical propositions[21]; and he implied that the philosopher's job is to

---

[20]Sir Karl Popper has defended falsifiability (in principle) rather than verifiability as a criterion for distinguishing scientific from non-scientific hypotheses. But he does not claim that all non-scientific hypotheses are " meaningless."

[21]As the totality of true propositions is identified with the totality of the natural sciences (4.11), and as philosophy is not one of the natural sciences (4.111), it follows that there are no philosophical propositions. Obviously, the *Tractatus* contains a large number of them. And Wittgenstein describes them as senseless or nonsensical (6.54).

exhibit the origins of "most" philosophical questions and statements in logical confusion.[22] Specific reference was made, in this connection, to metaphysical statements.[23] We can say, therefore, that in the *Tractatus* Wttgenstein proposed a view of the function of philosophy as "therapeutic," as directed to the clearing up of logical confusion.[24] As for the *Philosophical Investigations*, we find a number of somewhat different accounts of philosophy; but the suggestion is certainly made that the philosopher's job is not to reform or change in any way the actual use of language but only to describe it, thus leaving everything as it is.[25] To be sure, when Wittgenstein is not talking about philosophy but rather reflecting on concrete philosophical problems, he can hardly be said to be simply describing the use of language. But he does indeed propose what might perhaps be described as linguistic positivism.

Generally speaking, however, British philosophers are slow to dogmatize about the nature of philosophy. A good many years ago Gilbert Ryle (b. 1900) asserted his (somewhat reluctant) inclination to believe that philosophical analysis was the sole function of philosophy, and that it takes the form of " detection of the sources in linguistic idioms of recurrent misconstructions and absurd theories."[26] But J. L. Austin, who, if anyone, was devoted to " describing " or mapping out the actual use of language, was careful not to claim that his own way of philosophizing was the only way. On the contrary, he spoke of one possible way of doing what was possibly one part of philosophy. He doubtless hoped that people who pursued other

---

[22] 4.003. Wittgenstein uses the word " most," not " all."

[23] 6.53. In point of fact Wittgenstein's attitude to metaphysics is ambivalent. See what he has to say about solipsism (5.62 f.) and his remarks on problems of life (6.52 f.).

[24] In his preface to the *Tractatus* Wittgenstein says that the work is concerned with exhibiting the limits of language, of what can be said.

[25] 1.124. Wittgenstein's famous statement that his aim in philosophy is to show the fly the way out of the fly-bottle occurs in 1,309.

[26] *Logic and Language*, First Series, edited by A. G. N. Flew (Oxford, Blackwell, 1951), p. 36. The quotation is from an essay entitled *Systematically Misleading Expressions*, which first appeared in the *Proceedings of the Aristotelian Society* for 1931–2.

paths would try to avoid what he regarded as the slovenly and careless ways of a good many traditional philosophers; but he did not concern himself with issuing prohibitions against following other lines of inquiry. In general, British philosophers understand very well that the word " philosophy " can have a variety of meanings or can cover a variety of different lines on inquiry. The fact that a given philosopher devotes himself to what is commonly described as " linguistic analysis " does not entail the conclusion that he is prepared to identify the whole of philosophy with the sort of philosophizing which he himself practises.

In regard to the attitude of British philosophers towards metaphysics, I should like to begin by making some general remarks. In the first place, if metaphysics is taken to mean the construction of comprehensive systems or world-views, there is a general mistrust of this activity. It is not a question of claiming that nobody should construct a world-view. Nor is it a case of excluding the possibility of any synthesis. Rather is it a question of thinking that system-builders are given to making assumptions which should not be taken for granted, that the requisite spade-work is neglected, that psychological factors and the influence of untested beliefs are apt to play a conspicuous role, that a system constructed by one man can hardly be anything else than the expression of a partial and personal perspective, and so on. If someone feels the urge to construct a world-view, he is free to do so. But philosophical questions are likely to be answered by more pedestrian and humdrum and patient precedures.

This attitude has sometimes been associated with the idea that if a team of philosophers worked at clearly defined problems, such problems might be solved one after the other. J. L. Austin was a great defender of this laboratory technique. But the mistrust of system-building is not necessarily linked to the notion that philosophical questions can be solved one after the other. Gilbert Ryle, for example, has attacked the notion that philosophical problems " can and should be tackled piecemeal (a suggestion which) does violence to the vital fact that philosophical problems inevitably interlock in all sort of ways."[27] For the matter of that, Austin did not reject the idea of synthesis. The general feeling, however, whether justified or not, is that synthesis should arise naturally, so to speak, through the patient consideration of a variety of specific problems rather than through the construction of conflicting systems of philosophy. Of course, it can be objected that the making of implicit assumptions is not confined to the activity of constructing world-views but can be involved in the tackling of any philosophical problem. This is doubtless true. At the same time a certain mistrust of system-building in the traditional style is perfectly understandable. *The* truth about the world is apt to turn out to be the personal world-vision of X or Y.

In the second place it must be understood that a good deal of what used to be called metaphysics has passed under the name of analysis. It is obvious that the activity of conceptual analysis was carried on by such worthies as Socrates, Plato and Aristotle. Further, it formed part of what Aristotle described as " first philosophy " or metaphysics. To be sure, British philosophers show little confidence in the philosopher's ability to prove the existence of a transcendent God or of the Absolute. Many of them would claim that Kant successfully demolished " dogmatic " metaphysics, or at any rate its claim to cognitive value. But it by no means follows that they reject the whole field of what has traditionally been known as metaphysics.

In the third place such phrases as " linguistic analysis " can be extremely misleading. For they suggest that the philosophers who pursue this sort of activity are concerned " only with words." It may indeed be the case that some philosophers have claimed that all philosophical problems are problems of language. But this claim, if we leave aside the sense in which it is obviously valid,[28], would now generally be regarded as tending to obscure the fact that " when we examine what we should

---

[27]*British Philosophy in the Mid-Century*, edited by C. A. Mace (London, Allen and Unwin, 1957), p. 264.

[28]In an obvious sense every philosophical question is a question of what should be said. Further, it is pretty obvious that the philosopher does not add to our knowledge of facts in the same way in which an historian or an archaeologist can add to our knowledge of contingent facts.

say when, what words we should use in what situations, we are looking again not *merely* at words . . . but also at the realities we use the words to talk about."[29] In his *Concept of Mind*[30] Gilbert Ryle constantly draws our attention to what people are accustomed to say. But it would be absurd to say that the book is about words. It is about *man*. A. J. Ayer puts the matter clearly when he says that " when Ryle sets out to destroy what he regards as the myth of the ghost in the machine, he tries to make us fix our attention on the actual phenomena of what is supposed to be our mental life."[31]

It may be said, of course, that even if what is sometimes described as linguistic analysis is not concerned simply with words, the approach to extra-linguistic reality through language tends to obscure this reality by interposing a veil of language between the mind and things. But this objection, though understandable, raises an important issue. It is all very well to talk blithely about seeing the facts for what they are or letting the facts speak for themselves. The question arises whether what we call a fact does not represent an interpretation. To put the matter in another way, we cannot get at the phenomena without thinking them; and the question arises whether we can think them without symbolic expression, without language. It is not a question of claiming that " ordinary language " is sacrosanct and irreformable. Not even Austin claimed this. It is a question of the relations between thought and its object and between thought and language. Such questions are, at any rate, open to discussion

In the fourth place certain philosophers, when they talk about metaphysics, tend to use the term in a rather special sense. This is especially true, I think, of Professor A. J. T. D. Wisdom (b. 1904), who is accustomed to represent meta-

---

[29]*Philosophical Papers*, by J. L. Austin (Oxford, Clarendon Press, 1961), p. 130.
[30]London, Hutchinson, 1949.
[31] *The Concept of a Person*, p. 23.

physicians as making paradoxical or strange statements.[32] This may sound as though Wisdom was concerned to poke fun at metaphysics. But this is not the case. His point is rather that what appears at first sight to be nonsense may really exhibit penetration, even if the insight is expressed in a misleading manner. Suppose, for example, that a philosopher says that historical knowledge is impossible or that we do not know that there are material things existing outside our minds. On the face of it these are pretty silly statements. But if we take it, for instance, that historical knowledge is knowledge of the past, and if we admit that the past does not exist (for if it did it would not be the past), the question arises how we can properly be said to know it. There is a puzzle here. And it is worth clearing up. As for the statement that we do not know that there are material things existing outside our minds, this may be a way of expressing the fact that we cannot demonstrate the existence of a material thing in such a way that it is logically impossible that we should be mistaken in believing that it exists. We may object to the philosopher's statement. For it assumes a model of knowledge (perhaps that resulting from mathematical demonstration) and then refuses the name of knowledge to that which is commonly recognized as such but " fails " to conform to the model. At the same time the philosopher has drawn attention to a real difference. In brief, when philosophers say strange things, it is unhelpful to jump to the conclusion that they are talking nonsense. It is more helpful to ask them why they make the statements in question. For then we may be able to understand perfectly well what they are getting at. In fact the strangeness of their utterances may serve, by their very strangeness, to draw attention to something which we had not perhaps noticed.

---

[32]See, for example, *Philosophy and Psychoanalysis* (Oxford, Blackwell, 1953) and *Paradox and Discovery* (Oxford, Blackwell, 1965). Wisdom is not, of course, ignorant of the fact that metaphysicians have made statements which are plainly true or express familiar facts. But statements which would be recognized by most people as truisms would not be of much use to him in making the point which he wishes to make.

In the fifth place it is commonly recognized that the great metaphysical system of the past have embodied visions of the world which have proved influential, and that to describe such systems as consisting of nonsensical utterances simply will not do. As Friedrich Waismann pithily put it, " to say that metaphysics is nonsense *is* nonsense."[33]

The idea of world-visions, of possible ways of seeing the world, brings me to a distinction made by Professor P. F. Strawson (b. 1919) between descriptive and revisionary metaphysics.[34] The descriptive metaphysician, according to this distinction, explores or tries to lay bare the most general features of our conceptual structure, the basic concepts by which we think the world. That is to say, the descriptive metaphysician is concerned, as Aristotle was a to a great extent, in analyzing the basic concepts or categories of our actual thought, of the way in which we actually see the world. The revisionary metaphysician seeks to change our world-vision, to make us see things differently in some important way or ways. Strawson does not condemn revisionary metaphysics, though he remarks that any attempt to change the way in which we see things needs some justification, whereas descriptive metaphysics does not stand in need of any justification beyond that required for theoretical inquiry in general.[35]

Strawson does not claim, of course, that metaphysical systems as we know them can be neatly divided in terms of this distinction. In practice it is a case of a system being predominantly " descriptive " or predominantly " revisionary," not of being exclusively the one or the other. Similarly, when Professor W. H. Walsh (b. 1913) makes a distinction between immanent and transcendent metaphysics,[36] he admits that we rarely come across pure types. If a philosopher sets out to develop a system of basic categories in terms of which the world as we know it

---

[33]*Contemporary British Philosophy*, Third Series, edited by H. D. Lewis (London, Allen and Unwin; New York, Macmilan, 1956), p. 489.

[34]In *Individuals, An Essay in Descriptive Metaphysics* (London, Methuen, 1959).

[35]Strawson himself, in *Individuals*, concentrates on the concepts of person and material thing, by which we think " particulars."

[36]In *Metaphysics* (London, Hutchinson, 1963).

can be interpreted, this is more or less what Walsh calls immanent metaphysics. And he obviously sees no cogent objection to this sort of activity. If, however, a philosopher postulates or tries to prove the existence of a transcendent being or reality to explain this world or the events in the world, this is what Walsh describes as transcendent metaphysics. He associates it, not unreasonably, with religion.

Distinctions such as those made by Strawson and Walsh are of course open to discussion and criticism. But the fact that they have been made and thought helpful contribute to showing that even if the term " metaphysics " was pretty well a dirty word in the heydey of logical positivism, it is so no longer. Contemporary British philosophers may not be much addicted to what Strawson calls revisionary metaphysics, and still less to what Walsh describes as transcendent metaphysics; but they certainly do not rule out all metaphysics as meaningless nonsense on the ground that it will not satisfy the criterion of meaning proposed by the logical positivists.[37]

4

Turning now to the accusation of triviality which has been brought against contemporary British philosophy, I wish to approach the theme by making some remarks about ethics and philosophy of religion.

As has already been mentioned, G. E. Moore regarded " good " as a non-natural indefinable property. To define good in terms of a natural quality (such as " pleasant ") would be to commit the naturalistic fallacy. At the same time Moore believed that we can recognize what things possess this indefinable quality. Moreover, he defied obligation in terms of the production of good.[38] And from these premises it seems to

---

[37]It may be the case that some British philosophers who dissociate themselves from logical positivism nevertheless make tacit use of the principle of verifiability. Some give the impression of thinking that ' to exist " means to be a possible object of sense-perception.

[38]That is to say, our duty is to perform that action which will produce more good than would be produced by any alternative action. Obviously, apart from any other objection this criterion would be difficult to apply.

follow that the moral philosopher is able in principle to tell people how they ought to act.

The logical positivists, such as A. J. Ayer, agreed with Moore in rejecting attempts to define good in terms of, say, pleasure. But they were not prepared to follow him in asserting the existence of a non-natural quality. To say that something was good or that an action was right was not, in their view, to describe the thing or the action, by attributing to it an objective quality or relation. They regarded ethical propositions as expressing feelings or attitudes and as having the function of evoking similar feelings or attitudes in other people.[39] They could not therefore follow Moore in ascribing to the moral philosopher the job of ascertaining what things are good (what things possess the objective quality of goodness). In their opinion the job of the moral philosopher was to examine what people are doing when they enunciate ethical propositions. In other words, the moral philosopher is concerned with the nature of the moral judgment and with the function of ethical terms.

This general concept of moral philosophy has had a wide diffusion among philosophers who cannot properly be described as logical positivists. For example, Bertrand Russell has written about concrete ethical questions; but he does not regard this sort of writing as belonging to philosophy in the strict sense. The moral philosopher in the strict sense is concerned with the analysis of the judgment of value, not with telling people how they ought to act. Again, Professor R. M. Hare (b. 1919) made it clear in *The Language of Morals*[40] that he was concerned with ethical language, not with telling people what moral judgments they ought to make. To be sure, Hare's discussion of ethical language was much more careful, perceptive, elaborate and detailed than that of the logical positivists, who, for the most

---

[39]Moritz Schlick took a different line. But the emotive theory of ethics was characteristic of logical positivism.

[40]Oxford, Clarendon Press, 1952. This was followed by *Freedom and Reason* (1963).

part, were not much interested in ethics.[41] The point which I wish to make, however, is simply that there has been a marked tendency among British moral philosophers to concern themselves with the language of ethics, leaving concrete moral teaching and recommendations to " moralists " and preachers.

This restriction of moral philosophy proper to a study of the language of ethics is naturally a source of dissatisfaction to those who look to moral philosophers for enlightenment about difficult and important moral issues. Further, some philosophers have tended to illustrate the points which they wish to make by taking examples which seem to be remarkable for their triviality, such as omitting to fulfil one's promise to return a book by a certain date or taking more than one's fair share of a dish at table.

In regard to the last point, however, it must be remembered not only that selection of a trivial example may serve to illustrate a logical point just as well as any other example but also that the introduction of hotly disputed issues which everyone admits to be important may tend to divert attention from the logical questions under consideration If we insist on identifying moral philosophy proper with inquiry into the logic of the language of morals, a plausible case at any rate can be made for keeping the temperature low by using examples which appear trivial and boring.

In point of fact, however, the restriction in question shows signs of being abandoned. There has been a marked tendency in recent British ethics to take as axiomatic the Human thesis that no " ought " can be derived from an " is."[42] And this dogma has helped, I think, to restrict attention to ethical language. But it is obvious that we often offer factual assertions as reasons for ethical judgments. And though there have been

---

[41]Hare classified ethical language as a sub-class of prescriptive language. He also tried to show that logical relations (such as entailment) can be found between propositions in the imperative mood. In other words, logical argument is perfectly possible in ethics.

[42]In Hare's language this thesis would take the form of the assertion that from premises in the indicative mood we cannot deduce anything but a conclusion in the same mood. We cannot deduce a moral imperative.

ingenious attempts to reconcile this fact with the " no ought from an is " dogma, it is hardly a matter for surprise if in the end the dichotomy between fact and value should itself be called in question.[43] Further, it has been seen that the language of ethics cannot be adequately understood unless it is examined in the light of its function in human life, and that there is need of a philosophical anthropology.[44]

As for the philosophy of religion, here, too, there has been a marked concentration on religious language. Mediaeval theologians such as St. Thomas Aquinas considered problems relating to the meaning of terms predicated of God. In recent philosophy of religion, however, the scope of inquiry has been broadened to include other forms of religious utterance; and reflection on religious language has been conducted in the context of an examination of different types of " language-games." The complexity of religious discourse has been exhibited. And a good deal of useful work has been done.

There is no more reason for describing inquiry into the features of religious language a trivial pursuit than there is for describing reflection on ethical language as trivial. But just as those who expect a moral philosopher to tell them how to act are dissatisfied if they find him devoting his attention exclusively to analysis, so too is an exclusive concentration on religious language a source of dissatisfaction to those whose primary wish is to know whether there is a God or not.

This is understandable. At the same time it cannot be taken simply for granted that the philosopher is in a position to prove the existence of God.[45] Further, some philosophers have insisted that the problem of meaning is logically prior to the problem

---

[43]No less a person than J. L. Austin asserted his inclination to play Old Harry with philosophical " fetishes " such as the face-value dichotomy.

[44]This was suggested by Stuart Hampshire in *Thought and Action* (London, Chatto and Windus, 1959).

[45]Some Wittgensteinians, insisting on the autonomy of each language-game, have taken the line of saying that if religious language is a living language for a given man, and if the word " God " occurs in this language, then God is a reality for him, and that there is no " neutral " standpoint from which the existence of God can be discussed. This idea would fit in with a theological claim that God is known only through faith.

of reference, to the question of existence. That is to say, before we can usefully discuss whether there is a God, we must first clarify the concept of God. If it proves to be riddled with contradiction and incoherence, there is no more point in discussing the existence of God than in discussing the existence of a round square.[46] If, however, we can agree on a viable concept of God, we can then inquire whether there is any good reason for thinking that the concept is instantiated.

The religious man is likely to find this notion, namely that of looking round to see whether the concept of God is instantiated, extremely odd. He may see the point that we cannot profitably undertake a voyage of exploration to see whether there are any surviving specimens of the pterodactyl unless we know what the word " pterodactyl " means, what it would look like. But he may very well feel that there is something wrong in applying this procedure to God, even if he cannot put his finger on what is wrong. And in my opinion reflection on the reasons why the religious man is apt to have this reaction is well worth while. The point which I wish to make here, however, is simply that a concentration on religious language does not necessarily signify a trivialization of the subject of religious belief. For reasons can be given for this concentration, either that the existence of a transcendent God is, by the nature of the case, incapable of philosophical proof,[47] or that we cannot usefully discuss the existence of God until we are quite clear what we are talking about. These are serious reasons, whether we agree with them or not.

5

When, however, people bring a charge of triviality against contemporary British philosophy, they are generally thinking

---

[46]The view that the idea of God is contradictory and incoherent is maintained by Antony Flew in *God and Philosophy* (London, Hutchinson, 1966), though Flew does indeed criticize arguments for the existence of God.

[47]A Barthian theologian is likely to hold this view. At the same time he is unlikely to regard the philosopher as competent to shed much light on Christian religious language.

of what appears to them to be a wasteful expenditure of intellectual ability in the activity of supporting common sense views by appeals to ordinary language. They may recognize that in the meticulous examination of ordinary language a man such as J. L. Austin showed a very considerable virtuosity; but they do not see the point of this activity. It seems to them to get nowhere. And they see no good reason for supposing that ordinary language is an infallible criterion of truth, in a sense from which it would follow that what non-philosophers are accustomed to say ought always to be preferred to what philosophers have said.

First of all, a word must be said about use of the term " ordinary language." It is true that the term naturally suggests the idea of everyday, colloquial, non-technical language. But when used by philosophers, the term may cover all forms of language (including scientific language with its technical terms) except technical language invented by *philosophers*. And the phrase " the ordinary use of language " then implies a contrast not between non-technical and technical language but rather between the ordinary uses of expressions (whether technical or non-technical) and a non-standard or extraordinary use.[48] If Oxford philosophers such as Austin have steered clear of scientific language, one reason is doubtless that they felt a lack of competence in this field. Austin, for instance, had a classical, not a scientific, training.[49]

Now it is obviously very easy to interpret the distinction between " ordinary language " on the one hand and philosophical jargon on the other as implying that though scientists make discoveries and have to invent new terms, philosophers

[48]On this matter see Gilbert Ryle's essay on ordinary language in the *Philosophical Review*, Vol. 62, 1953 (reprinted in *Ordinary Language*, edited by V. G. Chappell, Englewood Cliffs, N.J., Prentice-Hall, 1964).

[49]It has sometimes been said that ordinary language philosophers seem to suppose that English is the only language, or, at any rate, that it is the standard language. Well, some people may have given this impression. But if a man wishes to map out the fine shades of distinction which are implicit in ordinary language, he would be foolish to select a language, Chinese for instance, which he knew only imperfectly, if at all. Analysis requires a mastery of the language selected for analysis.

can never have a good reason for inventing technical terms. Further, talk about standard and non-standard uses of words suggests that a decree is being issued forbidding philosophers to use words which occur in " ordinary language " in any other sense than that in which they are usually understood. In fine, it may appear that ordinary language philosophers are therapeutic positivists who reject all philosophical theories as fatuous, at any rate when they are at variance with what non-philosophers are accustomed to say, and who try to exhibit this fatuity by referring to ordinary language as a touchstone of truth.

Some philosophers may indeed have written in such a way as to imply that this was precisely their attitude. Appeals to Wittgenstein's statements that ordinary language is quite all right as it is and that the philosopher should not interfere with it but only describe it certainly suggest the attitude in question. And if this position is adopted, it is obviously open to the objection that so-called " ordinary language " is not a simple mirror of naked facts but an interpretation or complex of inter-pretations and that in its development it may come to embody all sorts of theories. It cannot therefore be taken as a touchstone of truth.

Though, however, some philosophers may have written in an unwary or unguarded manner, there is no justification for fathering such naive views about ordinary language on " Oxford philosophy " in general. Consider Austin, for example. He did not claim that ordinary language was sacro-sanct. " Ordinary language is *not* the last word; in principle it can everywhere be supplemented and improved upon and superseded. Only remember, it is the *first* word ".[50] He was perfectly prepared to admit that " superstition and error and fantasy of all kinds do become incorporated in ordinary language."[51] He did not claim that philosophers could never have a legitimate reason for inventing technical terms. He himself added to the number of such terms.[52] As for the use by

[50]*Philosophical Papers*, p. 133.
[51]*Ibid.*
[52]See especially *How To Do Things with Words.*

philosophers of words in deviant or non-standard senses, they are free to act in this way, if they make it clear what they are doing. The trouble arises when a philosopher takes a word from ordinary language, uses it in a sense of his own, and yet at the same time relies on readers understanding it in terms of its ordinary range of meaning.[53] When this occurs, comparison of the philosopher's use of the word with its range of meaning in ordinary language can shed light on an otherwise confused situation.

Well, why did Austin think that ordinary language has the first word? The answer which he gives can be illustrated in this way. Suppose that a philosopher concerns himself with questions about human freedom and personal responsibility. In ordinary language we can find a considerable number of subtle distinctions (relating, for example, to degrees of responsibility) which have been developed through the centuries in response to human experience and to meet felt needs in referring to human actions. It is most unlikely that such distinctions mark nothing. And philosophers would do well to attend to them. In ordinary language these distinctions are not, of course, stated in an abstract way. They are embodied in concrete utterances. Hence the philosopher, in Austin's opinion, should make them explicit by considering as wide a range of examples as possible and by describing them as accurately as possible.[54] In the end he might come to the conclusion that the views of human action which are implicit in

---

[53]This is not a new idea. For example, F. H. Bradley accused theistic philosophers of emptying the word " personal " (as applied to God) of its ordinary meaning and of then trading on the fact (for religious purposes) that the word would still retain for most people its original meaning and associations.

[54]In the lectures posthumously published as *Sense and Sensibilia* Austin argued, whether justifiably or not, that certain upholders of the sense-datum theory had constructed their theory on the basis of a few stock examples (such as converging railway lines, elliptical pennies, and sticks which appear bent when half immersed in water), which they had then proceeded to misdescribe, by speaking, for instance, of " delusion " when it was really clear that nobody was subject to delusion. He thought that a proper attention to ordinary language, involving consideration of a far wider range of examples and accurate description, would help to prevent this sort of hasty generalizing. He has been accused of misrepresenting the views which he subjects to criticism; but this is not an issue which we can consider here.

ordinary language are inadequate. He might think, for example, that there were scientific reasons for making this judgment. But he ought at any rate to start by examining the expression of man's experience of himself through a long period of time.

Austin thought that philosophy had got into a rut, the same old problems being raised and discussed on conventional lines, without any commonly agreed solutions being arrived at. He was determined to try a new approach, without bothering about traditional ideas of what philosophers should discuss and how they should discuss it.[55] He hoped that his inquiries might throw light on traditional problems, perhaps by dissolving them, but not necessarily so. But he went his own way without regard to the traditional conventions; and he became so interested in linguistic inquiries for their own sake that he regarded himself as possibly making a contribution to the development of a science of language, which would arise " through the joint labours of philosophers, grammarians, and numerous other students of language."[56] This science, once constituted, would no longer form part of philosophy.[57]

It is not unreasonable therefore to hazard the (admittedly unverifiable) hypothesis that if Austin had lived longer, he would have moved even further away from traditional philosophizing than in a good many people's opinion he was already. Though, however, Austin came to be a figure of very considerable influence at Oxford, it would be a mistake to think that the majority of British philosophers devote themselves to implementing his programme, except in so far as what he tentatively described as " linguistic phenomenology "[58] was part of the

---

[55]To represent Austin as having no respect of tradition is, however, misleading. He was strongly influenced by Aristotle, who was himself given to considering what people were accustomed to say, in areas in which he believed such reflection to be relevant. Among recent philosophers he admired Moore; and he was influenced by the Oxford philosophers of an older generation, such as H. A. Prichard.

[56]*Philosophical Papers*, p. 180.

[57]Austin did not claim, however, that philosophers would then have nothing to discuss. He said that there would be plenty, though he did not explain precisely what it would be.

[58]*Philosophical Papers*, p. 130.

conceptual analysis which, in various fields or areas, occupies the attention of British philosophers. But conceptual analysis is not specifically *Austin's* programme.

Is conceptual analysis trivial? The answer depends of course on one's standards of importance and on what one believes that philosophy is capable of doing. If someone thinks that it is the philosopher's job to give us information about the Absolute or to tell us how we ought to solve our social and political problems, he is likely to look on most contemporary British philosophizing as trivial. If, however, someone thinks that for the most part philosophers always have been concerned with conceptual analysis but that the job is now being done with greater care and less haste, he will obviously pass a different judgment of value. In any case we ought to remember that philosophers, like other men, have different interests and talents. If a man feels a genuine need or urge to express a vision of the world and of human life and history, let him do so. If his abilities and interests incline him to minute or meticulous analysis, he would be well advised to make a good job of this pursuit rather than a bad job of some other pursuit. This is only pedestrian common sense, it is true. But common sense is not, I think, to be despised.

CHAPTER II

SOME REFLECTIONS ON LOGICAL POSITIVISM

ONE does not need to know very much about the history of philosophy in order to realize that philosophy does not develop in complete isolation from other elements of human culture. Plato's philosophy was clearly influenced by the general cultural situation in which he was born and brought up. It was also influenced by Plato's interest in mathematics, the only science which had attained any remarkable degree of development in the Greek world. The direction of Aristotle's thought was influenced by his biological investigations. The political theory of both Plato and Aristotle has to be viewed in close connection with the concrete political life of contemporary Greece. Mediaeval philosophy cannot be understood in complete isolation from theology: indeed, Christian theology provided the mental background and atmosphere in which philosophers philosophized. One can legitimately say that it was theology which, to a large extent, set the problems for the philosopher and acted as a fertilizing principle.

In the modern era, however, that is to say, in the period after the Renaissance, the background of philosophy has been provided, to an increasing extent, by the empirical sciences, which have developed to such an astonishing extent since the pioneer work of the great Renaissance scientists. Indeed, a remote preparation for the later conception of the world can be seen as early as the fourteenth century. When philosophers like John Buridan and Albert of Saxony discarded the Aristotelian theory of motion and adopted the *impetus* theory of Philoponus, they were preparing the way for a conception of the world as a system of bodies in motion, in which impetus or energy is transmitted from one body to another, the total amount of energy remaining constant. The origin of motion or energy was ascribed to God : but once the machine had been started, to speak crudely, it proceeded mechanically. As the heavenly bodies, for example, do not encounter resistance, the original impetus given them by God at creation is sufficient to account for their movement; and it is unnecessary to postulate any Intelligences of the spheres. The principle of economy can be applied to the Intelligences postulated by Aristotle. In this way consideration of the problem of motion in the fourteenth century paved the way for a new cosmology, like that represented by the philosophy of Descartes in one of its aspects. It is unnecessary, for the general purpose of this chapter, to show how the development of the various sciences in the modern era has influenced philosophy: it is sufficient to remind oneself of the influence of mathematics and dynamics on the Cartesian philosophy, of the influence of the growth of historical science on Hegelianism, of the influence of biology, in a wide sense, on Bergson, of the influence of sociology and the rise of economics on Marxism, and of the influence of the newer physics on a philosopher like Whitehead. At the same time one should bear in mind the influence of the general historical and social situation on philosophers and their thought. The political theories of Hobbes and Locke, for example, and later that of Hegel, have to be interpreted in connection with the historical situation in which those philosophers severally found themselves. The German romantic movement was reflected in German idealism after Kant. Modern existentialism is not without its roots in the cultural milieu and general spiritual atmosphere, though one has to remember that the influence of the spiritual atmosphere in which a philosopher finds himself is not always " positive ": in many cases it produces a strong reaction. But to produce a reaction is, of course, to exercise an influence.

It is not the purpose of the foregoing remarks to encourage a purely relativistic interpretation of philosophy and its development. One should not allow the possibility of incurring a charge of " relativism " to blind one to the facts of history; but, apart from that, it is obvious, I think, that the fact of a given philosopher having been influenced in his adoption of some particular theory by non-philosophical factors does not mean that we cannot raise the question whether that theory is true or false or partly true and partly false. But my real reason for making these general remarks concerning the development of philosophy was to show that if one tries to give a partial explanation of the present vogue of the logical positivist outlook in England and certain other countries in terms of factors which lie outside philosophy itself, one is not attempting to treat logical positivism in a way that one is not prepared to treat other philosophies. On the other hand, what is sauce for the goose is sauce for the gander; and if, in the case of other philosophies, one can discern the influence of non-philosophical factors, it is only to be expected that one should be able to do the same in regard to logical positivism. There is no reason at all for supposing that the latter is a privileged exception. Nor is this sort of treatment necessarily a belittlement of philosophy. After all, it would be extremely surprising if the various elements of human culture were without influence on one another. And, if one admits the influence of non-philosophical factors on philosophy, this does not mean that one denies the influence of philosophy on other elements of human culture. It is not a case of one-way traffic only.

I have spoken of the amazing growth and development of the empirical sciences in the modern era. This rise of empirical science is, indeed, one of the major features of the post-Renaissance world. At the same time, if any one compares the development of empirical science and the development of speculative philosophy in the modern period, it may easily seem to him that, whereas the development of the former is an advance, that of the latter is nothing of the kind. It is very easy, and perhaps natural, to draw some such conclusion as the following. Scientific theories and hypotheses change indeed; but, by and large, there is advance in empirical knowledge; and hypotheses which have been recognized by later scientists to possess only a limited validity, or even to be incorrect, have nevertheless often proved fruitful as providing the stepping-off ground for a more inclusive or a more accurate hypothesis. In some cases speculative philosophers have suggested hypotheses or theories which have later been empirically verified, in some form at least[1]; but in such cases the truth of the hypothesis has been established, not by philosophic speculation, which often resembles brilliant guesswork, but by the empirical methods of scientists who have been able to verify the hypothesis, immediately or mediately. The advance in knowledge has thus been due to science rather than to speculative philosophy. And, when one comes to look at the theories of speculative philosophers that are not empirically verifiable, one finds a succession of highly personal interpretations of the universe of being, the truth or falsity of which cannot be established. They may have a certain value, for they express certain poetical or emotional reactions to the world and may provide for their authors and for like-minded individuals a scheme for the synthesis of their emotional life. And, as the emotions are a powerful factor in life, metaphysical systems, which express and co-ordinate emotional reactions, may also exercise a practical influence. But this does not mean that they represent " knowledge." If we seek factual knowledge, we must go to science. The reason why metaphysical systems constantly reappear is that man is something more than a cold and dispassionate observer; but, even if metaphysical speculation is as inevitable as lyric poetry, that does not mean that either gives us knowledge about the world.

Another factor which has to be taken into account if we want to understand how the logical positivist mentality has arisen, or perhaps rather how a mental climate favourable to logical positivism has arisen, is the tremendous growth of applied science in recent times and its influence in making possible our industrialized and technocratic civilization. I am talking now of the " masses " who live in highly industrialized and materially developed societies. These people are very conscious of the great benefits which have been brought to them and to society in general by applied science. They understand little of the nature of scientific hypotheses or of the provisional character of many scientific concepts; but they see clearly the practical benefits of applied science and they become accus-

---

[1]For example, the heliocentric, as opposed to the geocentric, hypothesis.

tomed to look to science for anything which makes " a difference " to life. Philosophic theories and speculations about the world seem to them, so far as they ever think of such theories, to be little more than a harmless pastime; they make " no difference " and they produce no tangible results. If one wants tangible results, one must go to the scientists; and it is tangible results which are the criterion of real knowledge about the world. The ordinary man does not think of questioning the assertions of the scientists, since the latter have proved their worth; but it would not occur to him to accept without question the assertions of theologians or philosophers. How can they know the truth of what they say? The only proof of the truth of their assertions would be a scientific proof; and no such proof has been forthcoming.

What I am suggesting is that the immense growth of empirical science and the great and tangible benefits brought to civilization by applied science have given to science that degree of prestige which it enjoys, a prestige which far outweighs that of philosophy, and still more that of theology; and that this prestige of science, by creating the impression that all that can be known can be known by means of science, has created an atmosphere or mental climate which is reflected in logical positivism. Once philosophy was regarded as the " handmaid of theology ": now it has tended to become the " handmaid of science." As all that can be known can be known by means of science, what more reasonable than that the philosopher should devote himself to an analysis of the meaning of certain terms used by scientists and to an inquiry into the presuppositions of scientific method? The philosopher will not increase human knowledge in the sense of extending our factual knowledge of reality; but he will perform the humbler, though useful, task of clarifying the meaning of terms and showing what they denote in terms of immediate experience. Instead of serving the theologian, the philosopher will serve the scientist, for science has displaced theology in public esteem. As science does not come across God in its investigations, and, indeed, as it cannot come across God, since God is, *ex hypothesi*, incapable of being an object of investigation by the methods of science, the philosopher also will not take God into account. Whatever can be known can be known by means of science. As to human survival after death, the philosopher will be willing to admit this precisely in so far as the statement that something of man survives can be verified empirically, by, for example, a critical and scientific investigation of the data of spiritualism and psychical research.

Before I proceed any further, I had better make it quite clear that I am not suggesting that all philosophers who adhere more or less to the logical positivist position are materialists, in the sense that they all lack belief in any spiritual reality. For there are logical positivists who are believing Christians. These would, however, lay emphasis on belief: they would say, I think, that they " believe " though they do not " know " that there is, for example, a God.[1] I am rather doubtful myself if a logical positivist can consistently be a theist at the same time; but it appears to be an empirical fact that there are people who are both, whether consistently or inconsistently. One is not entitled to say, then, that " logical positivist " and " materialist " are identical. Nevertheless, even those logical positivists who are believing theists or Christians are influenced by the common persuasion that it is science alone which can provide us with factual knowledge. In any case the existence of logical positivists who are prepared to make an act of faith in realities, the existence of which they do not think can be verified, does not alter the fact, or what appears to me to be a fact, that the soil out of which has grown the mentality favourable to logical positivism was prepared by that development of the empirical sciences which is characteristic of the modern era. Needless to add, to say this is not to say anything against the empirical sciences. Indeed, one of the problems of modern culture is that of combining technical industrialized civilization with religious faith, artistic sensibility, and perception of moral values: it is only cranks who wish to destroy machines

---

[1] A possible attitude, verified in a case known to me, is to say, " I would not use the word ' belief.' I regard Christian dogmas as myths, the function of which is to help me to lead a Christian moral life, to which I attach value." Allusion is made to this attitude in Chapter VII.

and return to the woods. But the fact remains that the growth of the empirical sciences has helped to produce a mental outlook which is unfavourable to metaphysics and to religion. How many people there are, as we know by experience, whose practically spontaneous attitude towards theology and metaphysics is that of believing that they are dreams and moonshine. In the last century people used to talk about a conflict between religion and science. We see now that there is not, and cannot be, any conflict between religion and science in the sense in which that conflict was understood in the last century; for no verified scientific statement can contradict a revealed dogma. We are no longer troubled by apparent discrepancies between scientific theories and *Genesis*; for we have a better idea now of the nature of scientific theories and hypotheses on the one hand, while on the other hand every sensible person realizes that the Bible was not designed to be a handbook of astronomy or of any other branch of science. But it is none the less true that the growth of our industrialized, technical civilization, governed predominantly by economic values, has produced a type of mind which is " naturally " closed to the Transcendent, to metaphysics and to theology. In my opinion, it is the existence of this type of mind, or of this mentality, which is largely responsible for the influence of positivist philosophy in such countries as England, Sweden and the United States. Positivism is, in large part, a reflection of that mentality. On the other hand it helps to intensify and strengthen that mentality. In regard to logical positivists who are theists or Christians one may remark that it is always possible to rise above one's philosophy, just as it is possible to sink below one's philosophy or one's religious creed.

I do not, however, wish to give the impression that, in my opinion, logical positivism can be dismissed as being simply the ideological reflection of a certain type of mentality fostered by what some people like to call " bourgeois civilization." There is more in logical positivism than that. Earlier on in this chapter, I remarked that if one tries to discern the connections between philosophies and factors which are not purely philosophical, and if one tries to indicate the influence of the latter on the former, that does not mean that one is unable to raise the question of the truth or falsity of the philosophies concerned. And it is quite obvious that men of acute intellect, possessed of a real power of philosophic thought, would not adhere to a philosophic movement or method unless they considered that there were good philosophic reasons for doing so. It would be quite illegitimate to suggest that all logical positivists were frivolous individuals playing a mere game or delighting in scandalizing the theologians, metaphysicians and moralists. It is important, then, to ask now it is that gifted philosophers can subscribe to a philosophy which might well appear to render practically all philosophy, at least in the traditional sense, superfluous. After all, even if the spirit of " bourgeois civilization " is favourable to the growth of positivism, it is possible for philosophers to free themselves from the influence of that spirit; and it must be supposed that if a considerable number of philosophers associate to a greater or less degree with logical positivism the reason why they do so is not simply that they succumb, in a quasi-mechanical fashion, to the spirit of their milieu. They must at any rate rationalize in some way their surrender to that spirit; and if we find among those who belong more or less to the ranks of the logical positivists some who are by no means hostile, or even indifferent, to spiritual realities, it is only common sense to conclude that they do not accept logical positivism without what seem to them to be good reasons for doing so. I want, then, to indicate how, in my opinion, it comes about that serious philosophers can subscribe to a philosophy which rules out a great part of what has been traditionally included in philosophy.

The usual way of presenting logical positivism is first of all to make a distinction between analytic propositions and empirical or synthetic propositions. The former are said to be certain, but not informative, in the sense that they do not give information about the world or existent things. For example, if I say, " If p entails q and q entails r, p entails r," I am simply illustrating, by the help of symbols or variables, the meaning of logical implication. Similarly, if I say, " Given a Euclidean triangle, the sum of its three angles is equal to 180 degrees," I am not stating that any thing which could properly be called a Euclidean triangle actually exists; nor is it necessary, in order that my statement should be true, that any Euclidean triangle should exist. I am simply stating what is necessarily implied in the notion or definition of a Euclidean triangle. Indeed, all systems of formal logic and all systems of pure mathematics consist, so to speak, in the unfolding of the implications of certain definitions and premisses. The pure mathematician does not state anything about the existent world: if we want to know what system of geometry, for example, " fits reality " or is useful for a specified purpose in science, we have to turn to the mathematical physicist or astronomer, i.e. to the applied mathematician. All the propositions of formal logic and pure mathematics are thus said to be " analytic " and purely " formal." They are sometimes said to be " tautologies," in the sense that they simply state the formal implications of certain definitions and premisses.

I do not propose to discuss this view of logic and mathematics; but I should like to point out two things in connection with it. First, it is a very common view and is not confined to logical positivists. To say that formal logic is " formal " is a tautology; and to say that all pure mathematics are formal and give no information about existent things is to say something which seems to me perfectly reasonable. This view would certainly be confirmed if Bertrand Russell's view of the relation of mathematics to logic were correct. Secondly, the fact that the logical positivists accept the view that the propositions of formal logic and pure mathematics are analytic and certain means that one has to make a reservation if one wishes to speak of logical positivism as " sheer empiricism." J. S. Mill tried to show that mathematical propositions are inductive generalizations from experience and that they are not certain; but the logical positivists very properly reject Mill's view in favour of Hume's, though they do not express their view in precisely those terms which were used by Hume.

However, if one leaves on one side their view of formal logic and pure mathematics, one can say that the logical positivists maintain a " radical empiricism." In my opinion, this empiricism is at once the strength and the weakness of logical positivism. Empiricism is always in a strong position, since it is only reasonable to accept the position of Locke, that all our normally acquired knowledge of existent reality is based in some way on sense-perception and introspection. Locke did not, of course, rule out metaphysics: indeed, in his own mild way he was a metaphysician. But he insisted, in a certain famous passage of the *Essay*, that " all those sublime thoughts which tower above the clouds, and reach as high as heaven itself, take their rise and footing here," in, that is to say, the impressions of sense and reflection on our mental operations. I do not say that the empiricism of Locke is an adequate account of human knowledge; but I certainly think that it is a *prima facie* reasonable view. What Locke did not realize, however, and what later empiricists did realize, was that the principles of empiricism could be turned against the metaphysics which Locke accepted. The strength and appeal of logical positivism are due, in large part, to the fact that it seems to take empiricism seriously; and empiricism, though by no means comprising the whole of the British philosophical tradition, is certainly congenial to the British mentality.

If one accepts empiricism, it would seem that one is compelled to ask, in regard to any existential statement, what it means in terms of the data of experience. For example, if the idea of " cause " is formed in dependence on experience, or, to put it another way, if the term " causality " denotes a relation which is given in experience, the question arises what it is that we experience which gives rise to the notion of causality or what " causality " means in terms of the data of experience. Does reflective analysis show that we speak of a causal relation between two phenomena when we have observed one phenomenon regularly following another phenomenon in such a way that the appearance of the latter enables us to predict, with a greater or less degree of probability, the appearance of the latter? If so, then " causality " is a term which denotes a relation between phenomena, a relation of regular sequence enabling us to predict. But, if this is what causality means, if, that is, it means a relation between phenomena, it does not mean a relation between all phenomena and something which is not a phenomenon. It may be that we naturally tend to extend the use of the principle of causality and apply it outside the sphere of the relation of one phenomenon to another; but this use cannot be theoretically justified, if the causal relation means precisely a relation between phenomena. This phenomenalistic analysis of causality makes hay, of course, of a considerable part of classical metaphysics. If we try to use the principle of causality to transcend phenomena, we are, if the foregoing analysis were correct, simply misusing language. I do not myself think that the metaphysician, when he speaks of " cause," means the same thing as the positivist: in fact, when they discuss the notion of causality, I think that they are often arguing at cross purposes; but, if one minimizes the activity of the mind and the reflective work of the intellect, and if, pressing the principles of empiricism, one tends to interpret the meaning of our ideas in terms of " sense-data," the phenomenalistic analysis of causality will appear eminently reasonable. What is more, this analysis gains support from the fact that scientists, for many purposes at least, can get along quite well on the basis of such a view of causality. If a physicist speaks of infra-atomic indeterminacy, what he means is that we are unable to predict the behaviour of electrons in certain connections. If, then, all he means by causality is regular sequence, enabling us to predict, he is entitled to say that the principle of causality does not " apply " in this connection, provided that he has good reason for thinking that the unpredictability in question is one " of principle," whatever that may mean. This would not, in my opinion, in any way affect the metaphysical principle of causality, which, as such, has to do with existence rather than behaviour; but my point is that the claim of the phenomenalistic analysis of causality to be a fully adequate analysis may easily appear to gain support from empirical science. And, in this sense, it may appear that empirical science lends support to the ruling out of metaphysics of the classical type. A further point is that the relation of finite to infinite being cannot be of exactly the same type as the relation of dependence of one phenomenon on another:

the former is, *ex hypothesi*, unique. To raise the question of the use of terms, or the problem of language, in this connection, as the logical positivists do, is thus a legitimate procedure.

But the difficulty concerning language or the use of terms, and the connection of this difficulty with the principles of empiricism, can be more easily seen, I think, in regard to such a metaphysical statement as " God loves us."[1] What love is or means is known through experience. The question therefore arises what " love," in the statement that God loves us, means. Does it mean that God has certain feelings in our regard, of the type that we feel when we love someone? Obviously not; for God cannot have " feelings "; and it would be sheer anthropomorphism to think of God as developing certain feelings when man came into existence. Does it mean that God wishes us well? If so, a similar difficulty occurs. The term " wishing " denotes something experienced, primarily our own wishing, and also, as interpreted by analogy, the wishing of other people. Do we mean to ascribe wishing to God in precisely this sense? The answer can only be that we do not. In what sense, then? If all that we have experienced in this connection is human wishing, and if the term " wishing " means human wishing (and what else can it mean, if we have experienced no other wishing?) the use of the term " wish " in regard to God involves us either in anthropomorphism or in the use of a term without any meaning. But a term without any meaning is a meaningless term; and the statement that God wishes us well will therefore be destitute of meaning. The fact that it seems to have a meaning may well be due to the fact that, uttered in appropriate circumstances, it has the function of expressing and arousing a certain emotional reaction. If a nurse tells a child that if it does some act God " will be angry," it need not be supposed that the nurse means to say that God is capable of what we call " anger ": what she wants to do, it might be said, is to work on the child's emotions in such a way that it will not act in the way disapproved of. Thus the statements made in a sermon, for example, may have

---

[1]For a development of this subject, see Chapter VII.

" emotional significance," even though they are in another sense " meaningless," in the sense, that is, that they cannot be interpreted in terms of the data of experience.

Needless to say, the view of metaphysical statements outlined or illustrated above is not my own view: my purpose was not that of giving my own opinions but of showing that a plausible case can be made out for the view that metaphysical statements are " meaningless." Further, what I have said shows, I think, that the problem of language is not simply an unnecessary complication of philosophical issues: it is a real problem. For a brief treatment of the question of the use of analogical language in metaphysics, with particular reference to theistic metaphysics, I may perhaps refer the reader to my paper on *The Possibility of Metaphysics*, in the *Proceedings of the Aristotelian Society* for the year 1950. I have there distinguished what I call " subjective meaning " from what I call " objective meaning." In the case of a statement like " God is intelligent " the theistic metaphysician cannot give the " objective meaning," in the sense that he cannot tell us what the divine intelligence is in itself. He cannot do this because he has never experienced or intuited the divine intelligence as it is in itself. By " subjective meaning " I understand the meaning in the mind of the speaker, the meaning that he can state. (Thus I do not use the word " subjective " here as equivalent to " subjective " or without objective reference. It is important to realize this fact.) The subjective meaning of statements regarding existent realities which transcend normal direct experience is necessarily analogical. Now, analogical language, as used in metaphysics, necessarily has a certain imprecision: in the terminology of Ockham, metaphysical statements about God always " connote " something in creatures. It is one of the tasks of the theistic metaphysicians so to purify the " subjective " meaning of his statements (for example, by the use of the " way of negation ") that he approximates as nearly as possible to the adequate " objective " meaning of those statements. But he will not be able to attain an adequate understanding of the objective meaning, not because there is no adequate objective meaning, but because of his psycho-physical make-up and the lack of the Beatific

Vision. We have to use " human language," because we have no other; and human language is not properly fitted to deal adequately with what lies outside the sphere of our normal experience; we have to use human language " analogically "; and the question is whether such analogical language is to be admitted as significant. It seems to me that the logical positivists interpret " meaning " univocally; and I see no adequate reason for doing so. But I willingly admit that the problem of " the meaning of meaning " is a real problem, and that it is not simply the instance of tiresome word-play that it has sometimes been represented as being.

When it comes to ethical statements, however, I must confess that I find it difficult to see how a really plausible case can be made out for saying that such statements are " meaningless," or, more accurately, that they have only emotional significance. It has been argued that ethical statements cannot be meaning-less, since we can argue, and do argue, concerning the rightness and wrongness of actions. To this the answer has been made that all we argue about is a matter of fact, not a valuation. We can discuss, for example, whether a particular line of conduct is likely to produce these or those results; but to discuss this question is not to discuss a properly ethical question, unless perhaps we are prepared to say that " right " means simply productive of certain consequences. But even then, if two people differ in their estimation of what are good or bad consequences, argument between them is possible only if they are already agreed concerning certain wider valuations. If two men are agreed that all consequences of type *t* are bad, then it is possible for them to discuss the question whether a given set of consequences exemplify type *t* or not. But this is a question of classifying empirical events, not of arguing about values. Ultimately the two men will either differ on a matter of fact or they will differ on a question of valuation in such a way that neither can prove to the other that his view is wrong. If John says that it is murder if a doctor gives a lethal overdose of a drug to a patient suffering from an incurable cancer, while James says that it is not murder but rather an act of charity, argument is possible if they can agree on a definition of murder. For all that remains then is to see whether the definition covers euthanasia or not. But if they differ in their definitions of murder, further argument is scarcely possible. John can try to " persuade " James, by working on his emotions, or James may have recourse to abuse of John, calling him, for example, " hard-hearted "; but working on someone's emotions or abusing him is not " argument," even if argument often tends to such degeneration. That ethical arguments not infrequently do degenerate into abuse or rhetoric simply confirms the view that values are, to use Hume's language, more properly felt than judged. This may sound plausible; and perhaps it is to a certain extent; but it is pretty obvious, I think, that in any sort of argument there must be some common ground between the disputants, if the argument is to be fruitful. The necessity for a common ground is not peculiar to ethics. It appears to me, whether rightly or wrongly, that the real reason why logical positivists say that ethical statements are " literally non-significant " and that they possess only emotive significance is that ethical statements cannot be " verified." We cannot indicate " what would be the case " if they were true, or we cannot derive observation-statements from them, which are empirically verifiable. But to say this is to say little more than that ethical statements are not statements of empirical science. Who supposes that they are? Again we are faced with the underlying assumption that all that can be known can be known by means of science.

I do not wish to pursue any further the complicated question of the meaning of ethical statements, for, in order to do so with profit, one would have to take into account a variety of ethical systems; and that cannot be done in the present chapter. But I should like to draw attention to the loose use of the word " emotional " or " emotive " by some logical positivists. If one properly speaks of feeling a pleasure and feeling a pain, then it would seem that to speak of " feeling " moral values is to use the word " feeling " analogically. Why not speak of " perceiving " moral values? If an exclamation like " Oh ! " uttered when I run a pin into myself, is an emotional utterance, a statement like " I ought to be more kind to X " is an emotional utterance in an analogical sense, in so far, that is to say, as it is proper to call it an emotional utterance at all. If we could speak properly of " feeling " values, we should have to admit, I think, that the " feeling " in question is a special kind of feeling; and it would be desirable to allow for this difference in what we say about ethical statements. To lump together as having " emotional significance " all statements which claim to be informative and which at the same time are not " empirically verifiable " indicates either a very cavalier attitude or an insufficient practice of analysis. In passing, one might also observe that it is somewhat strange to find a number of philosophers delivering excellent maxims concerning the value of the individual, the value of freedom, etc., when their phenomenalistic analysis of the self or their behaviouristic description of man would seem to lead to the conclusion that there is neither a self to have a value nor a human freedom to be prized.

I have mentioned " empirical verification."[1] As is well enough known, the logical positivists declare that " empirical verifiability " is the criterion of the meaningfulness of statements which purport to give information about existent reality. The question immediately arises how " empirical verifiability " is to be understood. Let us suppose that I make the statement that God exists. I am then challenged to show that the statement is empirically verifiable, by deriving from it an observation-statement, that is, some statement which is empirically verifiable, at least in principle. Let us suppose that I answer, " If God exists, there will be order in the world." We can then see if there is in fact order in the world. It is to be noted that I am not suggesting that the statement that God exists implies logically the statement that there is order in the world. The reason why I derive the statement that there is order in the world from the statement that God exists is that, as far as philosophic knowledge of God is concerned, I come to knowledge of God through reflection on some aspect of or factor in empirical reality. Supposing, then, that my philosophic reason

---

[1]For what appears to me to be a more satisfactory discussion of the principle of verifiability, see Chapter IV.

for accepting God's existence is reflection on the order in the world, I can offer the statement that there is an order in the world as an empirically verifiable statement, which is derivable (not logically, but in view of the empirical origin of our ideas concerning reality) from the statement that God exists. It is open, of course, to an opponent to say that one cannot justifiably conclude to God's existence from the order in the world; but we are not now discussing the truth of the statement that God exists so much as the meaningfulness of the statement. And if the logical positivist would accept this sort of interpretation of empirical verification, there would not be much reason for quarrelling with his criterion. If it were not for reflection on empirical reality I should never come, as far as philosophic thought is concerned, to postulate the existence of any being transcending direct experience; and, if anyone wishes to start with the statement of the existence of such a being and challenges me to " derive " an observation-statement, I can always offer him one of the propositions concerning empirical reality which originally led me to postulate the existence of the being in question. Indeed, the logical positivist would be quite right in demanding the production of an observation-statement or an empirically verifiable statement. And he would be right because human philosophic knowledge of the meta-phenomenal must be acquired by reflection on the phenomenal, and cannot be acquired in another way.

However, with the more rigorous type of logical positivist one is unlikely to enjoy any such plain sailing. Some would say, I think, that if I make the statement, " If God exists, there is order in the world," then all I mean by saying that God exists is that there is order in the world. That is to say, the meaning of the original metaphysical statement is identical with the meaning of the observation-statement or observation-statements derived from it. Frankly, this seems to be simply false. To state that a being exists which is responsible for order is not the same as stating that the order exists. Another way of tackling the metaphysician is to ask him what " difference " his metaphysical statements make. For example, if the metaphysician states that absolute being exists, he may be challenged to say what difference it makes to the world whether an absolute exist or not. The world remains the same in either case. Now, I think that one can detect in this attitude the influence of empirical science of which I have already spoken. It is assumed that the function of a scientific hypothesis, for example, is to predict future possible experience. The conclusion is then drawn that metaphysical statements, to be significant, must fulfil a like function. Here we are faced again with the influence of the *Zeitgeist*, of which logical positivism, is, in part, a reflection. In the face of this attitude the metaphysician could, I suppose, attempt to meet the demands of the positivist. More probably he would protest that his statement that absolute being exists was not meant to predict anything but to explain something, namely the existence of finite beings. His opponent will, of course, ask him what he means by explanation, and will challenge the validity of the metaphysician's " principles " or intuition, as the case may be. But at this point we move into a sphere of discussion which does not involve logical positivism as such. The challenge to the validity of metaphysical " inference " is not pecular to logical positivism; and a discussion of this challenge would carry one much too far afield.

In conclusion, I should like to repeat what I have said before, that the strength of logical positivism lies in its empiricism. Owing to psychological and epistemological facts, the problem, for example, of the meaning of metaphysical language is a real problem; and it is just as well that it should be brought to the forefront. On the other hand, it is, I think, a great weakness in logical positivism of the more rigorous type that it is so closely associated with the influence of a certain mental attitude characteristic of our industrialized and technocratic civilization. In our own country it is extremely difficult to escape the influence of this mental climate; and I cannot help thinking that this is, in part, the reason why many of us who would not subscribe to logical positivism feel none the less a certain sympathy for it. But, if human culture is not to descend into an arid wilderness of materialism, it is important to remember that there are other levels of experience and knowledge than that represented by empirical science. Moreover, the problems which are of the greatest ultimate importance for man are among those which are stigmatized by the logical positivists as pseudo-problems; and this is a fact which does not encourage one to suppose that logical positivism is an adequate philosophy. Happily, there have always been, and doubtless there always will be, people who concern themselves with these problems. A culture from which such problems had been banished would scarcely be a human culture.

CHAPTER III

A NOTE ON VERIFICATION

I

(i) In *Human Knowledge: Its Scope and Limits* (p. 167) Lord Russell makes a distinction between " meaning " and " significance." " The significance of a sentence results from the meanings of its words together with the laws of syntax. Although meanings must be derived from experience, significance need not." I agree with this; though I certainly do not wish to try to make Lord Russell responsible for any use I may make of this distinction.

(ii) That " meanings " must be derived in some way from experience seems to me to follow from the facts of human psychology. Not being prepared to accept the existence of innate ideas in the sense in which Locke attacked the hypothesis of innate ideas, I am prepared to accept the general position of Locke that the two sources of our empirical knowledge are sense-perception and introspection. (I am not prepared to dispense with the use of the latter term.) In the " concept " language I should say that our concepts are formed in dependence on, or through reflection on, the data of experience. Some experimental datum or data must be relevant to the formation of a concept, if that concept is to be intelligible to us. In this perhaps rather loose sense I accept Lord Russell's assertion that " meanings must be derived from experience."

(iii) The significance of a sentence need not be directly derived from experience. In other words a statement may be significant even though we do not know whether it is true or false. If I say that there are galaxies receding from us so fast that no light from them can possibly reach us, experience is certainly relevant to the formation of the ideas of " galaxies," " recession," " speed," " light," and the sentence has significance; but I may not *know* whether the sentence is true or

45

false. Let us suppose that the sentence states an hypothesis put forward in order to explain certain observed data. The hypothesis then rests on inference, *i.e.* on reflection on the data of experience.

(iv) In order that the sentence should be significant must it be verifiable? Obviously, it need not be verifiable in the " strong " sense of the word " verifiable." Must it be verifiable in the " weak " sense of the word? If the possibility of conceiving or imagining facts which would make the statement true will count as " verifiability in the weak sense," then I should say that the sentence, to be significant, must be verifiable in the weak sense. Perhaps I may refer to an example which I have used elsewhere, and which I think that I must have borrowed unconsciously from the above-mentioned work of Lord Russell. If I make the statement, " There will be a war in which atomic and hydrogen bombs will be employed and which will blot out the whole human race " this statement cannot be verified (*i.e.* cannot be known whether it is true or false), because there would be nobody to verify it, were the prophecy to be fulfilled. It may be said, of course, that I am unjustifiably disregarding the possibility of there being intelligent beings on, say, Mars, who might be able to verify the statement; but it is quite unnecessary to introduce consideration of such beings; the statement is intelligible to us because we can conceive or imagine facts which would render it true or false. I should not myself call this verification, because, in order to imagine the facts, I have to introduce myself, surreptitiously, as a background observer, whereas a condition of the fulfilment of the prophecy is that no human being should be alive. However, if anyone wishes to count the conceiving or imagining of the facts which would render the statement true or false as " verifiability in the weak sense," I should not wish to quarrel with him. I should regard it as a matter of terminology.

2

I wish now to examine one or two statements in the light of the remarks I have just made.

(i) Suppose that A says, " There is an invisible and in-
tangible football floating in the air exactly three feet above my
head," and that he intends to affirm by this that the football is
absolutely imperceptible.

(a) The meanings of words like " football," " floating,"
" air," and " head " are derived from experience. We know
by experience what it means to say of something that it is a
" football." Or, if we do not happen to have seen a football,
it can be explained to us what a football is, provided that the
explanation is given to us in terms of what we have experienced.

(b) This being so, A's assertion may appear at first hearing
to be significant; it is not obviously nonsensical in the sense
that " Bax, cax, bax " is nonsensical. We understand the
words " football," etc.; and it may seem to us, therefore, that A
has made a significant statement, the contradictory of which
would also be significant. Because the words have meanings,
the sentence seems to state something, something which could
also be denied. " Bax, cax, bax," however, states nothing;
and because it states nothing, it is impossible to deny it.

(c) But, if I apply the test of asking whether I can conceive
or imagine any facts which would render A's statement true or
false, the answer must be, I think, that I cannot. Why not?
Because the word " football " means something perceptible.
The Concise Oxford Dictionary defines a football as a " large
round or elliptical inflated ball "; and it is obviously nonsensical to say of an object of this kind, especially if one adds
that it is made of leather, that it is absolutely imperceptible.
If it is proper to say of something that it is a football, it cannot
be proper to say of it that it is imperceptible by any of the
senses. And if it is proper to say of anything that it is imperceptible, it cannot be a football. Therefore, since the phrase
" an absolutely imperceptible football " is analogous to the
phrase " a round square," I cannot conceive of any facts or
circumstances which would make it true to say that there is
an absolutely imperceptible football either floating in the air
or existing anywhere else. Therefore A's assertion is nonsensical, though it is not nonsensical in exactly the same sense
that " Bax, cax, bax " is nonsensical.

(ii) Suppose that B says: " In everything of which it is true to say that it is a human being, there is a spiritual soul."

(*a*) Is B's assertion nonsensical in the sense that " Bax, cax, bax " is nonsensical? If it were, this could only be because the phrase " spiritual soul " is a mere *flatus vocis*. If this were so, no explanation could be given of its meaning. But, if B says, " I think that every human being is capable of exercising certain activities, the existence and character of which can be known by experience; and I think that those activities must be attributed to something which does not fall into the class of those things of which it is proper to say that they are material; and that ' something ' I call a ' spiritual soul ' ", he has given a meaning to the phrase " spiritual soul." I am not in the least concerned now with the validity or invalidity of B's inference: what I wish to point out is that, whether the inference is valid or invalid, some experiential data are relevant to the formation of the idea " spiritual soul," and that the idea is formed through reflection on the data of experience. I think, then, that the idea or concept of " spiritual soul " fulfils the requirements for intelligibility or meaningfulness which I postulated earlier in these notes. If this is the case, B's assertion is not nonsensical in the same sense that " Bax, cax, bax " is nonsensical.

(*b*) Is B's assertion nonsensical in the sense that A's statement about the football is nonsensical? At first hearing perhaps it may be. For it might seem that if it is proper to say of anything that it is a " spiritual soul," it cannot be proper to speak of it at the same time as being " in " anything. But, when B asserts that *in* every human being there is a spiritual soul, he means that any given human being exercises certain activities, or can do so, which must be attributed to a spiritual soul, of which it is proper to say that it is the spiritual soul of that human being because it is the principle of activities exclusively associated with that human being. He does not mean that the soul is in the body in the same sense that the tea is in the pot, or that it is situated at the pineal gland. (If he is a Scholastic, he also means, of course, that the spiritual soul exercises vital functions, the relation of which to the soul makes it proper to say, given the limitations of language, that the soul is " in " the body.)

(c) Can one imagine or conceive facts which would render B's assertion true or false, or at least which would tend to confirm or disconfirm it? One cannot, of course, imagine a spiritual soul; for anything imagined must be pictured as material, even if it is pictured as " very thin," like Anaxagoras' *Nous*. But I at least can conceive the possibility of there being certain experienceable human activities, which would reveal the existence of a spiritual soul, or from which one might infer the existence of a spiritual soul.

At the mention of " inference " in this connection I can well imagine a raising of eyebrows. But my main point in these notes is to suggest that, though the modern discussion of " meaning " is certainly valuable, and though it has made clearer certain acute difficulties which confront the metaphysician in his use of language, it has not, so far as metaphysics is concerned, revolutionized the situation since Kant's criticism of metaphysics in the way that it is sometimes supposed to have done. I wish to illustrate my point.

3

(i) Let us suppose that someone, C, makes the two following metaphysical statements: " There is a spiritual soul in man," and " Absolute being exists." His friend D, who accepts the principle of verifiability, asks him what facts would verify or falsify, confirm on disconfirm, his statements. C answers that, if there is a spiritual soul in man, it will be found that man exercises, or can exercise, certain activities which must be ascribed to a spiritual principle; and he cites as examples of these activities mathematical reasoning and the passing of moral judgments. He also affirms that, if absolute being exists, it will be found that contingent beings exist or that at least one contingent being exists. A discussion ensues between C and D. If C takes as examples of " certain activities " mathematical reasoning and the passing of moral judgments, they will probably agree as to the fact that man is capable of mathematical reasoning and of passing moral judgments, even if there is some dispute as to the meaning of the words " man," " capable

of " and " moral judgments." When they come to discuss the
statement that at least one contingent being exists, they
may or may not agree; but they will be discussing a statement
the truth of which, C would claim, is verifiable by reference to
experience.

(ii) At this point D observes that, if C is offering the statement that at least one contingent being exists as an " observation-statement," then, whether it is an observation-statement
or not, he is equivalently saying that the statement that a contingent being exists can be logically derived from the statement that absolute being exists. C answers that he does not
mean to imply this. What he means is this. Our ideas are formed
in dependence on experience and through reflection on the
data of experience. Accordingly, if he makes the statement that
absolute being exists, this must, for psychological reasons
(omitting all consideration of immediate intuition or of revelation) be due to his recognition of some aspect or feature of
empirical reality, reflection on which leads him to make the
statement. If, then, the statement is made that absolute being
exists, one can, in a sense, " derive " the statement that at least
one contingent being exists, not because one can logically
deduce the latter statement from the former statement, but
because the existence of absolute being could not be normally
known or thought of unless the existence of contingent being
were first recognized. Similarly, if we suppose that there is no
direct immediate intuition of a spiritual soul, and if we leave
revelation out of account, the statement that there is a spiritual
soul in man would not, for psychological reasons, be made,
unless there were a previous recognition of the existence of
certain observable activities which the man who makes the
statement counts as spiritual activities. One can, then, in a
sense, " derive " the statement that man is capable of exercising
activities of a certain kind from the statement that there is
a spiritual soul in man; but this does not mean that one can
deduce logically from the statement that there is a spiritual
soul in man the statement that every man exercises in fact
certain activities. Nor does it signify that the statement that
there is a spiritual soul in man is precisely equivalent to the

statement that, for example, man is capable of mathematical reasoning.

(iii) C having explained in what sense he thinks that his verifiable statements can be " derived " from the metaphysical statements which he originally made, he and D continue to discuss these verifiable statements in the following form: " Man is capable of mathematical reasoning and of passing moral judgments," and " at least one contingent being exists." Let us suppose that C gives a definition of the meaning he attaches to the phrase " contingent being " which is acceptable to D, and that they finally agree on the truth of the statements that man is capable of mathematical reasoning and of passing moral judgments, and that at least one contingent being exists.

This measure of agreement having been attained, D goes on to say that he sees no reason whatsoever for concluding from these two statements respectively the statements that " there is a spiritual soul in man " and that " absolute being exists." The facts on which they have agreed are not such as to render true or false either the statement that there is a spiritual soul in man or that absolute being exists.

(iv) Leaving C and D to argue the validity of the inferences in question, I wish to give two syllogistic arguments, in order to show what I think C and D have been about, in the language of the syllogism, and in order to make clear my conclusion. The syllogisms, the validity of which I do not presuppose, as it is irrelevant to the point I want to make, are these.

(a) There is a spiritual soul in man if man is capable of exercising mathematical reasoning and of passing moral judgments:

But man is capable of mathematical reasoning and of passing moral judgments:

Therefore there is a spiritual soul in man.

(b) If at least one contingent being exists, absolute being exists:

But at least one contingent being exists:

Therefore absolute being exists.

(a) I supposed that C and D reached agreement as to the facts that man is capable of mathematical reasoning and of passing moral judgments, and that at least one contingent being exists. In other words, they reached agreement as to the truth of the minor premisses of the two syllogisms given above.

(*b*) We left C and D arguing about the validity of the existence of a spiritual soul from man's capability of mathematical reasoning and of passing moral judgments and the existence of absolute being from the existence of contingent being. In other words, we left them arguing about the truth of the major premisses of the two syllogisms given above.

(vi) From the foregoing I draw the following conclusions, using the language of the syllogism.

(*a*) When the logical positivist challenges the metaphysician to " derive " an " observation-statement " from his metaphysical statement, he is asking the metaphysician to provide the minor premiss which, given man's psychological make-up, is an indispensable condition of a valid metaphysical argument.

(*b*) When he challenges the metaphysician's inference, he is asking him to give a theoretical justification of an implied major premiss, which states an inference.

(*c*) It was Kant's conviction that inferences of this sort are not valid or theoretically justifiable. I submit, then, that Kant's problem, namely the problem of metaphysical argument, remains the fundamental problem for the metaphysician, and that the modern shifting of attention to the problem of " meaning " has not really superseded the older approach. I think that this conclusion is confirmed by what seems to me to be the fact that, when a metaphysician argues with a logical positivist, the discussion inevitably comes to turn round the question of inference or of " metaphysical argument." In the case of a metaphysician who admits that all our factual knowledge is in some way empirically grounded, this is inevitable. Moreover, if there is a certain " loosening-up " or an inclination to a greater degree of toleration in logical positivist circles in regard to the meaning of meaning, and if this process continues, it will gradually become more apparent, I think, that the Kantian line of attack on metaphysics remains the fundamental line of attack and presents the fundamental problem for the metaphysician. The language in which the logical positivist expresses his attack on metaphysics may not be the language of Kant; but the substance remains the same.

CONCLUSION

It may be said that all this is very trivial, on the ground that every philosopher nowadays must take the validity of Kantian criticism as a starting-point. But, apart from the fact that the statement that every philosopher must presuppose the validity of the Kantian criticism of metaphysics is not a self-evident proposition, the metaphysician cannot escape the necessity of metaphysical argument, even if he tries to conceal the use of such argument. It is of no real help to him to propound metaphysical theories simply as hypotheses and to say that he does not pretend to " prove " them. Unless a metaphysical theory accounts for some fact in or some feature of empirical reality, it can profitably be subjected to treatment with Ockham's razor. But, if it accounts, even if only with probability, for some fact in or some feature of empirical reality, the metaphysician may justly be called upon to show that this is the case. This means that he will have to give a " metaphysical argument," whether he supposes that the conclusion is established with probability or with certainty. If such argument is possible, well and good: if it is not possible, the principle of economy should be applied to metaphysical theories. It is not my purpose to discuss the question whether such argument is possible or not: my purpose has been to show that the problem of the validity of metaphysical argument remains the fundamental problem in regard to metaphysics.

CHAPTER IV

A FURTHER NOTE ON VERIFICATION

I

I STILL think that it is true to say that " when a meta-physician argues with a logical positivist, the discussion inevitably comes to turn round the question of inference or of metaphysical argument." It may appear that the discussion should centre round the significance of the propositions which the metaphysician enunciates. But I doubt whether the significance of a metaphysical proposition can be successfully discussed without any reference to the reason or reasons why the proposition is enunciated. The question inevitably arises, What is the metaphysician about or why does he say what he does say? If a philosopher were to say, for example, that everything is " ideal," the reason or reasons why he makes this statement may very well throw a light on its intended significance, a light which will not be shed if no reference at all is made to these reasons.

2

But I doubt whether it is true to say that " when the logical positivist challenges the metaphysician to ' derive ' an ' observa-tion-statement ' from his metaphysical statement, he is asking the metaphysician to provide the minor premiss which, given man's psychological make-up, is an indispensable condition of a valid metaphysical argument " (3, vi, *a*, Ch. III). For the positivist may demand an observation-statement which is not itself the reason or one of the reasons for which the metaphysical statement was originally made. And if the metaphysical state-ment is depicted as being the conclusion of an inference of the type alluded to above, the minor premiss is obviously one of the reasons originally assigned for making the statement.

3

If the positivist demands the derivation of what I may call a " fresh " observation-statement before he will be prepared to give favourable consideration to the meaningful character of a given metaphysical statement, he seems to be demanding that the latter should be shown to be in some sense a prediction before its claim to be meaningful can be admitted. And if this is the case, he appears to demand that the metaphysical statement should be shown to be a scientific statement (suppos-- ing, for the sake of argument, that scientific statements are predictions) or, in more general terms, an empirical hypothesis, before its meaningful character can be admitted. And if this condition cannot be fulfilled, the metaphysical statement will be excluded from the class of meaningful statements. But this procedure obviously lies open to the objection that a non-meaningful statement is here taken to be equivalent to a non-scientific statement. The metaphysician might then comment that he never intended to make a scientific statement and that if the positivist cares to assert that a metaphysical statement is meaningless because it is not a scientific statement, he is using the terms " meaningful " and " meaningless " in a technical sense which he is quite free to adopt if he chooses, but which nobody else can be compelled to accept and which gives rise to unnecessary confusion.

4

But it is now generally recognized, I think, that the procedure whereby one first analyzes the meaning of a particular type of statement (in the present context an empirical hypothesis) and then forms on this basis a general criterion of meaning, should be reckoned as a purely methodological procedure, useful perhaps for elucidating an important difference between statements of one particular class and statements which do not belong to that class but inadequate for establishing what statements are meaningful in a more general sense. But I should like to illustrate the point by utilizing some examples which I once cited in an (unpublished) broadcast talk on *Meaning*.

Suppose that a friend who is stopping in my house says to me: " I am looking for the evening paper. Do you know where it is? " And suppose that I reply: " It is on the table in the far corner of the room." As I was aware that my friend was looking for the paper, and as I wished to help him to find it, it is at least not unreasonable to say that the intended meaning of my reply was: " If you look on the table in the far corner of the room, you will see the paper." In other words, it is not unreasonable to analyze my reply as being equivalent to a prediction. Again, take the statement that the chemical formula for water is H_2O. It is not unreasonable to say that the statement is a prediction and that it means: " If anyone were to burn oxygen and hydrogen in the proportions mentioned, he would obtain water, and conversely, if anyone were to institute a chemical analysis of water he would obtain oxygen and hydrogen in the proportions mentioned."

But is there not perhaps some confusion here? If I tell my friend that the paper is on the table in the far corner of the room, my statement can be said to " mean " that if he looks on the table in question he will see the paper, in the sense that the first statement implies the second statement in a loose sense of the word " imply." But the meaning of the first statement cannot be identical with the meaning of the second statement. In view of my practical purpose in telling my friend that the paper is on the table, it is natural, if one wishes to analyze my statement as a prediction, to say that it means that if my friend looks on the table he will see the paper. But it requires no great ingenuity to see that it also means other things. In other words, that my friend on looking at the surface of the table will see the paper is not the only verifying statement which is implied by the statement that the paper is on the table. The latter statement can be verified in a number of other ways. Thus a number of other predictions could be " derived " from it. And it would certainly be a strange and paradoxical position if one were to maintain that the meaning of the statement that the paper is on the table cannot be understood until one knows all the possible ways of verifying it. Further, if this position is to be rejected, it can hardly be maintained that the meaning of my reply to my friend is identical with the meaning of the statement which enunciates one particular mode of verifying it.

I have spoken above of implying " in a loose sense of the word ' imply '." If the ordinary man were asked whether the statement that the paper is on the table implies that anyone who is not blind and who looks on the table will see the paper, provided that there is sufficient light in the room, he would doubtless answer " yes." But it is clear that the second statement introduces fresh ideas which are not contained in the original statement. And this is, of course, one reason why positivists have said, not that an empirical statement must be accounted meaningless unless an observation-statement can be derived from it alone, but rather that it must be accounted meaningless unless an observation-statement can be derived from it plus other statements. But how could we set about this process of deriving unless we first knew the meaning of the original statement? And if we must first know the meaning of the original statement, this meaning cannot be identical with the meaning of any observation-statement derived from it plus other statements. The most that we could legitimately say would be that it does not qualify for inclusion in the rank of empirical hypotheses unless it is possible to derive from it, together with other statements, an observation-statement. This would follow from the meaning given to the term " empirical hypothesis." But in this case nothing would immediately follow with regard to the meaningfulness of statements which do not fulfil this condition except that they are not " empirical hypotheses." To call a statement meaningless would be no more than to say that it is not an empirical hypothesis.

It may be said that I have been flogging a dead horse. And I am, indeed, well aware that those who make explicit use of the principle of verifiability acknowledge that they use it as a methodological principle. I am also aware that they admit that when they use this principle as a criterion of meaning they do not intend to assert that statements which fail to satisfy the criterion are devoid of meaning in every sense. They would not wish to say that ethical statements, for example, are " nonsensical," unless, indeed, the word " nonsensical " is given a technical significance which renders the assertion innocuous. Hence I am not under the illusion that I have been waging a victorious campaign against Professor X or Professor Y. None the less, I wished to indicate one or two of the reasons why the old positivist approach to the problem of meaning seems to me to be inadequate.

5

At the same time it is, I think, possible to free the principle of verifiability from its association with the analysis of scientific statements as predictions and to state it in such a way that it becomes acceptable as a general criterion of the meaningfulness of factual and descriptive statements.

Let us take the statement that the car is in the garage. I cannot be said to know the meaning of this statement unless I can understand what state of affairs is asserted. This is obvious. And I cannot understand what state of affairs is asserted unless I am in a position to understand what state of affairs is excluded. For if I thought that the statement that the car is in the garage was compatible with the statement that the car is in some other place than the garage, I could not be said to know the meaning of the statement that the car is in the garage. And if the statement that the car is in the garage was really compatible with the statement that the car is not in the garage but in some other place, we could not say that the statement possessed any definite meaning. This is not an arbitrary criterion of meaning. Reflection on the nature of descriptive language will show that a statement which asserts a certain state of affairs excludes a contradictory state of affairs. If it does not do so, it cannot be said to have any definite meaning. And if I am not capable of understanding what is excluded (even though I do not here and now advert to what is excluded), I cannot be said to understand the meaning of a descriptive statement.

Now, the statement is true if the state of affairs which is asserted actually obtains. It is thus true to say that we do not understand the meaning of the statement, unless we understand what would verify the statement. In order to understand the meaning of the statement it is not, of course, necessary that we should know whether the statement is in fact true. But we cannot be said to understand its meaning unless we understand what would make it true, if it were true. It follows that there is a sense in which we can legitimately claim that we do not understand the meaning of a factual or descriptive statement unless we know " the mode of its verification." But here there is no question of " deriving " observation-statements, with the consequent difficulty that we could not derive any further statement unless we first knew the meaning of the original statement. It is merely a question of understanding the state of affairs asserted.

6

If these considerations provide us with a general criterion or test of meaning, it must, of course, apply to metaphysical statements. But we obviously cannot apply it to " the metaphysical statement " in the abstract. It is generally recognized now that metaphysical statements have to be examined separately. To claim that such statements can be meaningful is not the same thing as claiming that all the statements ever made by metaphysicians are meaningful. Metaphysicians are probably much like other people, and they may sometimes make statements to which it is difficult to attach any clear meaning. After all, it is not entirely unknown for one metaphysician to question the meaningful character of a statement made by another metaphysician.

I should not, however, wish to press the term " clear meaning." The minimum requirement for the understanding of a factual or descriptive statement is that we should understand the state of affairs asserted to the extent of being capable of understanding at least something which is excluded. It is not required that we should have a perfect understanding of the state of affairs asserted before the statement can be recognized as meaningful. This is a point of some importance. Further mention of it in a particular context is made in the essay on *The Meaning of the Terms Predicated of God.*

A final point. Let us suppose that we do not understand the meaning of a factual or descriptive statement unless we understand the state of affairs which would verify it, if it were in fact true, to the extent at least of being able to distinguish between the state of affairs which is asserted and the contradictory state of affairs, which is excluded. By the word " understand " I do not necessarily mean " imagine." The examples of the paper on the table and of the car in the garage may suggest that I do mean this. But the conclusion would be incorrect. If by " understand " I simply meant " imagine," I should have to exclude from the rank of meaningful statements all metaphysical statements, for example, which concerned spiritual entities. Some would doubtless wish to do this, following in the footsteps of Hobbes. But I have been trying to free the " principle of verifiability " not only from a too close association with a particular analysis of scientific propositions but also from dependence on any particular philosophical presuppositions. If stated on the lines indicated above, it has, in itself, nothing to do with dogmatic materialism. One may add perhaps that if we substitute " imagine " for " understand " in all cases, we may very well find ourselves in considerable difficulty with regard to a number of the propositions of physical science, quite apart from the bearing of this substitution on metaphysics.

CHAPTER V

THE FUNCTION OF METAPHYSICS

I

ARISTOTLE stated that philosophy began with " wonder " and that men continue to philosophize because and in so far as they continue to " wonder." Philosophy, in other words, is rooted in the desire to understand the world, in the desire to find an intelligible pattern in events and to answer problems which occur to the mind in connection with the world. By using the phrase " the world " I do not mean to imply that the world is something finished and complete at any given moment: I use the phrase in the sense of the data of outer and inner experience with which any mind is confronted. One might say just as well that philosophy arises out of the desire to understand the " historical situation," meaning by the last phrase the external material environment in which a man finds himself, his physiological and psychological make-up and that of other people, and the historic past. One might discuss the question whether the desire to understand ought to be interpreted or analyzed in terms of another drive or other drives. Nietzsche, for example, suggested in the notes which have been published under the title " The Will to Power " that the desire to understand is one of the forms taken by the will to power. Or it might be suggested by some that the desire to understand is subordinate to the life-impulse, in the sense that it is the necessity of acting in a given historical situation which drives us to attempt to attain clarity concerning this situation. But I do not propose to discuss these psychological questions. I am concerned at the moment to point out that philosophy—and I include metaphysical philosophy—has its origin on the conscious level in the desire to understand the world. We are all familiar with children asking for explanations without any other obvious motive than that of resolving some perplexity, solving some difficulty or understanding some event or set of events; and I suggest that philosophy, as far as its original motive is concerned, is inspired by the same sort of desire which is observable in children.

What I have been saying may appear very obvious and trivial. But the original drive behind philosophical inquiry may possibly become obscured owing to the contention of some contemporary anti-metaphysicians that metaphysical problems are pseudo-problems which have their origin in linguistic confusion and error. Metaphysicians, it is said, were misled by language; they did not understand the proper use of terms; and they thus came to utter a lot of unintelligible sentences—or rather sentences which, though *prima facie* intelligible, can be shown by analysis to lack any definite meaning. That some metaphysical theories were due in part at least to linguistic confusion I should not attempt to deny, though I do not think that this can properly be said of metaphysics in general. But I am not now concerned with assessing the part played by linguistic confusion in the genesis of metaphysical theories. What I should like to point out is that we are not entitled to say of any question or theory that it is meaningless until it has been formulated. Otherwise we do not know what we are calling " meaningless." The questions must first be raised before analysis of them is possible. And they were raised in the first place because the people who raised them wanted to understand something, because they wanted answers; and this fact remains true even if it could be shown that they were mistaken in thinking that there was anything to understand or that any answers to their questions were possible. I think that it is as well to have drawn attention to this point, even if it appears to be a trivial point. For acquaintance with detailed disputes between metaphysicians may give the impression that metaphysics is a mere verbal game and obscure the fact that in its origin metaphysics arises simply out of a natural desire to understand the world or the historical situation.

2

It is evident that science, too, owes its birth to the desire to understand. Francis Bacon emphasized the practical function of scientific knowledge, and living as we do in a highly technical civilization we are not likely to forget this aspect of science. We are also aware today of the part played by hypothesis in scientific theory, while the development of mathematical physics in particular has led thinkers like Eddington to lay great emphasis on the rôle of *a priori* mental construction in the framing of physical hypotheses. But though on the one hand technics obviously has a practical function while on the other hand we are now aware of the hypothetical character of scientific theory, it is not, I think, unreasonable to say that philosophy and science had a common origin in the natural desire to understand the world. However much any one may be inclined to stress the practical function of science, he can hardly maintain that astronomy proper, as distinct from astrology, had any other origin than the desire to understand.

Originally, of course, there was no clear distinction between philosophy and science. Nor, indeed, could there have been. The distinction could not be drawn until science had developed far enough for the distinction to be brought clearly before the mind. It is sometimes difficult to say, therefore, whether a particular theory of a Greek philosopher should be classed as a metaphysical theory or as a scientific hypothesis, a primitive scientific hypothesis, that is to say. In a state of affairs when philosophy and science are not yet distinguished, it is a tautology to say that contours are vague and outlines obscure. For example, any philosopher today who wishes to defend the Aristotelian hylomorphic theory must of necessity present it as a metaphysical theory; for it would be absurd to present it as a rival physical hypothesis to, say, the atomic theory. And he will probably also wish to maintain that it was propounded by Aristotle as a metaphysical theory. If he does not maintain this, he lays himself open to the charge of holding the theory merely out of respect for tradition. He is determined to keep the theory, it would be said, because it was Aristotle's theory;

63

but since he sees that it cannot now be put forward as a rival physical hypothesis he changes what he admits to have been originally a physical hypothesis into a metaphysical theory in order to preserve it from attack on scientific grounds. A person, on the other hand, who does not wish to maintain the hylomorphic theory and who regards Aristotle's idea of " form," for example, as having been given definite content by the concepts of structure developed at a much later date by the various empirical sciences, may be inclined to speak of the Aristotelian theory as a primitive scientific hypothesis. And arguments could be adduced both for and against this way of speaking. One might say against it, for instance, that the theory involves mention of an entity, or rather of an essential constituent of entities, which is in principle unobservable. I refer to " first matter." On the other hand, an alchemist might say in favour of calling the theory a primitive scientific hypothesis that one could derive from it the testable conclusion that the so-called " baser " metals can ultimately be turned into gold. But it might also be claimed that the whole dispute is superfluous. It is only to be expected, it might be said, that at a time when the sciences had not yet taken shape speculative theories should have been put forward which it is difficult to classify in terms of distinctions which were made at a later date; and one should not attempt to make any rigid classification of this sort. To do so serves no useful purpose. All that one can profitably do is to distinguish, or to attempt to distinguish, those early speculative theories which represent answers to questions which have proved to be or are thought to be answerable by some branch of science from those other theories which represent answers to questions which are not answerable, or which we cannot see to be answerable, by any branch of science. The latter type of theory is properly called a " metaphysical " theory. As for the former type of theory, it does not matter much whether one calls it a metaphysical theory which has been succeeded by scientific theories or a primitive scientific theory, though the latter way of speaking may involve a misuse of the term " scientific." The main point is to recognize that theories of this type have been succeeded in the course of time by fruitful scientific theories which have formed the basis for further research, hypothesis and experiment. It is a matter of minor importance whether we say that the movement was from metaphysics to science or from " primitive science " to science proper. On the whole, however, it is preferable to speak in the first way, since the development and progress of the sciences have involved their gradual purification from metaphysics.

I do not want to discuss the terminological question any further or to make any definite recommendation about the proper way of speaking. But it seems to me undeniable that at least some lines of inquiry were once pursued by philosophers in a speculative manner which are no longer pursued in this way. It is significant that when Aristotle stated that philosophy began with wonder he went on to state that people wondered first about the more obvious difficulties and that they then gradually advanced and stated difficulties about greater matters, like the phenomena of the moon and sun and stars and about the genesis of the universe. Astronomical inquiries were once regarded as pertaining to philosophy. But this is not so today. If we want information about the sun or the moon, we do not turn to philosophers for that information. Again, if we want information about the physical constitution of matter, we turn to the physicists. Questions about these matters are now classed as scientific questions, not as philosophical questions. And this is not simply an affair of terminology. The point is that we do not think that questions of this sort can be answered by means of the pure reason, that is, by armchair reflection alone. We see that another method, or other methods, are required. (I say " we see "; but as a matter of fact it was more or less clearly recognized in the late Middle Ages that if we want to learn empirical facts, *a priori* deduction will not enable us to do so.)

It seems to me, then, that it is undeniable that the empirical sciences have gradually taken over some tracts of the territory which was once supposed to belong to philosophy. And in this sense it is true to say that the field of philosophy has been narrowed. On the other hand, it is undeniable that philosophers have asked questions which cannot be answered by any particular science. Some might, perhaps, take exception to the use of the word " cannot " in an absolute sense. They might prefer to say of these questions that we do not see how they can be answered by any particular science. But I fail to see how a question about the origin of all finite beings, for example, could conceivably be answered by any empirical science. So I am content to say quite simply that philosophers have asked a number of questions which cannot be answered by any particular science. And if anyone chooses to say that these questions are the properly philosophical questions and that questions about the sun and moon were never proper philosophical questions, he can go on to say that philosophy proper has *not* in fact been narrowed.

I do not mean to imply that all questions which cannot be answered by the empirical sciences are " metaphysical " questions. For I think that there are moral questions which cannot be answered by empirical science but which one would not normally call " metaphysical " questions. But I confine my attention in this chapter to metaphysical questions. And I think that both metaphysicians and anti-metaphysicians would agree that as far as words are concerned a number of questions are properly called " metaphysical " questions. Some anti-metaphysicians would then go on to say that these questions cannot be answered scientifically because they are unanswerable and that they are unanswerable because no intelligible question has been asked. Speculative questions about the " Absolute " or about the " Cause " of " the world " or about the spiritual soul would be classified as questions of this sort. But I want to leave aside for the moment this type of difficulty and to ask whether there are any inquiries which the anti-metaphysician would concede to be meaningful and which at the same time can sensibly be called " metaphysical."

3

A good deal of attention has been paid by modern philosophers to the analysis of statements about material things like chairs, tables and so on. And some have argued that objects like these are " logical constructions " out of sense-data or sense-contents. This might be taken to mean that a table, for example, is a fictitious entity, in the sense that there is no existent entity denoted by the word " table " but only a multiplicity of entities called " sense-data " or " sense-contents." We should then presumably have a form of idealistic phenomenalism, arrived at by philosophic reflection rather than by scientific hypothesis and verification. For it would be as difficult to prove scientifically that a table consists of sense-data as it would be to prove scientifically Berkeley's theory that material objects are " ideas " presented to us by God. In this case the theory might well be called a " metaphysical " theory. What other name could one give it?

But those analysts who maintain the truth of this theory refuse to allow that it means that a table, for example, is a fictitious entity. The statement that a table is a, " logical construction " out of sense-data or sense-contents is a linguistic statement, not a statement about the constitution of material things. What it says is that sentences which name a material thing like a " table " can be translated into sentences which refer to sense-data or sense-contents but which do not contain the word " table." This interpretation of the theory of " logical constructions " as a purely linguistic theory is highly ingenious; but I feel some misgivings about it. A table is a " phenomenon " in the sense that it is an object appearing to us; and if we say that statements about this phenomenon can be translated into statements of equivalent meaning about sense-data, it is difficult to avoid the impression that what we are saying is that this phenomenon is a collection of sense-data. I am not concerned with the truth or falsity of the contention that a table is a collection of sense-data. What I want to remark is this. The contention is not a metaphysical contention in the sense that anything is said about a substance in Locke's sense of the word " substance "; but it seems to me to be metaphysical in another sense, namely in the sense that it is not the result of any physical or chemical analysis of the table. It is the result of a philosophical analysis of meaning, and in this sense it can be called " linguistic "; but it is not linguistic in the sense that it concerns words exclusively. Philosophical analysis is not the same thing as grammatical analysis. I suggest, then, that the theory of " logical constructions " can sensibly be called a " metaphysical " theory[1] and that what it does is to replace the metaphysic of substance by a phenomenalistic metaphysic. Possibly this is felt by those analysts who tend to exclude the sense-datum theory and the theory of " logical constructions " in the name of " ordinary language."

Perhaps one can apply the same line of reflection to the analysis of causality. This is often represented as an instance of linguistic analysis. So it is in a sense. But in what sense? If it is simply an analysis of the meaning of the term as used by scientists, or by a number of them, or if it is simply an analysis of the meaning of the term as used by certain social groups at certain periods, it is linguistic analysis in a strict sense. But if it is possible by means of this analysis to establish what people " ought " to mean by causality, the procedure involved does not seem to me to be radically different from the procedure followed by those philosophers who would have regarded the analysis of causality as an instance of metaphysical analysis.

It may be objected that metaphysicians have imagined that they could find out fresh information about the world by reflective analysis, whereas in point of fact we cannot do this. We can analyze the way in which people speak about the world, but any facts we learn in this way are linguistic facts. But I think that a distinction ought to be made. There is certainly a sense in which philosophical analysis gives no fresh knowledge of " facts." For example, by analyzing relation-sentences we do not obtain fresh knowledge of actual relations: that is obvious. Nor do we obtain knowledge that things stand in relation to one another in some sense. For this knowledge is presupposed by the ordinary use of language involving relation-sentences. But we can obtain information of what it " means " to say that one thing stands in relation to another thing. As

---

[1]It may be said that I am neglecting Carnap's distinction between the " formal " and " material " modes of speech. But I am not at all happy about the way in which this distinction is applied.

this knowledge concerns " meaning " it can be said to concern
linguistic usage; but it can also be called a knowledge of what
relations " are "; it is not knowledge simply of what A or B
thinks is the meaning of relation-sentences. And it seems to me
that this kind of analysis can sensibly be called " metaphysical "
analysis. It is certainly not physical or chemical analysis. It
may be objected that it is precisely in order to distinguish it
from physical and chemical analysis that it is called " linguistic
analysis "; but what I am suggesting is that what is called by
philosophers " linguistic " analysis is not radically different
from what in the past has been known as " metaphysical "
analysis.[1]

There is, of course, an obvious comment which can be made
about what I have been saying. An anti-metaphysician might
reply as follows. " Leaving aside the question whether your
account of analysis is correct or incorrect, I am quite prepared
to admit that if you choose to call analysis ' metaphysics,'
metaphysics is possible and has a useful function. But to call
analysis ' metaphysics ' does nothing at all towards justifying
metaphysics in the sense in which I reject metaphysics. If an
astronomer rejects astrology, it would be futile to select some
part of astronomy and call it ' astrology ' under the impression
that astrology in the sense in which the astronomer rejects it
was thus being justified."

There is obviously truth in this line of reply. I entirely agree
that to call analysis as practised by the modern analyst " metaphysics " does little to justify metaphysics in the sense in which
the anti-metaphysical analyst rejects metaphysics. At the same
time I do not think that my line of argument is as futile as the
analogy about astronomy and astrology might suggest. In the
first place I have maintained that some at least of what passes
for " analysis " bears a marked resemblance to what used to
be called " metaphysics." The analyst might reply, of course,
that he does not deny the resemblance but that the kind of
inquiry referred to should be called " analysis " and not
" metaphysics " whether it is practised by Plato or by Berkeley

---

[1]One may note in passing that Carnap found himself compelled to distinguish " syntax " and " semantics."

or by a modern analyst. The point is, however, that the phrase " linguistic analysis " may be misleading; and to draw attention to resemblances of the kind mentioned may help to show how it can be misleading. In the second place it is not, I think, futile to point out that the interpretation of the word " metaphysics " which is fairly common today, that is, as a study of or talk about transcendent and unobservable entities, has not been the sense in which the word has been exclusively understood by metaphysicians themselves. If one analyzes, for example, the meaning of the word " thing," one is, I suggest, engaging in precisely one of those pursuits which metaphysicians have not infrequently engaged in and which they have regarded as pertaining to metaphysics. And it is just as well to realize this.

However, as I have said, the classification of analysis, or some of it, as " metaphysics," does little or nothing to rescue what the anti-metaphysical analysts call " metaphysics." And I want now to turn to this subject.

4

(1) If one looks at the history of metaphysical theories which involve reference to a being or to beings in some sense transcending empirical reality, one will see that in some of them the transcendent being is postulated in order to explain or to account for the world being in some respect like this rather than like that. In the myth of the *Timaeus* the divine craftsman is postulated (with what degree of seriousness it is unnecessary to discuss here) to account for the intelligible structure of the world, that is, for what Plato took to be the world's intelligible structure. Again, in Aristotle's *Metaphysics* the first unmoved mover is postulated as the ultimate explanation of " movement." In Whitehead's philosophy eternal objects and God seem to have the function of explaining how the pattern of the world comes to be what it is, while in Bergson's *Creative Evolution* the idea of the evolutionary process leads on to the idea of a creative power at work in the world. In the case of metaphysical theories of this kind their function seems to be that of explaining

what may be called the *how* of the world rather than the *that* of the world. This distinction certainly cannot be rigidly applied to philosophies like those of Whitehead and Bergson; but it applies very well in the case of Aristotle, who did not postulate the first unmoved mover in order to explain the existence of things, but rather in order to explain a feature of things, namely " movement " or becoming.

It is obvious, I think, that a metaphysical theory of this kind can claim to be taken seriously only if it is based on the conviction that any non-metaphysical explanation must be regarded as insufficient. An anti-metaphysician may think that all metaphysical theories are gratuitous hypotheses; but one could not expect him to give serious consideration to a metaphysical theory which even for its author was a gratuitous hypothesis. It is indeed unlikely that agreement will be reached in all cases whether a given feature of the world or a given set of empirical data can be adequately accounted for without the introduction of metaphysics. And I fail to see that the anti-metaphysician is entitled to issue a kind of advance prohibition against the introduction of metaphysics if he is unable to shake the conviction of another philosopher about the inadequacy of any non-metaphysical explanation. He is entitled, of course, to challenge the metaphysician to show that a metaphysical theory is required; for when any feature of the world can be adequately accounted for in terms of phenomenal causes, one should not drag in a metaphysical entity or theory to account for it. But, as I have said, agreement about the adequacy of non-metaphysical explanations is unlikely to be reached in all cases; and the metaphysician has as much right to his convictions on this matter as the anti-metaphysician has to his. In my opinion, there could be only one cogent ground for ruling out all metaphysical theories. This ground would obtain if it could be shown that the questions asked and theories propounded by metaphysicians are all meaningless, in the sense that to one or more of the terms no definite meaning can be assigned. But, as I said earlier in this paper, linguistic criticism of metaphysical questions and theories has to await their formulation. One has to allow the desire for understanding full play and permit it to lead to the formulation of questions and problems. Once a question has been asked, it is legitimate to ask what it means; but one is hardly entitled to say in advance: " Be silent! For if you speak, you will utter nonsense." One does not know *a priori* that nonsense is going to be uttered.

(2) Some metaphysicians might perhaps comment that I have misrepresented what they try do do. They do not take some isolated or selected feature of reality and build up a speculative theory on a narrow basis: they are more concerned with working out a general theoretical standpoint from which empirical data of various types can be seen as forming a coherent pattern. It is true that one type of metaphysician has tried to work out a system of philosophy, a comprehensive world-view, in a purely deductive manner, and that a procedure of this sort involves the application to empirical reality of a preconceived scheme, with the result that inconvenient data are slurred over or explained away. And it is true that some metaphysicians have emphasized one aspect of reality at the expense of other aspects. Schopenhauer is a case in point. But it is an exaggeration to suggest that metaphysicians in general attempt to force empirical data into a preconceived scheme or that they attend exclusively to one aspect of empirical reality. A philosopher like Bergson was not concerned with elaborating a " system." He considered problems separately, moving from one problem to another. And though his conclusions certainly converged on the formation of a unified world-view, this was the result, rather than a presupposition, of his reflections.

It is doubtless quite true that metaphysics does not stand or fall with the validity of Spinoza's method. And it is, I think, an exaggeration to depict all metaphysicians as endeavouring to prove a preconceived system. But a full understanding of reality has surely been the limiting goal of speculative metaphysics, even with those who have recognized from the start the practical unattainability of the goal. And though this does not involve the *a priori* assumption of any definite answers to questions, it does involve the assumption that reality is intelligible. But we should never attempt to understand anything unless we believed that there was something to understand. Whether subsequent confirmation of our initial belief is forthcoming is another question.

(3) The attempt to understand empirical reality involves at the end, even if not at the beginning, an attempt to understand the *that* of finite beings. In the *Tractatus* Wittgenstein has said, " Not *how* the world is, is the mystical, but *that* it is." I should not care to use the word " mystical " here. But, provided that I am not understood as contradicting what I have said earlier about metaphysics and analysis, one might perhaps say, " Not *how* the world is, is the metaphysical, but *that* it is." I should be inclined to say at least that the more prominent this existential problem is in a philosophy, the more metaphysical the philosophy is. The attempt might be made to dress up some metaphysical theories in the guise of scientific hypotheses, but it would be difficult to pass off any answer which might be given to the problem of the existence of finite beings as a scientific hypothesis in the common understanding of the term.

What I am concerned with is the question why this problem constantly recurs. Its prominence in western philosophy may be connected in part with Judaeo-Christian theology; but it is not peculiar to western philosophy. It is, indeed, easy to say that the problem is a pseudo-problem, which has its origin in linguistic confusion. We should ask, it may be said, only precise questions. If we ask for the cause or the causes of a given phenomenon, we can be given, in principle at least, a definite answer in terms of other phenomena. If we do not ask precise questions, we shall find ourselves talking about " all phenomena " or " all finite things " or " all empirical reality " or about " finite being as such." And all these phrases give rise to logical difficulties. The metaphysician trades on linguistic confusion, vagueness and imprecision; he is able to impress other people only in so far as they are already involved in the same confusion as himself or in so far as he can involve them by the use of obscure and probably emotively-charged language in this confusion. Yet the fact remains that the problem of which I am speaking continues to be raised. Indeed, if the

73

more important metaphysical problems are excluded from academic philosophy in a given period or in a certain region, what happens is that they are raised and discussed outside the confines of academic philosophy. It may be said that this is largely due to the fact that human beings are prone to wishful thinking, and that there are always a large number of them who endeavour to find some rational or pseudo-rational justification for what they believe or want to believe on other grounds. But what is the origin of this " wishful thinking "? That metaphysical speculation, when it is indulged in, is the fulfilment of a desire of some sort is obvious enough: nobody would practise it otherwise. But more than this can be said on the subject. And I want to suggest what seems to me a possible origin of the problem of the existence of finite beings.

The primary datum is not, I think, either subject or object but the self as existing in an undefined and unarticulated situation. Man finds himself " there," within the area of Being. The consciousness of the self as a reflectively apprehended centre and of definite external objects, a consciousness which grows with experience, presupposes a pre-reflective awareness of existing in encompassing Being. As empirical knowledge grows and as definite objects are marked off within a general field, that is, as " my world " is gradually constructed, these objects are still conceived, perhaps in a very vague way, as existing against a background of Being or as within encompass-ing Being. And accompanying the building-up, as it were, of a definite empirical world there is an articulation, an expression to the self, of the nature of this background. By a great many people it is thought of as " the world " or " the universe." There are, I think, many people who, perhaps without clearly recognizing the fact, conceive themselves and other things as existing within " the world," as though all definite things were phenomena existing within an all-encompassing and meta-phenomenal " world." In this sense there is an implicit metaphysic in the outlook of many people who are far from being metaphysicians. Again, the pre-reflective awareness (perhaps one might say the " felt " awareness) of things as standing in relation to an obscure Ground of existence may be expressed in the way in which we find it expressed in the writings of some poets. On the other hand, there may be an attempt to render explicit on the reflective level this pre-reflective awareness. And this attempt gives rise to various metaphysical systems. The attempt to state the " felt " dependence of finite things may give rise to a system like that of Spinoza or to a theistic philosophy or even to a philosophy like that of Sartre, with its conception of the *en-soi*. I do not want to argue here in favour of any particular philosophy or type of philosophy; but I do suggest that the question of the ultimate Ground of empirical existence would never be raised, were there not a primary implicit awareness of existing against a background of Being. To avoid misunderstanding I had better say that by using the word " Being " with a capital letter I do not mean to imply a direct awareness of God. A pre-reflective awareness of dependence or of what used to be called " contingency " is not the same thing as a direct awareness of God. If it were, there could hardly be those disputes between rival metaphysical systems of different types, to which we are accustomed in the history of philosophy.

It may be said that I have been putting forward a purely gratuitous hypothesis. I do not think that this is the case. I think that my hypothesis helps to explain a prominent feature of certain types of poetry, the origin, in part at least, of speculative metaphysics, a good deal of natural religion, and even the common though perhaps implicit conviction that things exist in " the world." I am perfectly well aware, of course, that what I have been saying is extremely vague: it could hardly be anything else when one attempts to discuss a matter of this sort within the limits of a few sentences. In any case, though one certainly ought to strive after clarity language can be used to draw attention to what lies on the pre-reflective level; and one function of speculative metaphysics is to make explicit the pre-reflective awareness of which I have been speaking and to state its implications. Once the attempt to do this is made linguistic difficulties arise, and the philosopher must consider them honestly. But one should not allow oneself to be paralysed by Wittgenstein's dictum that " what can be

75

said at all can be said clearly." It is indeed obvious that
" whereof one cannot speak, thereof one must be silent "; but
one is not compelled to choose between absolute clarity on the
one hand and silence on the other. Language can have various
functions: it can be used to " draw attention to." And when
one has drawn attention, one can then endeavour to express in
clear language, so far as this is possible, what one has drawn
attention to. This, I think, is what speculative metaphysics
tries to do in regard to the primary awareness of Being. One
cannot bypass linguistic analysis, but one must first strive to
state. Otherwise there can be no analysis.

What I have been saying will be regarded by some as a
relapse into " mysticism," as an exhibition of the inherent
weakness of metaphysics, as confirmation of the theory that
metaphysical propositions possess no more than emotive
significance, and even perhaps as an indication that metaphysicians stand in need of psychoanalysis. But many quite
ordinary people possess an implicit metaphysic; and the real
reason why the central metaphysical problem constantly recurs
in different forms in spite of critical analysis is, I think, that it
springs from man's existential situation, accompanied by an
awareness of dependence or " contingency," and not from
linguistic confusion. It is open to anyone, of course, to deny
this. But one might, perhaps, reverse Wittgenstein's saying,
" the limits of my language mean the limits of my world," and
say, " the limits of my world mean the limits of my language,"
" my world " signifying here the experience which I am willing
to acknowledge. Inability to find any value in metaphysics
may very well be an indication of the limits of a man's " world."

NOTE

One obvious objection to the line of thought suggested in the last section
is that I have introduced psychological considerations when I ought to
have devoted my attention to logical and linguistic problems. But I prefer
to leave the essay as it stands rather than to anticipate reflections which I
hope to develop when I have time to do so. However, something further on
this topic will be found in Chapter XII.

CHAPTER VI

ON SEEING AND NOTICING[1]

THE metaphysician as a metaphysician does not see more things than other people see. This proposition is quite general. I do not mean simply that the metaphysician as a metaphysician does not see a greater number of physical objects than the non-metaphysician sees. I mean also that he does not enjoy a mental vision or intuition of spiritual things or beings, which the non-metaphysician does not enjoy. Possibly some people might wish to challenge the truth of this general proposition. Is there not mysticism to consider? I do not deny the possibility of mystical experience; but I do not think that mysticism falls within the extension or denotation of the term " metaphysics." I cannot insist on anyone else using this term in the way in which I use it; but in the sense in which I use it, it excludes mysticism. This is one reason why I said that the metaphysician " as a metaphysician " does not see more things than the non-metaphysician sees. Smith may be both a metaphysician and a mystic, but this no more means that mysticism is synonymous with or a part of metaphysics than the fact that Jones is a tennis player and a doctor means that the practice of medicine is synonymous with or a part of tennis-playing.[2]

On the other hand, some metaphysicians claim that metaphysics rests on or presupposes what they call an " intuition of being." Thus a contemporary philosopher claims that it is the intuition of being which makes the metaphysician. And I propose to inquire what meaning can be attached to the claim that there is an intuition of being. Can any meaning be attached to the phrase " intuition of being," which would

---

[1]Address given at the Annual General Meeting of the Royal Institute of Philosophy at University Hall, 14 Gordon Square, London, W.C.1, on Monday, July 20, 1953.

[2]One can philosophize about mysticism; but philosophizing about mysticism is not mysticism.

make it possible to admit the claim in some sense and yet to assert at the same time that the metaphysician as a metaphysician does not see more things than the non-metaphysician sees?

My inquiry will take the particular form of asking whether a distinction between " seeing " and " noticing " or " adverting to " is of any use in shedding light on what is claimed to be the starting-point of metaphysics.[1] And I should like to emphasize here that my procedure is tentative and exploratory. What I am going to say is put forward as an attempt at elucidation. That is to say, I am not trying to expound what seems to me to be clear: I am trying to attain clarity in a matter which appears to me to be obscure.

I

To begin with, I want to use the distinction between " seeing " and " noticing " in two non-metaphysical contexts.

John says, referring to Peter, " Yes, I saw him and spoke with him, but I did not notice what he was wearing." I assume that Peter was not standing on the other side of a wall or hedge with only his head protruding over the top. For if this had been the case, John would hardly have said, " I did not notice what he was wearing." He would probably have said, " I could not see what he was wearing." I assume also that John did not keep his eyes fixed so steadfastly and unwaveringly on Peter's face that though it would be in order for him to say that he saw Peter it would not be true to say that he saw Peter's clothes. I assume, therefore, that John saw Peter's clothes. But he did not notice what they were. Peter was not wearing something extraordinary which would inevitably have attracted John's attention. Nor was John a detective and Peter a suspected criminal whose description had been circulated by the police. The fact of the matter is that John wanted to discuss a certain matter with Peter, and he was interested in the

---

[1] I propose, therefore, to apply the distinction between " seeing " and " noticing " to one particular case. It is capable, of course, of being applied to other cases.

conversation: he was not interested in Peter's clothes. And so he did not advert to them. But they were there and he saw them. And it is possible that later, under cross-examination by his wife, he can recall with an effort more or less what Peter was wearing.

" I saw the snake, but I did not notice that it was an adder." This statement seems to imply that I am capable of recognizing an adder, that is, that I know the use of the word " adder." For if I was unaware that a snake with certain characteristics is called an " adder," I probably ought to have said, " I saw the snake, but I did not know that it was an adder." If I say, " I saw the snake, but I did not notice that it was an adder," I am probably understood as meaning that if I had noticed the characteristics of the snake, I should have said to myself, " Hullo! There's an adder." But I did not notice the size and colour and markings of the snake. Did I see them? In other words, was I in a position to notice them? If I only caught a glimpse of a snake-like object slipping away through the grass, I might very well have been unable to notice its characteristics. But in this case I should hardly say, " I saw the snake, but I did not notice that it was an adder." I might say something like this, " I only caught a glimpse of the snake, and I could not tell whether it was a grass-snake or an adder." But what I actually said was, " I saw the snake, but I did not notice that it was an adder." Perhaps I was walking through a wood with a companion, my mind intent on the conversation, when my companion suddenly said to me, " Did you see that adder? You passed just by it." And I replied, " I saw the snake, but I did not notice that it was an adder." Yet in some sense I may have seen the adder-characteristics, though I did not notice them or advert to them. For looking back on the incident I may say to myself, " Yes, I think that it must have been an adder. Now that I come to think of it, the colour was not quite right for a grass-snake. And I have a vague impression of having seen the markings of an adder, though I did not notice them at the time."

John did not notice Peter's clothes, but the clothes were there, and he saw them. I did not notice that the snake was an adder, but the snake was there, and I saw it, including, I assume, its colour and markings. I could hardly see the snake apart from its colour, though I might very well fail to notice its colour. Why did not John notice what Peter was wearing, and why did I not notice that the snake was an adder? Partly at least because John was interested in his conversation with Peter, and I in my conversation with my companion. And what would have been required for John to have noticed what Peter was wearing, and for me to have noticed that the snake was an adder? Attention, stimulated by some interest, would have been required in both cases; and, given the necessary assumptions, it would have sufficed. For the verbal expression of this noticing a knowledge of the correct use of words would be required. I should wish to distinguish between noticing and its verbal expression.[1] In any case, however, if John had noticed what Peter was wearing and if I had noticed that the snake was an adder, neither of us would have seen what was invisible to other people, though it might be true that we noticed what other people did not notice.

I turn now to consider the claim that metaphysics rests on or presupposes an intuition of being.

In the first place, the philosophers whom I have in mind as claiming that metaphysics rests on an intuition of being do not mean to say that the metaphysician as a metaphysician has an intuition of Being, spelt with a capital letter and meaning either God or the Absolute. Nor do they mean that the metaphysician has an intuitive knowledge of a finite thing called " being " which exists alongside other finite things. It would be absurd to speak of John, being and Peter receiving invitations to a party or of seeing cows, sheep, beings and cowslips in a field. Cows, sheep and cowslips are things or beings, but being is not a thing, it is not itself a being. We cannot, therefore, be said to see being in the sense in which we can be said to see a cow or a sheep. If, then, the metaphysician is said to have an intuition of being, this cannot mean that he sees a thing which other people do not see. The word " being " in the context cannot be a name designating a thing. If we take

_____

[1]By " verbal expression " I do not mean *spoken* words, of course.

" being " in the sense of " existence," it is obvious that it is
not a thing. Things exist, but existence does not exist as a thing
among other things.

In the second place, if being is not a thing, neither is it a
characteristic of a thing in the same sense in which the colour
and markings of an adder are characteristic of an adder. We
should think that there was something wrong if we were told
by someone that he had seen a snake which was so many
inches long, of a certain colour, existing and possessed of
certain markings. It would be absurd to say that William is
tall and existing and tanned by the sun. For if he did not exist,
he could be neither tall nor tanned by the sun. Unless there
were a thing called William, William could have no characteristics at all. Existence or being-ness, therefore, cannot be a
characteristic among other characteristics. It cannot be a
predicate in the sense in which " white " and " black " are
predicates.

If, therefore, we can be said to notice being in the sense of
existence, this cannot mean that we notice it, if we do notice it,
in the same sense in which we notice the markings of an adder
or the blackness of black sheep. If I advert to the fact that the
sheep in the field are black, I advert to the fact that they are
black and not white or any other colour. If I advert to the fact
that the snake which I see is an adder, I advert to the fact that
it is an adder and not any other kind of snake. But there would
be something queer about saying that the sheep in the field
are black and not white, existent and not non-existent. Of
course, if someone says to me, " You merely imagine that
there are sheep in the field," I might go up to them and touch
them and say, " Not at all! The sheep exist all right." But I
am not thinking of cases like this. I am concerned with making
the following point. I notice that the sheep are black because
not all sheep are black, and I notice that the snake is an adder
because not all snakes are adders. Some sheep are white, and
some snakes are grass-snakes. But it would be very odd to say,
" There are some sheep in that field, and I notice that they
belong to the class of existent sheep," as though there might
have been sheep in the field which did not belong to the class

of existent sheep. Existence is certainly not a characteristic which some sheep and some snakes and some human beings possess, and which other sheep and other snakes and other human beings lack.

2

To say of anyone that he has an intuition of being cannot, therefore, be the same sort of thing as saying that I saw a snake in the wood. Nor can one be said to notice being in exactly the same sense in which one can be said to notice the characteristics of an adder or the blackness of black sheep. What, then, can it mean, presuming that it has a meaning?

One might perhaps be tempted to say that understanding of the fact that existence is not a predicate in the sense in which " white " and " black " are predicates is itself the intuition of being, considered as existence, inasmuch as it involves adverting to existence as the basis and fount of all characteristics and qualities. But there are plenty of philosophers who recognize that existence is not a predicate but who would add that to recognize this is to recognize the truth of a proposition about language, which cannot legitimately be used for metaphysical purposes or understood as having metaphysical implications. This raises the question of the relation of language to extra-linguistic reality, and I cannot embark on this topic here, though it seems to me that to recognize that existence is not a predicate in the sense in which " white " and " black " are predicates is to recognize something not only about language but also about the things of which we speak. And I think that this can be shown by examining the sort of reasons offered for saying that existence is not a predicate. However, as there are in fact philosophers who recognize that existence is not a predicate but who would not be prepared to go on to make any metaphysical statement about existence or, indeed, any metaphysical statement at all, if they could avoid doing so, one could hardly be justified in saying that the intuition of being which is said to make the metaphysician is identical with the realization of the fact that existence is not a predicate.

But is the so-called intuition of being perhaps a noticing or adverting to or realization of existence or being in a sense analogous to that in which a man can be said to notice or advert to or realize the beauty of a landscape or the significance of another person's actions? Let us suppose that a man has seen a certain landscape many times, so that it has become familiar to him. If he wants to see beautiful scenery he takes his car and makes a journey into the next county. Then one day he suddenly notices or adverts to or realizes the beauty of the familiar landscape. Again, a man may have seen another person acting in a certain manner on several or perhaps on many occasions. Then one day he notices or adverts to or realizes the significance of this way of acting; that is to say, he adverts to the relation between this way of acting and the person's character, he notices for the first time how it reveals the person's character. In both cases the man sees what he has seen before, a certain landscape in the first case and certain actions in the second, but he notices what he has not noticed before.

I think that analogies of this type suggest considerations which are relevant to the experience of adverting to or noticing existence. For they illustrate the fact that familiarity may lead us not to notice or advert to. It seems to be true to say that one reason why we tend to notice or advert to the fineness of fine days is the variability of our weather. And in the first case which I mentioned it was the familiarity of the landscape which led the man not to notice or advert to its beauty. Hence when he does notice or advert to it, this noticing comes to him with the force of a sudden vision or revelation. Now, the existing of things is much more familiar than a familiar beautiful landscape. For there are landscapes which are dull or even ugly, whereas there are no landscapes which are non-existent. There are, of course, landscape-paintings, and the words " exist " and " existent " can be used in analogous senses; but though a section of the Cotswolds can be beautiful or dull it cannot be non-existent, and though the painting of a landscape might be beautiful or dull or ugly, it cannot be non-existent. As we have already seen, existence is a necessary condition of the possession of any characteristics; and it is thus more familiar than any particular characteristic. Therefore, if it is possible at all to notice or advert to existence, one can say that the familiarity of what is noticed is one of the main reasons why it is comparatively rarely noticed or adverted to.

This consideration about the influence of familiarity is, I think, relevant to our theme. At the same time what I have just been saying about the analogies which I mentioned suggests the following reflection. If I notice the beauty of a landscape, I can express this noticing by saying that the landscape is beautiful and, by implication, not ugly. Similarly, if I notice or advert to the significance of a person's actions, I can say to myself that the actions exhibit this or that definite trait of character and, by implication, no other. But if I can be said to notice or advert to the existence of existent things, how is this noticing or adverting to be expressed? If it is not an incommunicable experience, it ought to be capable of being stated. Would it not be odd to speak, for example, of James, who is in love with Mary, as noticing or adverting to Mary's existence, in the sense of noticing the fact that Mary exists and is not non-existent? Is not this way of talking ruled out by what I have already said in the course of this essay?

If James told us that he had suddenly realized Mary's existence, we should probably have some inkling of what was meant. But we might be inclined to conclude that he had been suddenly filled with joy at the thought of Mary, and that if he had said to himself (a possible, though perhaps improbable event), " Mary exists," this apparent statement would have been no more than an expression of emotion. The words " Mary exists! ", with an exclamation mark after them, would possess only emotive significance. But I do not think that this analysis would be adequate. If James suddenly realizes Mary's existence, what he is realizing or adverting to or noticing may be this, that in certain circumstances things might not have included the person called Mary (if, for example, Mary's parents had had no children or if Mary had died some time ago) but that in actual fact they do. He knew this before, of course; but now he suddenly realizes or notices or adverts to it. This adverting to or noticing may be accompanied by an emotion of joy, but it is not identical with the emotion. And if he were to express his realization by the statement, " Mary exists," or, very improbably, " I notice that Mary exists," these sentences would be incomplete sentences. James may very well advert to the fact, for example, that Mary might have been killed in the last raid but that she was not killed. And if he says, " Mary exists," this may be in part an expression of an emotion; but it is also an abbreviation of the longer sentence which would express what he adverted to.

3

I suggest, therefore, that what is called the " intuition of being " is a noticing or adverting to the fact that this particular thing is a member or that these particular things are members of the class of things or physical objects, though in certain circumstances it might be or have been false to say that the class contains or contained a thing or things possessing the characteristics which could be mentioned in a description of this thing or of these things. To notice or advert to this fact is not to see things which other people do not see; it is to advert to or notice what many people rarely advert to explicitly, partly because of the familiar and it-goes-without-saying character of what is noticed, partly because their predominant interests do not facilitate their noticing it. But I do not think that this noticing by itself makes the metaphysician. John's attention, canalized by his affection for Mary, is concentrated on a particular instance; he does not abstract from this particular instance; he does not undertake any work of reflective analysis, nor does he inquire into the general implications of what he notices. At the same time I think that this noticing is a condition of metaphysics. It is, of course, possible to have different ideas of philosophy and different ideas of metaphysics. It is possible to identify philosophy with the analysis of language and at the same time to try to assimilate language in general to the special language of mathematics by eliminating, or attempting to do so, existential propositions. It is possible to build a system of metaphysics which has as little as possible to do with existent reality. It is possible to attempt to build metaphysics on scientific hypotheses. But if metaphysics is concerned with real being, it must, I think, start with adverting to existence in particular cases. And though I am certainly not prepared to go to the stake for the adequacy of the foregoing analysis of what this means, I do not think that the fact that it ends in drawing attention to what everyone already knows, at least implicitly, constitutes by itself any valid objection. For I am convinced that metaphysical problems rise out of common experience or, rather, out of adverting to what is in some sense perfectly familiar to all. Metaphysicians are sometimes inclined to use language which suggests, especially to those who are already unfavourably disposed to metaphysics, that they are using it for a primarily emotive purpose. But one should not come to this conclusion without a serious attempt to discover what is meant. And I have tried to do this in a particular instance. Whether it has been well or badly done is another question; and I doubt whether my analysis would commend itself to the metaphysicians whom I have in mind. But I think that the attempt at analysis was worth making.

CHAPTER VII

THE MEANING OF THE TERMS
PREDICATED OF GOD

WE all know that language can be used for different
purposes or have different functions. And in determining
the primary function of any proposition or set of consecutive
propositions we have, of course, to take into account the
general context, including the intentions of the speaker or
writer. In a propaganda speech, the function of which, we
will suppose, is primarily evocative (I mean, evocative of
emotional attitudes or dispositions) many propositions may be
included which convey factual information. Indeed, their
inclusion may well be necessary for the fulfilment of the general
purpose of the speech as a whole. But this would not prevent
the general purpose of the speech being that of evoking an
emotional response.[1]

Now, one must admit, I think, that propositions about God
can be used to stimulate emotional reactions. It appears that
they have been so used in certain types of sermons. It is also
clear that they can be used, and not infrequently are used, to
evoke what I may call a conduct-response, the emotional
response, if there is one, being teleologically subordinated to
this purpose. If little Tommy jumps in all the puddles and
dirties his shoes and clothes, his devout mother might possibly
say: "If you don't stop doing that, God will be angry with
you." If she does say this, her primary purpose is not that of
conveying a piece of factual information to the child; nor is it
that of evoking an emotional reaction; her primary intention
is that of inducing the child to alter its mode of behaviour.

---

[1]If I say, " I have recently been in Sicily, and I find the tail-end of the
English winter highly uncongenial," my primary purpose might be that
of awakening sympathy with my distress, but, if so, I use factual statements to attain my end.

Similarly, the preacher of an exhortatory sermon, as distinct from an " instruction," is primarily concerned with evoking or confirming attitude-responses and conduct-responses in his hearers rather than with giving them information. No doubt, he will make informative statements in the course of his sermon, but this giving of information will probably be subordinate to the general or primary purpose of the sermon. He wants to awaken, or to confirm, a " change of heart."

Now, it may appear that the problem of the meaning of terms predicated of God can be got rid of if one is prepared to say that statements about God are made simply and solely to evoke emotion- and conduct-responses which, rightly or wrongly, are considered desirable and that they are not intended to assert a state of affairs. For example, if one says that God is wise and loving, one's aim is to induce in oneself or others an attitude of mental tranquillity and resignation. The effect would scarcely, indeed, be produced if the words meant nothing at all; but it is quite sufficient that they should be taken in their natural *prima facie* sense, as meaning, that is to say, that God is wise and loving in pretty well exactly the same way as a wise and loving human father, though doubtless in a magnified manner. There is then no reason for making a problem out of the meaning of the words. All that is required for them to be capable of producing the desired practical effect is that they should have a meaning which is intelligible in terms of the experience of the hearers; whether it is precisely stated or can be precisely stated, does not matter. If it is said that God repented of having made man, it is quite sufficient to take the statement in its ordinary sense. The logical status of such statements is akin to that of Plato's statements at the end of the *Gorgias* about judgment after death, supposing that Plato's purpose in making them was not to assert that the judgment described in the myth actually takes place or will take place but simply to induce his readers to have an esteem for the soul and always to practise justice rather than injustice.

But if we say that Peter is white, we presumably imply that Peter exists, or that there is someone called Peter; for if there were not, Peter could not be white. And if we say that God is intelligent, we presumably imply that there is a being which can be called " God." And if " intelligent " in the context means intelligent simply in the human way, we seem to imply that there is a being called " God " and that this being is at most a superman. Yet though one might not be prepared to state dogmatically that there is no such being, I doubt whether anyone would be seriously concerned to argue that there is. It appears, then, at first sight at least, that anyone who wishes to uphold the interpretation of propositions about God which I have mentioned and at the same time to maintain that they have a useful and beneficial function to perform must be prepared to defend the view suggested by Plato in the *Republic* that it is sometimes a good thing to teach the people what one does not oneself believe. It may be said that this does not necessarily follow; for a man who makes statements about God may not only believe them to be mythical in character but may also say that they are mythical in character. The question then arises whether such statements can have any persuasive and evocative power unless they are believed to be true. I should hesitate to affirm that a statement can have no evocative power unless it is accepted as true at least by the hearers or readers. For if a Communist radio-speaker calls Sir Winston Churchill a Fascist cannibal, not only he but also his hearers may know very well that Sir Winston is not in the habit of eating human flesh; and yet the statement may serve to evoke or confirm an emotion-response, because of the associations of the word " cannibal." But the statement that Sir Winston is a Fascist cannibal does not seem to be merely an injunction to the hearers to dislike Sir Winston; it seems to imply, and would presumably be understood as implying, some factual statements, for example, that Sir Winston is not a Communist, that he is opposed to the policy of the Soviet Union, and so on. If, then, statements about God are interpreted as being purely mythical in character and yet at the same time as useful for a practical purpose, one might ask whether any factual statements are in any sense implied other than statements about emotions and attitudes, and, if so, what they are. In any case even though I hesitate to say that a statement can have no evocative efficacy unless it is believed by the hearers or readers, it seems to me to be clear that most people are interested in propositions about God only to the extent in which they think that they might be true or false, in the sense of asserting a state of affairs which does or does not obtain. And as it seems to be only in the light of a claim to factual truth that a real problem arises about the meaning of the terms predicated of God, I omit further consideration of an interpretation of theological propositions which follows rather than precedes a discussion of the problem, for the simple reason that, though these propositions undoubtedly have an evocative function in certain contexts, they have been put forward as informative propositions. It is obviously true that the Christian must subordinate the amassing of information about God to a practical purpose. What does it profit a man if he know the whole of theology and suffer the loss of his own soul? But this does not alter the fact that theological propositions purport to be informative. And this is why the problem of meaning arises.[1]

Now, if I propose to discuss the problem of the meaning of terms predicated of God, it might reasonably be demanded that first of all the problem should be clearly and precisely formulated. But this is not so easy as might at first sight appear.

For the mediaeval writers the problem arose subsequently to the affirmation of the existence of God. They found in the Scriptures and in Christian tradition certain terms predicated of God. And they recognized clearly enough that there is a problem in connection with the meaning of these terms. Convinced, for example, that our idea of intelligence is founded on our experience of human intelligence, and convinced that we cannot predicate of God human intelligence as such, they asked in what sense or in what way the word " intelligent " is being used when it is applied to God. Believing already in

---

[1] The conscious and deliberate interpretation of theological propositions as mythical seems, as far as Christianity is concerned, to *follow* their enunciation as factual statements. Can we seriously imagine that anyone would consciously *invent* the Christian theology as a myth designed to stimulate certain conduct- and attitude-responses?

God, and believing, for instance, that the Scriptures are the word of God (and this is true even of an " empiricist " like Ockham), they assumed that terms predicated of God in the Scriptures must have some meaning. They asked what their meaning is rather than whether they have any meaning; they asked, in modern parlance, what is the logical status of such terms rather than whether they have any logical status at all.

A modern writer, however, would be inclined to treat the problem of the meaning of the terms used to describe God as a problem to be settled before an inquiry into God's existence. He would be inclined, I think, to speak as follows. " If you ask whether God exists, you are asking whether it is the case that there is a being, and one only, which is infinite, personal, omniscient, omnipotent . . . or whatever the terms are which are used to describe God. Now, before I can help you to ascertain whether this description fits anything or not, I must know what the terms mean. It is not, of course, necessary that I should be given the precise meaning of the terms, but at least I must be given a meaning sufficiently clear to enable me to recognize God, so to speak, that is to say, to distinguish the divine being from other beings."

I have expressed this second approach in a very bald way. But it was not my intention to caricature it by suggesting that it necessarily implies a refusal to recognize God's existence unless God is discoverable in the same way that tigers are discoverable, that is, by going and seeing if there are any animals in the jungle answering to a certain description. For our speaker might say: " I do not demand that God should be a visible thing. If He were, He would not be God; that is to say, He would not correspond to your account of what you mean by God. But before I can undertake to inquire whether there is rational evidence for the existence of a being possessing attributes described in certain terms, I must have some idea at least of the meaning of those terms."

Now, both approaches seem to me natural if they are viewed in their historical contexts. The mediaevals believed before they philosophized. Indeed, all the great mediaeval philosophers, including Ockham, were theologians. And it was natural for them to approach the matter in the way they did. On the other hand, after centuries of theism, when most people have some idea of the meaning of the word " God," it is natural that the question should be asked, " Does God exist? " That is, is there a Being which corresponds to the idea of God? And it is also natural, though it demands a greater degree of sophistication, that some should ask for an explanation of the meaning of the terms used to describe God before they are willing to inquire whether there is a being answering to the description.

For a reason which may become apparent later I do not, however, think that the problem of meaning can well be treated in entire abstraction from the question of existence. On the other hand I do not want simply to presuppose the existence of God. So I put the problem in this form. " If finite things are conceived, whether truly or falsely, as depending existentially on an infinite transcendent Being, what is the meaning of terms like ' personal,' ' intelligent ' and so on when they are predicated of this Being? " The comment can be made, of course, that not only am I apparently excepting from analysis the terms " infinite " and " transcendent " but also that the term " being " itself stands in need of analysis. But I have already remarked that it is more difficult than appears at first sight to formulate the problem at issue when one starts from the meaning end. However, you would probably find it unsatisfactory if I spent all my time trying to formulate the question without any attempt at all to discuss the answer. And so I must claim to be allowed " transcendent " and " infinite." The retort may be made that it is useless to discuss the answer to a question unless the question has first been given a satisfactory formulation. But as the problem of meaning really only arises in the form in which I propose to discuss it in connection with terms predicated of a Being conceived as transcendent and infinite, it is perhaps not so unreasonable to express the question in the way in which I have. If by " God " one meant a Greek anthropomorphic deity, who, as Schelling remarked, was really a part of Nature and not a transcendent being at all, there would not be a problem in connection with the meaning of a term like " intelligent " when predicated of such a being. It is only because one is not talking about Greek or Roman deities that the problem arises.

It is obvious that when we predicate attributes of God we do not invent entirely new symbols; we use terms which already have meanings. And these meanings are primarily determined by our experience. For instance, the term " intelligent," to speak rather loosely and without wishing to prejudge analytic issues, is predicated primarily of a human being and refers to his or her proximate capability of or disposition for thinking, speaking and acting in certain ways. We then extend the field of application and say, if we do say it, that God is intelligent. But the meaning of the term cannot be precisely the same when it is predicated of God as when it is predicated of a human being. At least, if we want to say that it is precisely the same, we are faced, as I have already remarked, with two alternatives. Either we must say that God is simply a glorified human being or we must say that propositions about God are put forward simply as myths or fairy stories which are useful in helping us to lead a life which we consider worth living. As neither of these views commends itself to me, I shall assume that terms which are predicated of God and human beings cannot be used in precisely the same sense when they are predicated of God as that in which they are predicated of finite things. On the other hand, if they are used in a completely different sense when they are predicated of God, they lose all meaning for us in this field of application. If the meaning-content of terms like " personal " and " intelligent " is determined by our experience of human personality and human intelligence, and if they are used in an entirely and completely different sense when predicated of God, they can have no meaning for us when they are used in this second way. For we have not observed God. For the term " intelligent," therefore, in the proposition " God is an intelligent being " we might just as well substitute a symbol like X or Y. And these symbols would express no idea at all. Sheer agnosticism would result. A botanist who discovers a hitherto unknown flower in Africa or Asia can give it a new

93

name; he can even invent a new word to name it. And this word will have meaning, a meaning which can be learned either ostensively or by description. For the flower can be exhibited, or at least it can be described in terms of its unlikeness and likeness to other flowers with which we are acquainted. But we do not and cannot see God. And if all the terms used in descriptive propositions about God were used in entirely different senses from the senses which they bear in the context of human experience, God could not be described; no attribute could be significantly predicated of Him. I conclude, therefore, that the terms which are predicated of both finite things and God must be used analogically when they are predicated of God, if they have any meaning at all. That is to say, a term which is predicated of God and of finite things must, when it is predicated of God, be used in a sense which is neither precisely the same as nor completely different from the sense in which it is predicated of finite things. And this means that it must be used in a sense which is similar and dissimilar at the same time to the sense in which it is used when predicated of finite things.

Now, to say that a term like " personal " or " intelligent " must be used analogically when it is predicated of God is to lay down the condition under which the term can be significant while at the same time gross anthropomorphism is avoided. (By " gross anthropomorphism " I mean the assertion that God is simply a glorified human being. We cannot help thinking of God " in human terms "; but it is one thing to think of God in an inadequate way and at the same time to recognize its inadequacy, and it is another thing to maintain that God is a superman.) But to lay down the condition under which a term can be significant, while saying something about the use of language or about the logical status of such terms, is not the same thing as to give the meaning of the term. If I call my dog " intelligent " and someone asks me what I mean by this statement, it is no adequate answer to reply that I am using the term analogically. For this reply, though it says something about the use of the word, does not give the meaning of the word.

Moreover, this example about the dog can help us to see a peculiar feature of the use of analogy in theological propositions. When I call my dog " intelligent " I can explain the meaning of the word by pointing to the dog and its activities. We can observe human beings and their activities, and we can observe dogs and their activities; and we can point out similarities and dissimilarities. All the terms of the analogy are knowable in experience. But we can scarcely say that this is so in the case of the analogies under discussion. For though we can observe certain phenomena which we may regard as the effects of God's activity and as manifesting it, we cannot observe God. And this renders the problem of meaning in this context all the more acute.

Now, one of the traditional ways of approaching the meaning of terms predicated of God is the so-called " negative way." The use of this way of negation is, indeed, inevitable, for the simple reason that the meaning of terms like " personal " or " intelligent " is primarily determined for us by observation in ourselves or others of activities which cannot be ascribed to God in precisely the same sense. If I say that God is an intelligent Being, and if someone then asks me whether I mean that God is quicker than we are at drawing conclusions from premisses, that He sees the points of arguments more swiftly than human beings do and that He is accustomed to size up situations very quickly and see what should be done in the circumstances, I must answer that I do not quite mean any of these things. I therefore set about eliminating what are called the " imperfections " of human intelligence. But as I proceed in this way I become conscious that I am gradually eliminating the positive meaning which the term has for me. For the positive meaning of the term is determined for me by experience. And my experience is of human and not of divine intelligence. And human intelligence manifests itself in precisely those ways which I afterwards eliminate as imperfections. I return, therefore, to a positive affirmation. God, I say, is intelligent, but He is intelligent in an infinitely higher sense than human beings are. But when I am asked to give a positive account of this higher sense, I very soon find myself back

95

again in the way of negation. It would appear, then, that the theistic philosopher is faced with a dilemma. If he pursues exclusively the negative way, he ends in sheer agnosticism, for he whittles away the positive meaning which a term originally had for him until nothing is left. If, however, he pursues exclusively the affirmative way, he lands in anthropomorphism. But if he attempts to combine the two ways, as indeed he must if he is to avoid both extremes, his mind appears to oscillate between anthropomorphism and agnosticism.

At this point I introduce a distinction which seems to me to be important, the distinction between what I shall call "objective meaning" and "subjective meaning." This distinction might be expressed in other terms of course. But these are the terms which I propose to employ. And I understand them in this way. By "objective meaning" I understand that which is actually referred to by the term in question (that is, the objective reality referred to), and by "subjective meaning" I understand the meaning-content which the term has or can have for the human mind. The distinction should not be understood as a distinction between the true or real meaning of a term and a purely "subjectivist" interpretation. It is a distinction between that which is objectively referred to or "meant" by a term and my understanding or conception of what is referred to. My conception may be inadequate; but it does not necessarily follow that it is false.

If this distinction is applied, for example, to the proposition "God is intelligent," the "objective meaning" of the term "intelligent" is the divine intelligence or intellect itself. And of this I can certainly give no adequate positive account; for the divine intelligence is God Himself, and I have no direct apprehension of God. The "subjective meaning" of the term is its meaning-content in my own mind. Of necessity this is primarily determined for me by my own experience, that is, by my experience of human intelligence. But, seeing that human intelligence as such cannot be predicated of God, I attempt to purify the "subjective meaning." And it is at this point that the line of reflection which I have outlined above comes in. To avoid anthropomorphism of a gross sort the mind takes the way of negation, departing from its starting-point, namely human intelligence, while to avoid agnosticism it returns to its starting-point. It tries to hold together similarity and dissimilarity at the same time. But this is simply one of the characteristics of our understanding of descriptive statements about God. In our language about God we always move within the sphere of analogy. We have no direct natural apprehension of God, and we can have no natural knowledge of Him save by way of reflection on the things which do fall within our experience. Hence the use of analogy. What I have called the " objective meaning " of the terms predicated of God transcends our experience. Hence it cannot be positively and adequately described. All we can do is to attempt to purify the " subjective meaning." And in doing so we are caught inextricably in that interplay of affirmation and negation of which I have spoken.

At this point I want to try a new tack. Earlier in this paper, after mentioning the mediaeval and what I take to be a not uncommon modern approach to the problem of the meaning of the terms predicated of God, I remarked, with reference to the second approach, that I did not think that the problem of meaning could well be treated in entire abstraction from the question of existence, while on the other hand I said that I did not want simply to presuppose the existence of God. And I now want to explain what I had in mind when I said this.

If I am asked what I mean when I say that my dog is intelligent, I mention certain of the animal's habits and activities. But these habits and activities are at the same time the reasons why I call the dog " intelligent." And this suggests that there is a close connection between asking for the meaning of a factual proposition and asking for the reasons why the proposition is enunciated. Perhaps it comes to the same thing.

Now, suppose that I were to say that God is intelligent simply because, given the idea of an existentially dependent world, I think that there is order or system in the world, which I ascribe to a Creator. This would be my reason for saying that God is intelligent. Would it not also be what I mean when I say that God is intelligent, so far as " subjective meaning " is concerned? For if this is my sole reason for saying that God is intelligent, when I think of God as intelligent I necessarily think of Him as the sort of being capable of creating the world-system or order. And in this case the meaning of the proposition that God is intelligent cannot well be treated in entire abstraction from the reasons why I enunciate the proposition. At the same time it is not necessary that the reasons should be objectively valid in order that the proposition should have this meaning. My reasons for saying that the world depends existentially on a Creator, as also my reasons for saying that there is a world-system or order, might be invalid; but they would still govern the subjective meaning of the proposition that God is intelligent. In order to consider the subjective meaning it would not, therefore, be necessary to presuppose dogmatically the existence of God; but at the same time the problem of meaning could not well be treated in entire abstraction from the question of existence.

Now, the reasons for saying that God is intelligent are obviously also the reasons for using one analogy rather than another, for speaking of God according to an analogy based on human intellectual life rather than on an analogy based on the life of, say, a plant. And if the reasons were bad reasons, one would have no objective justification for using the one analogy rather than the other. Further, if the reasons were bad reasons, one would to that extent be without any objective justification for thinking that the term " intelligent," as predicated of God, possessed any " objective meaning." But it would still be true that the reasons governed the " subjective meaning," and that this could not well be analyzed without any reference to the reasons for making the statements in which the term occurred.

And this suggests that it is perhaps preferable to ask why this or that statement about God is made rather than to ask simply what is meant by making the statement in question. For if we ask simply what is meant by some statement about God, we may put the question with some standard or criterion of clarity in our minds which is not applicable in the case. If, for example, an agnostic asks a theologian what is meant by some obscure statement about the Trinity in dogmatic theology, it is unlikely that the theologian will be able to give an answer which is considered by the questioner as being in any way satisfactory; and if the theologian refers to the need for first learning the technical vocabulary and use of terms in dogmatic theology, his remarks are apt to seem like an evasion of the point at issue. But if the theologian is asked why he makes the statement, the questioner should be better prepared to consider sympathetically the answer that the " why " cannot be understood without a previous study of the particular context and realm of discourse.

Furthermore, if one tries substituting the question " Why do you say that? " for the question " What does that statement mean? ", it may become easier to see how a descriptive statement about God can satisfy the minimal requirement for a significant descriptive statement, namely that it should not be compatible with every other conceivable descriptive or factual statement.

That this requirement is a necessary condition seems to me to be clear. For I can hardly be said to know what is meant by a factual statement unless I am able to recognize that something at least is not asserted. It is not required that I should know whether the statement is true or not; nor is it necessary that I should actually advert to what is excluded. But unless I am able to recognize that something is excluded I do not know what is asserted. If someone tells me that Jane is a good cook and I think that this statement is compatible with the statement that Jane habitually prepares food which is unfit for human consumption, no one would say that I understand what is meant by calling Jane a good cook. And if the statement that Jane is a good cook really were compatible with every other conceivable statement about Jane's cooking, it could hardly be said to have any definite meaning. Similarly, if someone tells me that Martha loves her child, and if I think that this statement is compatible with the statement that Martha deliberately starves her child in order that she may have more money for spending on the cinema, I simply do not understand what is meant by saying that Martha loves her child. And if the statement really were compatible with all other possible statements about Martha's attitude towards her child, it would have no definite meaning at all.

Now, it has been argued that a statement like " God loves all human beings " excludes no other factual statement, and that on this account it has no positive meaning. The Christian, it is said, will not allow that any other factual statement counts or can count against the truth of the statement that God loves human beings. Whether one mentions war or disease or the sufferings of children, the Christian will still go on saying that God loves human beings. It is not denied, of course, that it belongs to the Christian faith to say this. But the statement is raised whether the statement that God loves human beings can in these circumstances be said to have any definite meaning at all. It may, indeed, have emotive significance. For the word " love " has meaning in other contexts, and this meaning is so familiar that it can stimulate an emotional response even when it is used in a context where it is deprived of definite significance. But though the statement that God loves human beings may possess emotive significance, any factual significance which it may at first sight appear to possess evaporates under the influence of analysis. If the statement that God loves human beings is compatible with all other statements that one can mention and does not exclude even one of them, it no more possesses a definite meaning than the statement that Jane is a good cook or that Martha loves her child would possess a definite meaning, were it compatible with all other possible statements.

The difficulty is clear, I think. But suppose that one asks the Christian theologian why he makes the statement that God loves human beings. He may answer that he says this because he believes that God offers all men through Christ the grace to attain eternal salvation. So interpreted, the statement is incompatible with, and therefore excludes, the statement that God wills the eternal damnation and misery of all human beings. And this account of the matter serves also to show that the statement as made by the theologian is not, as the line of criticism mentioned seems to suggest, an empirical hypothesis arrived at by adding up the joys and sorrows of life and seeing which is the larger total.

In this paper I have, of course, discussed the problem of the meaning of the terms predicated of God in the setting and in the way that the problem presents itself to me. And I have no hesitation in admitting that the precise way in which the problem presents itself to me is determined to a certain extent by " presuppositions," in the sense of convictions already held. But those responsible for according me the honour of an invitation to address this society[1] obviously did not expect me to pretend to be other than I am or to hold positions other than those which I do in fact hold. So I hardly think that any apology is needed on the score of implicit " presuppositions." Indeed, is it possible to discuss a particular problem of this nature without making some implicit assumptions? It seems to me that some assumptions at least will necessarily be involved in a person's general position in regard to philosophy and religion, in the light of which the problem will present itself to him or her in a certain light and possess whatever degree of interest he or she may find in it.

Mention of religion suggests one final remark. I can quite well understand that the way in which I have discussed this theme may appear highly uncongenial to some minds on the ground that it seems to have nothing to do with what we call " religion." Surely, it may be said, the whole paper is an illustration of the gulf which yawns between the God of the philosophers and the God of Abraham, Isaac and Jacob. But though I can understand this feeling, I should like to point out two things, as far as the Christian is concerned. The Christian recognizes in the human nature of Christ the perfect expression in human terms of the incomprehensible Godhead, and he learns from Christ how to think about God. But at the same time it is certainly no part of the Christian religion to say that God in Himself can be adequately comprehended by the human mind. And that He cannot be so comprehended seems to me to be at once a truth vital to religion, in the sense

---

[1]As stated in the preface, this paper was read to the Moral Sciences Club at Cambridge.

that it prevents us from degrading the idea of God and turning Him into an idol, and a truth which follows necessarily from the fact that our natural knowledge begins with sense-experience. For my own part, I find the thought that the reality, the " objective meaning," far exceeds in richness the reach of our analogical concepts the very reverse of depressing. St. Paul tells us that we see through a glass darkly, and the effect of a little linguistic analysis is to illuminate the truth of this statement.

CHAPTER VIII

THE HUMAN PERSON IN CONTEMPORARY PHILOSOPHY[1]

I

IN the early part of the sixth century A.D. Boethius defined the person as " an individual substance of rational nature " (*rationalis naturae individua substantia*). This definition, which became classical and was adopted by, for example, St. Thomas Aquinas, obviously implies that every human being is a person, since every human being is (to employ the philosophical terms of Boethius) an individual substance of rational nature. If one cannot be more or less of a human being, so far as " substance " is concerned, one cannot be more or less of a person. One may act as a human person ought not to act or in a way unbefitting a human person; one may even lose the normal use of one's reason; but one does not in this way become depersonalized, in the sense of ceasing to be a person. According to St. Thomas, a disembodied soul is not, strictly speaking, a person, since a disembodied soul is no longer a complete human substance; but every complete human substance is always and necessarily a person.

If in the philosophy of Aquinas the emphasis is laid on the human substance, consisting of rational soul and body, the emphasis was laid by Descartes on self-consciousness, on the self-consciousness of the spiritual substance, the whole essence of which is to " think." With Descartes the human person tends to become a self-enclosed consciousness. (I use the word " tends " because one could scarcely state without qualification that the person, for Descartes, is simply a self-enclosed

---

[1]This paper represents a lecture given at the Royal Institute of Philosophy in February, 1949. The section on the personalism of M. Mounier was made the basis of an (unprinted) broadcast talk.

consciousness.) Moreover, it is true to say, I think, that in what one may call, in a very wide sense, the idealist current in modern philosophy the tendency has been to look on consciousness, or rather self-consciousness, as the chief characteristic of personality. In the system of Hegel, for example, we find the progress of mind or spirit consisting predominantly in the advance of self-consciousness, though self-consciousness did not mean for Hegel precisely what it meant for Descartes.

But in the case of the modern thinkers whose philosophies of personality I wish briefly to discuss the emphasis is laid on freedom rather than on self-consciousness. Freedom becomes recognized as the chief characteristic of the human person. Perhaps, however, it would be preferable to say that human freedom is regarded as the efficient cause of personality, or at least as its necessary condition, for personality is looked on as something to be won, something to be created and maintained with effort. In the eyes of certain thinkers one can become a person and one can cease to be a person; one can descend, for example, into being a mere " individual " or a mere " self." I shall return to these distinctions; but I mention them now in order to show that the philosophers whom I propose to discuss do not use the word " person " in precisely the same sense that a thirteenth-century Scholastic would have used it. For them it is not equivalent to " human being "; it frequently has a moral connotation and denotes what a mediaeval philosopher might have thought of as a person who not only exists as a person but also lives and acts and chooses as a person, that is, in a way befitting a person. Aquinas would, I suppose, have regarded it as absurd to talk of a human being becoming or ceasing to be a person or becoming more or less of a person; but if the word " person " is understood in the sense given it by certain groups of modern thinkers, then such a way of talking could hardly be called absurd. It is as well to draw attention to this point, as some terminological confusion may thus be avoided.

The philosophers whose views on personality I want to discuss are the personalists, the existentialists and Professors Lavelle and Le Senne. The personalists in the narrow sense are Emmanuel Mounier, editor of *Esprit*, and his circle; but one can speak, I think, of all these thinkers as belonging to a personalist movement in modern philosophy, even if their views are by no means identical. That such a movement should have arisen is, of course, easily understandable. The personalist type of philosophy tends to recur as a protest or reaction against the recurrent forms of monism or " totalitarian " philosophy which are felt to threaten the dignity, independence and individual value of the human person. One might call it the periodic protest of the personal against the impersonal. It should be added, however, that the use of the words " protest " and " reaction " is not meant to imply that the personalist type of philosophy is simply negative: on the contrary, it involves the positive affirmation of the person and positive interpretations of personality.

2

One scarcely needs to recall to mind the fact that Kierke-gaard, the father of modern existentialism, rejected the Hegelian conception of the Absolute, which seemed to him to reduce the individual human person to a mere moment in the life or self-unfolding of the Absolute. Kierkegaard drew attention to the category of the " individual " and ridiculed the absolute idealist who forgets himself, the individual thinker, and tries to become impersonal, abstract thought or mind. " The thinker who can forget in all his thinking also to think that he is an existing individual, will never explain life. He merely makes an attempt to cease to be a human being, in order to become a book or an objective something, which is possible only for a Munchausen."[1] " If a thinker is so absent-minded as to forget that he is an existing individual, still, absent-mindedness and speculation are not precisely the same thing."[2] I am certainly not prepared to defend up to the hilt Kierkegaard's interpretation of Hegelianism and in any case the reaction against Hegelianism was only one of the factors

[1] *Unscientific Postscript*, p. 85.
[2] *Ibid.*, p. 108.

which influenced him in the formation of his idea of the
" individual." However, regarding Hegelianism, rightly or
wrongly as involving moral irresponsibility and the substitution
of speculation or thinking about the Absolute for a personal
attitude to God, Kierkegaard emphasized the individual's act
of free submission to the moral law and his free acceptance or
choice of his personal relationship to God. A man becomes an
" individual " (contemporary thinkers would say " person ")
by the exercise of his free choice, by freely giving form and
direction to his life.

An analogous development can be observed in the case of
Gabriel Marcel. While discarding empiricism, Marcel found
himself unable, owing to his " sense of the concrete," to accept
the absolutist philosophy of Bradley; and his study of experiences like belief led him to lay emphasis on the individual,
concrete subject, which is neither identical with the empirical
ego nor a moment in the subjectivity of a transcendental ego.
" I can honestly say that I arrived at it (this position) by
myself, for it was before I had read Kierkegaard, in whom I
might so easily have found it."[1] Again, Marcel speaks with
disparagement of what he regards as the modern functionalization of life, the tendency of the individual " to appear both to
himself and to others as an agglomeration of functions."[2]
Marxism functionalizes man in one way, Freudianism in
another; in either case the spiritual freedom and uniqueness
of the human person are overlooked. But the same sort of thing
can be seen, according to Marcel, in ordinary life. A man is
a ticket-puncher on the Underground, for example. That is
his function; and all other functions, sleep, eating, recreation,
and so on, are subordinated to this main social function. In
modern life a man is not primarily a human person; he is an
embodied function, a railwayman, a clerk, a civil servant, a
schoolmaster, a trades-union official, or whatever it may be.
When he retires, he is still regarded and regards himself in
terms of his function; he is a retired civil servant, a retired
doctor, a retired detective.

---

[1] *The Philosophy of Existence*, p. 89.
[2] *Ibid.*, p. 1.

Marcel is a convinced Christian; but a like theme is emphasized by Camus, who is an atheist, and, to a certain extent, by
Sartre. Against this functionalization of life Sartre sets the free
man, creator of values, Marcel the unique human person,
capable of a spiritual relationship to other persons and to
God. For Sartre the human person transcends his " function "
in virtue of his complete freedom; for Marcel he transcends
it in virtue of his " openness." For both philosophers man is
more than an embodied social function, just as he is more than
a mere biological urge.

But, well before Sartre and Camus, Jaspers had spoken of
the " anti-bourgeois " character of the existentialist movement,
that is to say, of its opposition to the crowd mentality and to
superficiality of outlook: in place of man as a mere member of
the social complex existentialism sets the individual human
being, aware of his personal freedom, his potentialities and the
incommunicable and unique in himself. I do not think that
the reason why existentialists tend to dwell, not only on man's
liberty, but also on his fragility as a finite, contingent being
and on the constant menace of " unauthentic existence,"' is
simply a love of the sensational and morbid or a desire to
scandalize the " bourgeois," though this desire may, of course,
be operative. The desire to draw attention to what it actually
means to be an individual human person is also operative,
even if Sartre is inclined to do this by administering a shock
to what is termed, probably unhappily, the " bourgeois "
mentality and spirit.

However, opposition to this spirit is by no means the only
factor which helps to explain the rise of the contemporary
personalist philosophies. There is also the reaction to positivism
to be taken into account. In his preface to the volume of essays
entitled *Personal Idealism* (1902) Henry Sturt spoke not only of
the neglect of personality by some of the leading thinkers of
his day but also of the attack made on it by the naturalists.
" One adversary tells each of us: ' You are a transitory resultant
of physical processes '; and the other: ' You are an unreal
appearance of the Absolute.' Naturalism and Absolutism,
antagonistic as they seem to be, combine in assuring us that

personality is an illusion." The personal idealists and the pragmatists reacted against both positivism and absolutism. For example, the American philosopher Borden Parker Bowne (d. 1910) published a work entitled *Personalism*, in which he developed a personal idealism under the influence of Leibniz and Lotze; and William James, the famous pragmatist, who had been strongly influenced by Charles Renouvier, employed the word "personalism" to express his philosophy. That Kierkegaard and Marcel reacted against absolute idealism has been already noted. It is also true that existentialism expresses a reaction against positivism, a reaction which may be characterized as personalist in a wide sense, even if the existentialist slogan is "existence" rather than "person."[1] The existentialists depict man as existing in a literal sense, as standing out from the background of nature; and they emphasize the difference between the human person and the things of nature which man uses. For the existentialist there is a sharp difference between the *Umwelt*, the world of things or objects, and the *Mitwelt* or world of persons. Thus, in a manner rather reminiscent of Fichte, Heidegger represents the world of things as the field of action of the human person. Again, Jaspers insists on the peculiar character of the human being, on his liberty or power of "self-transcendence," which is the peculiar foundation of human personality. Moreover, both Heidegger and Jaspers, I think, maintain that, since man can raise the problem of being in general, the metaphysical problem, he thereby shows that he transcends the sphere of immediate vital needs and impulses to which the animal is confined. Even Sartre, who has been accused, perhaps with justice, of materialism, makes a sharp distinction between the sphere of the human, the self-conscious, and the non-human.

I have tried to show, in a rather sketchy manner, how the personalist movement, so far as the existentialists are concerned, has arisen; but perhaps I ought to have made it clearer that the theistic current in existentialism emphasizes man's openness

---

[1] With Marcel the idea of person is, I should say, much more in evidence than that of existence. But then Marcel resigns himself to being called, rather than claims to be, an existentialist.

to the Transcendent. This emphasis can be seen in the philosophies of Kierkegaard, Jaspers, Marcel, Berdyaev, and in
certain other philosophies like those of Lavelle and Le Senne,
which can hardly be classed as existentialist philosophies
though they show certain affinities with existentialism. From
the negative point of view one can regard this emphasis on
man's openness to the Transcendent as partly a reaction against
positivism and, in some cases, as partly a reaction against the
reduction of religion to social morality. From the positive point
of view one can regard it as a rediscovery of the Transcendent
through a consideration of personal experience and its implications and, in the case of a thinker like Lavelle, as involved in
the reassertion of a metaphysical philosophy of being.

3

Turning now to the personalists in a more restricted sense
(I refer to Emmanuel Mounier and his circle) one is confronted with the distinction between " individual " and
" person." The term " individual " is used in a pejorative
sense: it is used to denote man considered as a centre or spring
of egotistic desire; the individual is the purely egocentric man.
According to Mounier, the individual is " the diffusion of the
person on the surface of his life and his satisfaction in losing
himself therein."[1] " Matter isolates, cuts off. . . . The individual
is the dissolution of the person in matter." The individual thus
corresponds to the man who stands on the lowest level of the
Spinozistic ethic; he is the man who regards himself as the
only pebble on the beach, the man who, from a practical point
of view, absolutizes his own ego. At least this is one of the
aspects of the " individual " as described by the personalists.
One might also say that he is man considered on the biological
level, the man in whom the biological urge to self-preservation
is all-dominant. He is not unlike the atomistic individual
depicted by Thomas Hobbes, in abstraction from society. The
individual is also the practical materialist, as well as the man
who has no sense of moral vocation: he is the man who has

---

[1] *Révolution personnaliste et communautaire*, p. 67.

no moral or spiritual independence, the superficial man, the man who lives as a mere member of the crowd, who has no inner life of his own. Thus according to Denys de Rougemont the individual is " a man without destiny, a man without vocation or reason for existing, a man from whom the world demands nothing."[1]

The " person," on the other hand, is conceived by the personalists in close connection with the idea of moral vocation. According to M. Mounier, the person is " mastery, choice, formation, conquest of self"; the person can be described according to its three dimensions, " vocation, incarnation, communion." In his personalist *Manifesto* M. Mounier declares that, while no rigorous definition of the person can be given, a " sufficiently rigorous " definition is as follows. " A person is a spiritual being constituted as such by a manner of subsistence and of independence in being; it maintains this subsistence by its adhesion to a hierarchy of values, freely adopted, assimilated and lived, by a responsible self-commitment and by a constant conversion; it thus unifies all its activity in liberty and develops, moreover, by means of creative acts, its own unique vocation."[2] Denys de Rougemont also links together the ideas of person and vocation, interpreting " vocation " in a frankly Christian manner. Person and vocation are possible " only in this unique act of obedience to the order of God which is called the love of the neighbour. . . . Act, presence and commitment, these three words define the person, but also what Jesus Christ commands us to be: the neighbour."[3]

The personalists make a great point of applying their doctrine of personality in the social and political field. In political theory we find two extreme positions. First, there is extreme individualism which makes the private interests and purposes of the individual supreme. I suppose that a representative theory of this type would be that of Herbert Spencer,

---

[1] *Politique de la personne*, p. 56.

[2] *Manifeste au service du personnalisme; Esprit*, October, 1936.

[3] *Politique de la personne*, pp. 52–53. De Rougemont is, incidentally, a Protestant, while Mounier is a Catholic.

according to whom the state exists simply in order to enable individual human beings to pursue their private interests in peace. The individual is everything, and the more the importance of society or of the state is minimized the better. Secondly, there is extreme collectivism or totalitarianism. This may take various concrete forms; but in essence it means the complete subordination of the individual to society and of the private interests of the individual to the interests of the group, whether the group is conceived as the state or the economic class or as the race.

It might appear that we are forced either to choose between these two extremes or to attempt a synthesis. According to the personalists, however, both individualists and collectivists are agreed in looking on man as an " individual," in the personalist sense of the term, and not as a " person." Both individualists and collectivists look on man simply as the biological man, the man who is no more than an individual member of the species. For, according to the personalists, man, considered as an " individual " and not as a person, is no more than a part of a greater whole. Individualism absolutizes the " individual "; it endeavours to make absolutes of the parts at the expense of the whole—just as though an individual cell in an organism were to assert itself at the expense of the organism. Collectivism, on the other hand, represents the organism's reassertion of its own greater value and importance against the undue self-assertion of the cell or the part. In other words, in so far as man is considered simply as an " individual," collectivism or totalitarianism is truer than atomistic individualism. But man is not simply an " individual," a member of the group; he is also a " person," an independent being with a spiritual nature which surmounts the biological and economic levels. It follows that both atomistic individualism and totalitarianism are wrong, since neither allows for the person's moral and spiritual nature and vocation.

The personalists may sometimes tend to give the impression that they mean by " person " and " individual " two separate things: and it might appear to follow from this that personalism is an anti-social philosophy or that it at least belittles objective social institutions like the state. However, the apparent separation of "individual" and person must not be taken literally: as one personalist has explained, they denote two aspects of one human reality, aspects which should not be separated as though they denoted two things nor confused as though there were no real distinction between the aspects. It is not a question of choosing between the aspects but of uniting them hierarchically. The person is a social being; but at the same time he is more than a mere member of the group. He is orientated towards society, but not like a cell in an organism; he is orientated towards a society of persons, and a society of persons is a society of free, morally responsible human beings, no one of which is completely absorbed in or exhausted by his social relations. Mounier insists, therefore, that if personalism is opposed to Marxism this is not because Marxism is anti-individualist but because it tends to interpret man simply in terms of its initial economic categories. For example, the Marxist, as Marxist, is bound to regard religion as escapism or as clerical politics, because he insists in interpreting all levels of experience in terms of his initial politico-economic categories.[1] But, though Mounier rejects Marxism as a system, he regards his own doctrine as the very antithesis of individualism and capitalism. Indeed, his dislike of individualism, coupled with his desire for a concrete, non-utopian attitude towards the contemporary political and social situation, has made him in recent years somewhat surprisingly sympathetic towards the Marxists.[2]

Somewhat similar ideas about "individual" and "person" have been propounded by the Thomist philosopher Jacques Maritain. Accepting the Thomist notion of matter as the principle of individuation he describes individuality as "that which excludes from oneself all other men" and as being "the narrowness of the ego, forever threatened and forever

---

[1] *Equivoques du personnalisme* and *Tâches actuelles d'une pensée d'inspiration personnaliste; Esprit*, February, 1947, and November, 1948.

[2] In attempting to understand the well-meant efforts of certain French Christians to find a bridge between Christianity and Marxism one must, of course, bear in mind the difference between the French and English political scenes, however one may finally evaluate these efforts.

eager to grasp for itself."[1] Personality, on the other hand, is " the subsistence of the spiritual soul communicated to the human composite ": it is interiority to self, but it is character-ized not by grasping for self but by the giving of self in love and freedom. Individual and person are not, however, separate beings; it is absurd to cry " Death to the individual, long live the person !" The human being is a unity, and if, as an individual, he requires society to satisfy his private needs, he requires it, as a person, for " communication," to give or to overflow. The person is, then, a social being, and human society is, or should be, a society of persons. But it can degenerate. " Only yesterday, across the Rhine, we saw to what atrocities a purely biological conception of society can lead." In Maritain's view " bourgeois individualism," " com-munistic anti-individualism " and " totalitarian dictatorial anti-communism and anti-individualism " all disregard the person in some way or other and substitute simply the material individual. When this has been done, the common good must be subordinated to the private, egotistic interests of individuals or individuals must be submerged in the collectivity. The only way of escaping this dilemma is to recognize man as person and society as a society of persons.

<h2 style="text-align:center">4</h2>

It is interesting to notice the hostility felt by personalists like Mounier and Thomists like Maritain for what they call " bourgeois individualism " and, indeed, for the " bourgeois " spirit in general. It seems to me rather difficult to define what is meant by " bourgeois " in this connection; but it is clear that the word is used to denote a certain spirit rather than membership of any precise economic or social class. In this hostility to the " bourgeois " spirit the personalists show an affinity with the existentialists. The existentialists regard man as capable of what they call " authentic existence " but at the same time as ever menaced by the tendency to " unauthentic existence." The personalists regard man as capable of becoming

---

[1] *The Person and the Common Good*, p. 27.

a " person " but at the same time as threatened by the tendency to surrender either to egocentric individualism or to submersion in the totality. But though there are affinities between personalism and existentialism, there are also considerable differences. In the latter one can discern a tendency to belittle objective social institutions. It can hardly be denied, I think, that in Kierkegaard's philosophy there is a marked individualist trend, and M. Sartre has had to defend his doctrine against the charge of being anti-social. Jaspers and Marcel certainly lay great emphasis on " communication," but one receives the impression, perhaps wrongly, that this means for them primarily an intimate relationship between kindred souls. The personalists, however, emphasize the person's orientation towards society; and some of them appear to go as far as they can with the collectivists, stopping short at the point at which the person's spiritual nature is either obscured or denied. Perhaps one reason for this difference between existentialists and personalists is, as M. Mounier has suggested, that the former tend to describe authentic existence in negative terms. It involves a tearing oneself away from the mentality of the crowd, a separation, a refusal. For the personalists, however, the person and the society of persons are taken as the positive standard: the " individual " is simply a degraded condition of the person, just as the totalitarian state is a degraded form of the true state.

Both personalists and existentialists possess a sense of the dramatic aspects of man's existence, the former insisting that personality, the latter that authentic existence is something constantly to be won and maintained, that it is for ever threatened. The theme of self-creating is common to them both; and " self-creating " is the achievement of freedom. As I said earlier in this paper, in the contemporary theories of man which I am discussing there has been a shift of emphasis from self-consciousness to freedom as the chief characteristic of personality. (I do not mean to imply, of course, that the thinkers in question envisage freedom without self-consciousness.) I have already indicated some reasons for this change of emphasis. One might go on to recall the heralds of this change within the field of philosophic thought. One could recall, for instance, Fichte's insistence on freedom or Maine de Biran's substitution of *Volo, ergo sum* for Descartes' *Cogito, ergo sum*; one could recall the doctrines of philosophers like Ravaisson, Guyau, Boutroux or Bergson. The last-mentioned actually spoke of " self-creating." But I wish rather to keep to the idea of freedom as found in the philosophies of the existentialists, the personalists and thinkers like Lavelle and Le Senne. I will say at once that in my opinion the main division is between those who look on freedom as orientated and on man as having a moral and spiritual vocation and those who deny objective values and who refuse to recognize in freedom any teleological function. This division cuts across the lines of demarcation between personalists and existentialists. For example, Marcel would have to be grouped with Mounier, and also with Lavelle and Le Senne, whereas Sartre would fall outside this group.

5

I am very doubtful if any strict definition of freedom can be given which would give a clear idea of it to anyone who was not already experimentally acquainted with it. One might, of course, describe the conditions of freedom, or some of them, and one might say what freedom is not; but it would seem that a definition of freedom must either presuppose some awareness of freedom or misrepresent it by defining it in terms of what it is not. However, most upholders of human freedom speak as though it is something which man is capable of exercising, not as something which characterizes all man's actions or as something which is identical with man. But M. Sartre assures us that freedom is the being of man. His actual words are difficult to interpret. " Freedom is not *a* being: it is the being of man, that is to say, his not-being."[1] Self-consciousness, which, as I have said, M. Sartre, under Cartesian influence, strongly emphasizes, means presence to oneself; therefore distance from oneself. But what separates oneself from oneself is nothing. Man, as *pour-soi*, perpetually

[1] *L'Être et le Néant*, p. 516.

" secretes " his own nothingness; by his very structure he is perpetually torn away, as it were, from what he was and what he is: he is a perpetual movement away from what he was to what he will be. We can never say of him, without qualification, that he *is*; he is perpetually constrained to make himself: he is *projet*. Now, freedom is precisely the nothingness which is at the heart of man and which " constrains the human reality to *make* itself, instead of *being*." " For man, to be is to choose oneself: nothing comes to him either from within or from without that he can receive or accept. He is entirely and helplessly abandoned to the insupportable necessity of making himself be, even down to the least detail."[1] So far as one can make sense of these assertions, it appears that Sartre regards freedom as identical with man's being (or the " not-being " which is his being), that it is unconditioned and that it extends to all man's acts. It is understandable that Marcel accuses Sartre of debasing and cheapening freedom by flooding the market with it.[2] M. Sartre speaks of an original gushing-up (*jaillissement*) of freedom in each human being, an initial free determination of the man's ultimate direction of will. " It is, then, the determination of my ultimate purposes which characterizes my being and which is identical with the original gushing-up of my freedom."[3] Values are not recognized by man but determined by him: I am the being by whom values exist. Freedom is thus unorientated, in the sense that there is no objective value correlative to the human will. This point of view is perhaps not altogether consistent with what Sartre has to say on " authentic existence," which seems to be presented as something objectively valuable. In any case, Sartre's doctrine of freedom, taken in itself, seems to me to be nihilistic in character and to make of the human person a kind of monster in the world of being, in the sense in which a grossly deformed human being is called a " monster." The human person is " the baseless basis of values."[4]

---

[1] *L'Être et le Néant*, p. 520.
[2] *The Philosophy of Existence*, p. 63.
[3] *L'Être et le Néant*, p. 520.
[4] *Ibid.*, p. 76.

Marcel takes a different line. He distinguishes the ego (*le moi*) or self-enclosed consciousness, the " individual," that is, man considered simply as a member of the anonymous " one " (*l'on*) from the person. The person is characterized by commitment. " I affirm myself as a person in the measure that I assume the responsibility of what I do and what I say. But before whom am I or before whom do I recognize myself as responsible? . . . both before myself *and* before others; this conjunction is characteristic of personal commitment."[1] Effective commitment is an act of freedom; but though the ideas of freedom and commitment are emphasized by both Marcel and Sartre, the former does not regard freedom as irresponsible or as total. Although the person realizes himself as person only in commitment (in a work, an action, in the course of a life), it belongs to the essence of personality not to be exhausted in any one particular commitment, because it participates in Being, its beginning and end.[2] In other words, personal freedom is an orientated freedom, orientated towards others and, finally, to God: it is founded in Being and is orientated to Being. For Marcel, the ideas of person, commitment, community, Being, go together and must be apprehended together. Sartre seems to be, to all intents and purposes, a materialist: at least his philosophy seems to be deeply influenced by the materialism of the French Enlightenment, in so far as the latter was materialistic in spirit: but Marcel interprets personality in the light of a philosophy of spiritual being. On this point he is at one with Mounier. There is, indeed, a difference between Marcel's philosophy and personalism in the narrow sense; but it seems to me to be a difference in the respective interests of the philosophers concerned rather than in their actual tenets. The personalists concern themselves extensively with problems arising out of the present conditions of society, particularly with the relation between the person and the common good, whereas Marcel is concerned rather to show how one " becomes " a person by transcending one's self-enclosedness in love for other persons and in the free

[1]*Homo viator*, p. 26.

[2]*Ibid.*, pp. 32–33.

acceptance of a personal relationship to God. If Marcel does not interest himself particularly in the political problem, this is not because the person, as conceived by him, is self-enclosed.

Marcel is a Catholic; and one may receive the impression from reading his books that he presupposes Christian doctrine. As a matter of fact, however, he does not presuppose it in the sense of explicitly assuming its truth; and he had developed the main line of his thought before he became a Christian. On the other hand, he insists that Christianity is an historical datum (which is obviously true) and that " it favours the development of certain ideas which we might not have conceived without it."[1] We can no more be expected, he says, to reason today as if there is no such historical datum as Christianity than we can be expected to pretend, when discussing the theory of knowledge, that there have not been some centuries of positive science. But, just as positive science does not supply a philosophical theory of knowledge, though it may act as a fertilizing principle, so Christianity, considered as an historical datum, may act as a fertilizing principle in regard to certain lines of thought, even though it does not supply the philosophical ideas and theories themselves.

There are other philosophers, however, who are, in certain respects, what one might call trenchantly Christian. Thus the late Russian philosopher Nicholas Berdyaev, who looked upon himself as a true existentialist, declared not only that " spirit is freedom," but also that " apart from Christianity there is no freedom, and determinism is supreme."[2] For Berdyaev, freedom is not natural to man; it is something to be won; and it is to be won only by entering into an order of being which is superior to the natural order. I do not agree with Berdyaev's statement that " apart from Christianity there is no freedom " (unless " freedom " is understood in a very special sense); but I have mentioned him in connection with Marcel in order to illustrate the religious orientation of a large section of personalist thought. This religious direction of thought is, I think, only to be expected. An anti-positivist

---

[1] *The Philosophy of Existence*, p. 30.
[2] *Freedom and the Spirit*, pp. 117 and 121.

movement tends, by its natural impetus, to reintroduce a metaphysic; and, in particular, to reintroduce the idea of transcendent being. One can see this happening not only in the case of someone who, like Marcel, is actually a Christian, but also in the case of Karl Jaspers. (No doubt exceptions can be found; M. Sartre is one of them; but the question might be raised, of course, how far M. Sartre has really freed himself from positivism.) But in an anti-positivist philosophy which proceeds to transcendent being not so much by way of metaphysical argument in the traditional sense as through consideration of the " openness " and free commitment of the person the idea of transcendent being will naturally tend to become the concrete idea of God rather than to remain a purely abstract notion. It is true that Jaspers has stressed the tension between religion and philosophy; but the way in which he speaks about the Transcendent suggests a religious attitude far more than the attitude of purely abstract thought. This is inevitable in view of the fact that, for Jaspers, the apprehension of the Transcendent is a matter of personal faith, not of " objective " thought. It may be " philosophic faith "; but it is faith of a kind; it is not the sort of thinking whereby Aristotle concluded to the existence of an unmoved mover. There is nothing to be surprised at, then, in the fact that Jaspers now seems to speak habitually of " God."

6

This religious orientation of thought is implicit also in the philosophies of two French thinkers, Lavelle and Le Senne, who are both, I think, professors at the Collège de France. Lavelle emphasizes freedom as the characteristic of the person: it is " the heart of myself and the act by which I make myself . . .":[1] it is creative initiative or the power of creative initiative. But freedom is something received. I am responsible for the exercise of freedom; but a potentiality for this creative initiative is presupposed, and it is something given, received. Further, freedom is orientated. First of all, it is orientated to

---

[1] *De l'Acte*, p. 189.

society, that is, a society of persons. Passing over the metaphysical reasons for the existence of a plurality of persons, one may mention Lavelle's argument, which reminds one somewhat of Fichte's teaching, that the existence of a moral order demands the existence of a plurality of persons or free beings. " Duty cannot be fully realized by any one of them, but only by all."[1] Moreover, " I have need of other freedoms because my freedom can take as object only another freedom. We are well aware that it is truly exercised only in presence of a free being and not at all in presence of a thing. It is the encounter with a freedom which is not mine that obliges my freedom to question itself, to become deeper and even to actualize itself."[2] But though different freedoms or free beings are discontinuous and, in a sense, mutually exclusive, they enjoy a mutual solidarity in virtue of their common relation to " pure Act," the transcendent free Being. Freedom is, then, by its very nature, directed towards the creation of a society of persons; and, beyond the society of persons, it reaches out to the plenitude of being, to pure Act or, to use a more concrete term, to God.

Lavelle's doctrine of the person and of human freedom is thus dependent on his metaphysic of being. It would not be relevant to the theme of this paper, were I to discuss this metaphysic; but it is as well to draw attention to its primacy in Lavelle's thought, in view of its influence in determining the character of his interpretation of human personality and freedom. Whereas in the philosophy of Sartre the " human reality " is an unexplained *monstrum*, in that of Lavelle human freedom is interpreted as a " participation " in infinite creative freedom. Therefore, while for Sartre freedom is neither received nor directed towards any objective value, for Lavelle it is received and also orientated. In other words, the philosophy of Lavelle belongs to what one may call, in a generously wide sense, the Platonic metaphysical tradition.

If Lavelle lays emphasis on the two ideas of being and of participation, Le Senne emphasizes the idea of objective

---

[1] *De l'Acte*, p. 185.
[2] *Ibid.*

values. Personality is " neither a substance, or a state, nor a category; it is existence, as it is formed by the double cogito, hindered by obstacles, elevating itself by and towards value."[1] According to Le Senne, personality grows in proportion as the self apprehends or discovers value and in proportion as it freely realizes value. " In the measure that value triumphs " consciousness " personalizes itself."[2] In other words, personality is something to be won; it grows together with the apprehension and realization of value, in proportion, that is to say, as the moral consciousness overcomes the obstacles to its discovery of value and to its free moral activity. One can speak, then, of the existence of personality as an existence " in suspense "; it exists only on condition that it constantly makes itself, though it cannot complete itself in such a way that no further effort is needed in order to maintain itself.[3] It thus involves constant effort, and a person who ceases to make any effort towards further self-personalization " immediately ceases to make any effort at all."[4] Moreover, this effort must take the form not merely of moral self-culture but also of realizing in the objective world particular intentions based on the intuition of value. Le Senne thus interprets personality in terms of moral vocation. But he does not remain within the sphere of determinate values, for he insists that determinate values depend on the principle or ground of value, the good as such or value as such. " Bradley has shown definitively that every judgment has reference to the Absolute. The Absolute is value."[5] Moral experience and moral achievement are the ways in which men experience " the presence and the activity of God," value being " the existential relation between God and myself."[6]

---

[1]*Obstacle et Valeur*, p. 321. The " double cogito " refers to the *moi public* and the *moi intime*.

[2]*Ibid.*, p. 322.

[3]*Obstacle et Valeur*, p. 321.

[4]*Traité de morale générale*, p. 481.

[5]*Obstacle et Valeur*, p. 194.

[6]*Ibid.*, pp. 345 and 344.

7

I am only too well aware that some of the ideas I have mentioned must appear extremely vague and lacking in precision. On some occasions, of course, the immediate difficulty is predominantly terminological in character. For example, if a writer speaks of " freedoms " confronting one another he is obviously speaking of persons considered as free. At other times, however, it is really very difficult to understand precisely what meaning a given statement is intended to convey; and I can well imagine some British philosophers rejecting many of the theories which I have narrated as meaningless nonsense. But I think that it would be a mistake to allow one's natural impatience with vague or unfamiliar language to lead one into rejecting the modern Continental philosophers unheard, that is, without one's making any real attempt to understand what they are getting at. Of course, it is possible to adopt a criterion of significance which will exclude, from the outset, a great many of the characteristic utterances of these Continental philosophers from the rank of significant propositions; but does this procedure amount to much more in the end than showing that, if one philosophy is true, another philosophy is false, in so far as it differs from or is opposed to the first? If one is willing to investigate what Mounier, for example, means by his distinction between " individual " and " person " and if one is content to ask whether there is anything in human experience which is relevant to the formation of these ideas, I think that one will see that these ideas are not devoid of significance. It might, indeed, be preferable not to make this dichotomy between " individual " and " person "; but it could hardly be maintained, I think, that there are no types of human behaviour which are relevant to the formation of the ideas expressed by these words.

One should also take into account the possibility that the philosophers whom I have discussed find difficulty in discovering appropriate words and phrases for certain ideas rather than that they are merely playing with words. It may be said that, if they cannot express their ideas linguistically, they have no ideas. But I am doubtful whether the conclusion necessarily follows. Unless these thinkers wish to invent words, they will have to use words already in existence. But terms already in use have an already accepted meaning or set of meanings. To invent new terms, just as the scientist may invent terms like " photon " or " positron," would have serious disadvantages and would not be of any great utility, for the philosopher would then have to go on to explain what he meant by these terms, unless he were prepared to leave this task to future commentators. But if the philosopher, eschewing the invention of new terms, tries to draw attention, by means of terms already in use, to something which he thinks has not been expressed before, adequately at least, his statements will inevitably be involved in a certain vagueness or ambiguity. " Existence," for example, as commonly understood, does not mean what the existentialist means by it; nor has the term " individual," as commonly employed, always the precise pejorative sense given it by the personalist. In this case the philosopher might perhaps be expected to explain as carefully as possible the precise sense in which he is using a word which is ordinarily used to denote something else. Unfortunately this is not always done. When it is not done, one can either decline to make the effort to distil his meaning, because one has other things to do or because one thinks, for reasons good or bad, that the effort so expended will not be adequately recompensed, or one can set oneself patiently to discover the intended meaning. If one can discover no meaning, then one may decide that the meaning is " beyond one " or one may decide that the words have no meaning. But to decide from the outset that there is no discoverable meaning, simply because the writer uses more or less familiar words in an unfamiliar sense, would be a rather high-handed procedure.

These reflections are not meant to indicate that I feel in a position to elucidate all the statements of these Continental thinkers; still less that I agree with all of them. It would scarcely be possible to agree at the same time with both Marcel and Sartre, for example. But I think that the general direction of thought in what I have called the personalist movement (including, that is to say, the existentialists) is fairly clear. The philosophers of this movement endeavour to draw attention to the particular aspects of the human personality which seem to them to differentiate it most sharply from all that is non-personal. All of them, as we have seen, agree in stressing freedom, the person's free "self-creating," and most of them stress also the person's orientation towards other persons, his need of other persons not only in order to receive but also in order to communicate or give. To deny that orientation in favour of atomistic individualism is to neglect one of the most important aspects of man. On the other hand, as the personalists and at any rate the theistic existentialists (including Jaspers) would maintain, the human person's potentialities are not exhausted in his social relationship; he can discover and accept his relationship to the Transcendent, showing thereby that he is more than a mere member of society, a mere part of a whole. It follows that to interpret the person as a mere part of the state or of the race or of the class or even of humanity is to misinterpret him.

One may or may not agree with such statements; but I do not think that they are meaningless or even that they are very difficult to understand. I would also suggest that they are not without some practical relevance. It is always open to man, of course, to analyze himself into a series of fleeting phenomena; but the picture suggested by such a procedure is, to my mind, somewhat comical.

CHAPTER IX

EXISTENTIALISM: INTRODUCTORY

THE term "existentialism" does not connote any one particular philosophical system. It might indeed be convenient to reserve the name for the philosophy of M. Sartre, since he has explicitly called it "existentialism," and to refuse it, for example, to the philosophy of Gabriel Marcel who, after having once resigned himself to being called an existentialist, has now repudiated the title. This procedure would also have the advantage of allowing for the fact that Martin Heidegger has dissociated himself from M. Sartre and has drawn attention to the differences between their respective philosophies. Further, one has to make a distinction between the *Existenzphilosophie* of Karl Jaspers and the *Existenzialphilosophie* of Heidegger; and this distinction tends to be slurred over if one applies the term "existentialism" indiscriminately to both philosophies.

But I cannot in these lectures reserve the term "existentialism" for the philosophy of Sartre. You will quite rightly expect me to talk about those philosophers who are generally called "existentialists." And they certainly include not only Sartre but also Kierkegaard, Jaspers, Heidegger and Marcel. There are other writers too who might well be included, such as Abbagnano, Merleau-Ponty, Berdyaev and Camus, though the only one of these of whom I propose to say anything much is Camus. In other words, I intend to take the conventional line of talking about those philosophers who are customarily discussed in books about existentialism. I certainly do not intend to go back to Socrates, or even to St. Augustine; and still less do I propose to discuss Thomism which, according to some Thomists, is the true existentialism. For I take it that what you expect from me is a discussion of the modern existentialist movement.

Now, I have said that there are very considerable differences between the various philosophies which are customarily classed as existentialist philosophies. And I hope that some of these differences will become clear when I deal in turn with individual thinkers. But if the habit of grouping these different philosophies together and treating them as members of a class is not simply the fruit of misunderstanding and misinterpretation but has an objective justification in the nature of these philosophies, there must be, besides differences, some common elements. And this is the subject which I wish first to discuss. It might be more natural to discuss the elements which these philosophies have in common only after describing their various contents; but if there is such a thing as an existentialist movement in modern philosophy, of which these various systems are different products, it is perhaps possible, and even desirable, to begin by discussing some common impulses and themes.

In the first place I do not think that we can successfully define and mark off existentialism, considered as a general movement, in terms of a particular abstract proposition such as " existence precedes essence." It is quite true that M. Sartre has stated categorically that this is the chief tenet of existentialism and that it is common to all existentialist philosophies. But the question arises, What is meant by the proposition? If it meant simply that nothing can belong to any class or have any characteristics unless it exists, it would be accepted by many philosophers who are not existentialists. Anyone who is convinced that existence is not a predicate in the sense in which " white " is a predicate would accept it. But Sartre does not intend the proposition to be understood simply in this sense. He connects it with atheism, by declaring that it means, or that part of its meaning is, that there are no eternal essences, present as " ideas " in the mind of God, which precede the existence of things. He also appears to mean that there are no objective essences at all, essences being determined in terms of human interest and choice. And on both counts the proposition would be rejected by Gabriel Marcel. If Marcel stresses. the primacy of the existential, he means, I think, for example, that my insertion into the world through my body or my participation in being through " incarnation " is an existing and lived insertion or participation before I objectify the distinct concepts of " ego " and body, so that it is a mistake to start with the idea or " essence " of, say, the body, and then try to prove theoretically that there is something corresponding to it, as though without such a proof the matter would be doubtful. Marcel certainly does not deny that there are common structures or " essences " which are discovered, and not simply invented or constructed by the mind. Again, according to Heidegger, what Sartre does is simply to reverse the proposition which might have been enunciated by Plato, namely that essence precedes existence, and this piece of metaphysics has nothing to do with his own, that is Heidegger's, system. Further, the proposition " existence precedes essence," as understood by Sartre, would be acceptable neither to Kierkegaard nor to Jaspers. Of course, if the proposition is taken to mean that man has no character given from the beginning which determines his actions but that he is free, it would serve to distinguish existentialism from the doctrine of character-determinism. But it would not serve to distinguish existentialism from other philosophies which also deny determinism, unless, indeed, it is given some more precise sense. And the more precise the meaning which is given it, the closer will be the connection between the proposition and some particular brand of existentialism.

It seems to me very difficult, therefore, to find any set of clearly defined propositions or theses which will serve to mark off existentialism from all other forms of philosophy. But at the same time it may be possible to give some general considerations which will serve to indicate the spirit and common inspiration of the movement, without, however, enabling us to define existentialism in any strict sense of " define " and without these considerations being equally applicable to every writer who is generally classed as an existentialist.

In his work *Existentialism from Within* (Routledge and Kegan Paul, 1953) Dr. E. L. Allen describes existentialism as an attempt to philosophize from the standpoint of the actor rather than, as has been customary, from the standpoint of the spectator. And I should like to consider for a few moments whether this distinction will help us to understand existentialism.

The general nature of the distinction can, I think, be easily elucidated with the aid of examples. The attitude of Aristotle, as manifested in the esoteric or pedagogical works, is predominantly the impersonal attitude of the scientist. He is the spectator of the world, and he analyzes, for instance, the different senses in which the word cause (*aitia*) can be used, the basic categories exemplified in things and the different levels of life and of psychical activity. True, another attitude shows itself at times, particularly in the fragments of the exoteric works and even in certain passages of the esoteric writings; but for the most part he is the impersonal analyst and spectator. He writes more as a representative of " Mind " than as the concrete Aristotle, concerned with personal problems arising out of his own inner struggles to shape the course of his life. Kierkegaard, on the contrary, philosophizes in function of his own personal problems. Philosophy and biography go together in the sense that the former arises in response to personal problems in which Kierkegaard is involved and which are solved on the existential level, by choice, rather than simply on the abstract and theoretical level. He does not stand back from problems as an impersonal analyst and spectator; he grapples with them as one who is involved in them with his whole being; they are for him not merely objects of intellectual curiosity but rather matters of vital concern which he cannot regard with a purely detached interest. He is not spectator, but actor.

But though there is no great difficulty in seeing there is a real distinction between the philosophical attitude of an Aristotle and that of a Kierkegaard, it is not at all so easy to define or to describe accurately the spectator-actor distinction. We cannot very well make it a matter simply of the presence or absence of passionate interest. It is conceivable, for instance, that Hegel was in some sense passionately interested in working out the details of the dialectic. Yet Hegel is generally considered, and was certainly considered by Kierkegaard, to be the very antithesis of an existential thinker. Nor is it easy to define the distinction simply in terms of certain problems. Take, for example, the problem of human immortality. It is possible for a man to consider this problem in a very detached manner. He examines the evidence for and against human immortality; but he feels perhaps that the answer is of little importance to him personally. He considers the problem in much the same way as he might consider a problem in pure mathematics or in linguistics. Another man, however, may feel that the solution of the problem is of vital concern to him as an individual human being and that the value of his life and of his moral struggles is at stake. The problem is in a sense the same for both men. But the former is detached and adopts the attitude of the spectator, whereas the latter is not detached but involved and adopts the standpoint of the actor. It may be said, of course, that no philosophy is possible without detachment. Philosophizing inevitably involves standing back from the sphere of immediate experience; it involves reflection, communication, or at least communicability, and so universalization. In so far as Kierkegaard philosophizes, he passes inevitably from the existential level to the level of reflection, and to this extent he becomes spectator. This seems to me to be true. But the distinction with which we are concerned is not a distinction between actor and spectator: it is a distinction between philosophizing from the standpoint of a spectator and philosophizing from the standpoint of an actor. And the contention with which we are concerned is that existentialism is an attempt to philosophize from the standpoint of the actor rather than from that of the spectator. This presumably means several things. First of all it means that the problem considered by the philosopher presents itself to him as one which arises out of his own personal existence as an individual human being who freely shapes his destiny but who seeks clarification in order to be able to do so. Secondly it means, I think, that the problem is of vital concern to him because he is a human being, and not simply as a result of accidental circumstances. It might be, for instance, a matter of vital concern to a Soviet scientist to solve a scientific problem which he had been appointed to solve; but however vital it may be for his future welfare and happiness to discover the solution of this scientific problem, the problem, considered in itself, is not one which arises out of and owes its importance simply to the fact that he is an individual free human being. Thirdly, the attempt to philosophize from the standpoint of an actor demands that one does not attempt to solve the problem by forgetting oneself and one's personal involvement by trying to adopt, for instance, the standpoint of the Absolute for which individual human beings are conceived as being of no importance.

I cannot say that I am satisfied with this elucidation of the distinction. But I do not wish to spend time on further refinements. I prefer to ask whether we can say that the existentialists really do attempt to philosophize from the standpoint of the actor.

We can say, I think, of both Kierkegaard and Marcel, that they are personal thinkers, in the sense that their reflection springs from personal experience which possesses for them a profound significance and importance and that they are both concerned primarily with problems in which they feel themselves to be personally involved. I have already remarked on the connection between biography and philosophy in the case of Kierkegaard. And it is true, I think, of Marcel that his philosophy is the expression of, or rather that it is part and parcel of, his own spiritual itinerary. As we will see later, he makes an explicit distinction between a " problem " on the one hand, in which the being of the questioner is not involved, and a " mystery " on the other, which requires, not the application of a universal technical method in a purely detached manner, but rather reflective penetration of data which involve the being of the questioner himself. Marcel tries, for example, to penetrate the metaphysical significance of love or hope from within the experience itself rather than by treating it in the detached " objective " manner that a psychoanalyst might. In other words, he tries to combine the immediacy of experience with philosophical reflection. And the themes on which he chooses to reflect are clearly those which are of importance and significance to him in his own spiritual life. He is, of course, a philosopher; and, as such, he advances on to the plane of reflection and of universality. At the same time he is a personal thinker, and it can be said, I think, that he attempts to philosophize from the standpoint of the actor, provided that we make allowance for the fact that the contemplative and reflective attitude of the metaphysician is much more evident in his case than it is in that of Kierkegaard.

When, however, we turn to Jaspers and Sartre, the connection between man and philosophy is not at all so evident. I do not for a moment wish to say that it is absent; but it seems to me that it is not at all so evident as in the case of Kierkegaard and Marcel, especially the former. The element of systematization, for example possesses an importance which it does not have for Kierkegaard. The latter was a passionate personal thinker, and it is only with difficulty, if at all, that one can imagine him occupying a university chair of philosophy. Jaspers on the contrary is very much the professor of philosophy. Yet we find both Jaspers and Sartre, in spite of the striking differences between their philosophies, united in their concern to reveal to man what he is and what the concrete possibilities of human choice are, with a view to illuminating and promoting authentic choice. And thus even if they do not philosophize from the standpoint of the actor in the same way that Kierkegaard does, their concern with the illumination and promotion of authentic choice shows that they are concerned with the actor and not simply with satisfying the intellectual curiosity of the spectator.

As for Heidegger, his philosophizing would seem to be that of the spectator rather than that of the actor if we go by his declared intentions in *Sein und Zeit*. For he is concerned with the construction of an ontology, with examining and solving the problem of Being, or of the meaning of Being; and he insists that the existential analysis of man is a preliminary stage in the treatment of the general ontological problem. Again, his analysis of, for instance, authentic and unauthentic choice is not meant to be an exhortation to anyone to choose and act in a particular way. It may appear, therefore, that to include Heidegger among the existentialists is simply to surrender to a convention based on misunderstanding and misinterpretation. However, even though he claims to be an ontologist and not an existentialist, and even though we may admit this is in fact his intention, it can hardly be denied that in his choice of themes and in his manner of treating them Heidegger gives ample ground for the common view of his philosophy. There seems to me to be in him a forcing of the inspiration of the existentialist movement into the framework and scope of an ontological inquiry, and that while this makes it necessary to distinguish carefully between his philosophy and that of Jaspers, who has a much closer relation to Kierkegaard, it also justifies his inclusion in any general examination of the existentialist current of thought. I very much doubt whether Heidegger's protestations will serve, even in the future, to secure his dissociation from the existentialists. What is more likely, as it appears to me, is that historians will see in his philosophy a marriage, as it were, between existentialism, which is found at its purest in a thinker like Kierkegaard, with the classical ontological theme of inquiry into Being. However, we may admit that as far as philosophizing from the standpoint of an actor is concerned, this belongs more to the popular Heidegger, that is, the view of Heidegger's philosophy which has been most influential and against which he has protested, than to Heidegger as he conceives himself to be.

I have mentioned that Jaspers, for example, is concerned with revealing the possibilities of human choice and with promoting authentic choice. And I have alluded to themes in Heidegger's philosophy which link him with existentialism. I wish, therefore, to omit further consideration of the actor-spectator distinction and to inquire whether there are any themes or subjects for reflection which can be said to be common to the existentialists.

It is often said that the existentialists are primarily concerned with man. A critic can, of course, immediately object that this statement does not fit the facts. It will not, for instance, fit the case of Heidegger who, as we have seen, set out to take up afresh the problem of the meaning of Being (das Sein), so that for him the ontological problem of Being is more central than any discussion of man. Nor, it may be objected, will the statement fit the case of Jaspers who has explicitly declared that the philosophy of the present day is, like that of former times, concerned with Being. Further, even though it may fit Marcel to some extent, it is apt to give a wrong impression of his philosophy; for it suggests that he offers an anthropocentric philosophy to which metaphysics is alien. And such criticism ought, indeed, to be made; for it brings out important facts which the generalization, namely the statement that the existentialists are primarily concerned with man, is apt to slur over or conceal from view. Yet it remains true that even if the existential analysis of man is subordinated by Heidegger to the investigation of the meaning of Being, it occupies such an important and prominent place in his philosophy that it has inevitably attracted to itself the attention of readers. And in so far as he qualifies for inclusion in the ranks of the existentialists, it is this analysis of man which justifies his inclusion. As for Jaspers, though it is true in a sense that his philosophy centres round the affirmation of the Transcendent, the accent is placed on human choice and on man's realization of his own possibilities or potentialities. Again, it is not unreasonable to say that Marcel's thought centres round the human person; round the person as related to other persons and to God, it is true, but still round the human person. Marcel is certainly not concerned with analyzing, for example, the most general categories exemplified in things: he does not pursue the type of ontological reflection carried on by Aristotle in the ancient world or by Nicolai Hartmann in the present century. Nor does Heidegger; nor does Jaspers. Finally, when we come to writers like Sartre and Camus, it is clear, I think, that their philosophies centre round man.

In my opinion, therefore, the statement that the existentialists are primarily concerned with man can be allowed to stand, provided that we recognize that it is a generalization which labours under the defects which so often attend on generalizations. But it is important to understand what is meant by saying that the existentialists are concerned with man. And in the first place they are not concerned with man in so far as he can be treated as an object like any other object and studied with the aid of scientific method. Man can turn himself into an object and consider himself as one kind of thing among other types of things which together form what we call the world and each of which can be studied from different points of view in the impersonal and objective spirit of the scientist. Man can study himself from, for example, the point of view of the biochemist or of the anatomist or of the psychologist or of the sociologist. But though man can objectify himself, he is also subject, a fact which is shown, indeed, by his very capacity to objectify himself. And it is with man as subject that the existentialists are concerned.

But here again misunderstanding is possible. For to say that the existentialists are concerned with man as subject may suggest that they are concerned with the self-enclosed human ego. And this would be to give a false impression. For the existentialists certainly have this in common that for them the primary datum is man-in-the-world and not the self-enclosed ego of Descartes. Heidegger has said, with reference to the Cartesian problem of the existence of the external world and of other minds, that the scandal is not that no demonstrative proofs have been offered but rather that they were ever thought to be required (*Sein und Zeit*, I, pp. 124–25). Marcel avoids the gulf between the self-enclosed consciousness of Descartes and the external world by insisting on the primary fact of *incarnation*, embodiment, and by concentrating on those spiritual activities of man such as hope and love and fidelity which involve the relationship of person to person and reveal the subject as essentially " open," not self-enclosed. Sartre, it is true, has declared that his starting-point is subjectivity and that the first and basic truth is the *Cogito, la verité absolue de la conscience s'atteignant elle-même* (*L'existentialisme est un humanisme*, pp. 63–64). But he goes on to say that *Par le je pense, contrairement à la philosophie de Descartes, contrairement à la philosophie de Kant, nous nous atteignons nous-mêmes en face de l'autre, et l'autre est aussi certain pour nous que nous-mêmes* (*ibid.*, p. 66). Man, therefore, as considered by the existentialists, is the concrete human person, not an abstract epistemological subject. But at the same time he is considered under a particular aspect, namely as a free, self-creating and self-transcending subject.

By using the terms " self-creating " and " self-transcending " I do not mean to imply that according to the existentialists a man brings himself into existence in the sense in which we speak of God creating finite things or that he can get outside of his own skin and become something other than man. Man creates himself in the sense that what he becomes depends on his freedom, on his choices. And man transcends himself in the sense (though not exclusively) that, as long as he lives, he cannot be identified with his past. Through the exercise of freedom he transcends the past, the already-made. True, it might also be said of a tree that it transcends its past, in virtue of the fact that it develops and changes. But in the case of the tree its past, together with other factors beyond the tree's control, determine its future. In a sense its future is something already given. Man, however, is capable of freely transcending the weight of the past. And, at least for Jaspers and Marcel, man is also the self-transcending subject in the sense that he can not only enter the sphere of personal communication with other human beings but also affirm his relationship with the Transcendent, that is, with God.

But it would be a mistake to suppose that the existentialists are concerned simply with an academic analysis of man as free, analogous to the scientific analysis performed, for example, by the physiologist. Rather do they try to illuminate human freedom and its implications with a view to promoting authentic choice. Kierkegaard drew attention to what it means to be an existing individual, above all to what it means to be a Christian. And he did so in order to illuminate and facilitate choice. Whether a man drifts with the crowd and hardly merits to be called an existing individual or whether he becomes by free affirmation what he is, a finite individual related to God, is a question which can be answered only existentially, that is, by free choice; and no amount of theorizing or of purely intellectual dialectics can take the place of choice. To think that it can was, in Kierkegaard's opinion, one of the main faults of the absolute idealists. But though theorizing cannot solve a man's existential problems, reflection can illuminate and facilitate choice. Again, according to Jaspers, existentialism as a general theory is the death of the philosophy of existence. It is not the function of the philosopher to teach a *Weltanschauung*. The philosopher should be concerned with making clear to man the possibilities of choice and showing what authentic choice is. To be sure, no philosophy is possible without reflection, analysis and description in universal terms; but at the same time the object is to illuminate human existence with a view to the decision and choice which the individual has to make for himself. And if we turn from theists like Jaspers to atheists like Sartre and Camus, we find analogous attitudes. For Sartre the philosopher cannot determine a universally valid set of objective values, nor can he tell the individual what his moral choices should be. But he can make clear the inevitability of choice of some kind, the nature of choice, and the difference between authentic and unauthentic choice, so that a man may realize what he is about and commit himself with open eyes. Again, while Camus would not maintain that the philosopher is in a position to dictate to the individual precisely how he should behave and act in an absurd world, a world without any given rhyme and reason, he can draw a man's attention to the nature of the world and to the possibilities of choice and behaviour.

Marcel, it is true, may appear to constitute an exception to these generalizations. The idea of freedom occupies a less prominent place and plays a less dramatic rôle in his philosophy than it does in that of Sartre or even in that of Jaspers. And the spirit of his thought, as revealed in his concern with exploring the realm of " Being," is more contemplative, more " metaphysical," than the spirit of Sartre's thought, which is turned dramatically towards action. Nevertheless we can hardly read Marcel's writings without realizing his concern with exhibiting what it means to be a human person in the fullest sense of the term and with bearing witness to what he regards as the truth with a view to enabling others to appropriate it freely, not only by intellectual recognition, but also on the plane of being.

I must admit, however, that the statement that the existentialists are concerned with promoting the exercise of authentic freedom is not applicable to Heidegger, if, that is to say, one takes into account, as one should, the philosopher's own explanation of his intentions. For though Heidegger draws a distinction between authentic and unauthentic existence, and though he has been interpreted as intending to promote the former, he has protested that the distinction was purely a matter of analysis and that he was not concerned in any way with exhortation. If, therefore, one persists in applying to Heidegger what I have just been saying about existentialists in general, one does violence to his thought. The only justification for doing so, if it is a justification, is that it is Heidegger the " existentialist," the misinterpreted Heidegger, if you like, who has exercised the widest influence. In its effective influence his philosophy has outrun the professed intentions of its author.

Reservations apart, however, we can say that existentialism in general is the form taken in a particular historical epoch by the recurrent protest of the free individual against all that threatens or seems to threaten his unique position as an ex-sistent subject, that is to say, as a free subject who, though a being in the world and so part of nature, at the same time stands out from the background of nature. From time to time we find in philosophy the tendency to treat man simply as " object," as an item in the physical cosmos, to reduce him, as far as this is possible, to the level of every other object in the world, and to explain away the consciousness of freedom. But we find also that this tendency is offset by a counter-affirmation, which is more than a mere protest, since it draws attention to aspects of man which have been slurred over or neglected. The " spiritualist " movement in French philosophy can be said to constitute a counter-affirmation to materialism and determinism and to embody the free human being's reassertion of himself. But it is not only materialism which can threaten to engulf the free individual: absolute idealism can appear to do the same. And this theme is particularly relevant to the case of Kierkegaard. Owing to the circumstances of his university education philosophy meant for him primarily the Hegelian system; and he revolted against the Hegelian exaltation of the Idea or Absolute at the expense of the individual and against the Hegelian insistence on mediation and on the dialectical synthesis of opposites. The primary fact is the individual, and it is simply comical if the individual strives to strip himself of his individuality by the exercise of thought and to merge himself in the universal consciousness or cosmic reason. Absolute idealism may be a philosophy for the study and for the professor's chair; but it is not a philosophy which has much relevance to the existential problems of human life. In absolute idealism we find the tyranny of the universal and the attempt to transcend sharply defined contrasts by an intellectual tour-de-force which betrays mental ability and ingenuity but little appreciation of existent reality. Kierkegaard never tired of denouncing the submerging of the individual in the collectivity or universal and of stressing the need for becoming more, and not less, of an individual. According to him, the specific immorality of the age consists precisely in the depreciation of the individual. "Each age has its own characteristic depravity. Ours is perhaps not pleasure or indulgence or sensuality, but rather a dissolute pantheistic contempt for the individual man" (*Concluding Unscientific Postscript*, p. 317). And in the long run to become the individual means to affirm freely what one is, a finite being related to God, who is not the Hegelian Idea but the personal and transcendent God of Judaism and Christianity.

In the present epoch, of course, the submerging of the individual takes other forms than that of absolute idealism. We have seen, for example, and indeed still see, the powerful tendency towards political and social totalitarianism with its reduction of personal responsibility and its evaluation of personal value in terms of service to the collectivity. And existentialism, in some of its forms, can be considered, in part that is to say, as a reaffirmation of the free individual in the face of this powerful tendency. This is one reason, of course, why Marxists have represented the existentialism of M. Sartre as being the philosophy of the dying bourgeoisie, the last convulsive effort of an outmoded individualism. Again, existentialism, by insisting on the individual, on the free subject, is also a protest against the general tendency in our civilization to resolve the individual into his social function or functions, such as taxpayer, voter, civil servant, engineer, trade unionist, etc. This theme has been developed by Gabriel Marcel in particular, who believes that the tendency towards the functionalization of man involves a degradation of the human person. In general, therefore, we can say that existentialism represents the reassertion of the free man against the collectivity or any tendency to depersonalization, and in this respect it is akin to personalism and has some affinities, with pragmatism.

But existentialism is more than a protest of the free individual against totalitarianism and impersonal functionalization. For in certain of its forms it seems to me to be presented, tacitly at least, as a way of salvation. This is only partly true of Marcel's philosophy; for, as a convinced Catholic, he believes that man's salvation is achieved by other means than by philosophizing or by man's unaided effort and choice. But it seems to be verified not only in the case of Jaspers' philosophy but also in those of Sartre and Camus. It may, indeed, appear to constitute a gross paradox if one speaks of a way of salvation in connection with an atheistic philosophy such as that of Sartre. But I wish now to explain what I mean.

In the ancient world we find people looking to philosophy for a way of life, for reasoned guidance in conduct and belief, which was not provided by the official cult. I do not mean, of course, that great numbers of people turned to philosophy for moral guidance and for religious belief. Serious philosophy is scarcely a popular pastime; and the number of people who pay much attention to philosophers is at any time comparatively restricted. But even in the earlier phases of Greek thought we find the tendency to look to philosophy for a way of life: we have only to think of the Pythagorean " society." And in the Hellenistic and Roman periods we find the tendency taking definite forms as in Stoicism and Neo-platonism. The former offered a moral doctrine which was supported by rational argument: the latter offered, besides ethical teaching, a deeply religious view of the world and of human life, a view which was capable of attracting those who had no real belief in the ancient anthropomorphic mythologies and who at the same time looked, in the uncertainty and bewilderment of human existence, for some message of personal salvation which was at once intellectually respectable and satisfying to the religious impulse. The individual, thrown back on himself in the great cosmopolitan society of the Empire and only too conscious of the forces threatening his personal security, could find in Stoicism the ideal of the self-sufficient virtuous man or in Neo-platonism a religious doctrine of liberation and salvation.

In the mediaeval world the situation was very different. The way of salvation was provided by the Christian religion, and, whether they practised it or not, men accepted the Christian code as the norm of moral action. Philosophy, therefore, tended to be a purely academic pursuit, a matter for university professors and their students. I do not say that it was always and only this; but it is natural, in view of the general circumstances, that mediaeval man should not have expected from philosophy, as distinct from Christian theology and Christian moral and ascetic teaching, what Marcus Aurelius, for instance, had looked for in Stoicism.

Modern Europe is not, however, mediaeval Europe. Belief in the Christian religion has waned, and this has been followed, as Nietzsche saw that it would, by doubt concerning the absolute character and universal applicability of Christian values and of the Christian moral teaching. At the same time it is now realized more clearly than it was in the last century that we cannot expect science to provide us with a normative morality or with religious belief. And it is no matter for surprise that some at least should look to philosophy to provide them with what, in their opinion, neither Christianity nor science can give them. Whether we think that existentialism meets the need or not, it seems to me that it is one of the forms of philosophy which attempt to do so.

140

Now, as we have seen, existentialism lays special emphasis on the free individual. And I think that this emphasis is relevant to the theme of which I have just been treating.

Many people find it very difficult to believe in God. Some seem to themselves to be conscious of the absence rather than of the presence of God. Even if He exists, He appears to hide Himself rather than to reveal Himself. Even those who would not be prepared to say that " God is dead " and that the idea of God has lost all significance may feel that human existence and history are in some way alienated from the divine. On the other hand the physical cosmos, though its existence is evident enough and though its nature is progressively revealed by the natural sciences, is alien to man in the sense that it is indifferent to man's ideals and hopes and strivings. It is not the geocentric, and indeed anthropocentric, cosmos of earlier days, but a vaster universe in which human existence and history appear as transitory and casual events. Yet if man, apparently alienated from God and set in an alien world, turns for reassurance to human society, he finds a riven society, a society divided and in ferment. He sees powerful forces threatening him as a free individual and striving to subject him to a crushing tyranny extending even to the mind. And it is not simply a question of a gulf between the Communist world and the democratic world. In the democratic world itself there are not only differences of belief, of moral standards, of political ideas and aims, but also forces at work which threaten the breakdown of the social structure as we know it. Man can hardly find in society at large and in social tradition a sure answer to the questions which perplex him concerning belief, values and conduct. The old traditions seem to be crumbling; and even in the family fundamental differences of allegiance may reveal themselves. Furthermore, the individual has become a riddle to himself. He has been told, for example, that his conscious life is the expression of hidden subconscious drives, impulses and urges, and the self, as it exists for consciousness, may appear to be disintegrated. Man has to act; but the goal and standards of action are obscure. God, if He exists, is hidden: the physical cosmos is indifferent:

society is divided and stands always on the brink of an abyss: man is a riddle to himself and can find in himself no final reassurance. He has been described as alienated man, or as man in a state of alienation.[1] And it is to this alienated individual, thrown back on himself and yet unable to find in himself the answers to the problems which beset him, that the message of the existentialists seems especially to be addressed. Jaspers, for example, tries to show how even in face of the shipwreck of all earthly hopes and ideals man can still affirm his relationship to the Transcendent. He offers us a religious philosophy, but at the same time a post-Christian religious philosophy. For, as will be seen, his " philosophic faith " is not the same thing as Christian faith; and for him the affirmation of the Transcendent is made even in face of the breakdown of belief in the Christian religion. He addresses himself more to those who have lost any definite dogmatic belief than to believing Christians. Sartre on the other hand addresses himself to those for whom " God is dead." He speaks to those who have no belief in God and no belief in any absolute universally-obligatory moral law, to the individual who is thrown back on himself and who yet has to act in the world and to commit himself. Camus addresses himself to the man for whom the world is " absurd," for whom human history and existence have no given significance or purpose, but who is yet faced with the problem of acting in this absurd world. Heidegger is, indeed, again the exception. For in so far as he is engaged in ontological inquiry and analysis he can be said to be writing for professors of philosophy and serious students with what one may call an academic interest in philosophical analysis. But the Heidegger who has exercised the most influence is without a doubt the philosopher who describes man as " thrown " into the world and as faced with the choice between authentic and unauthentic existence in a world from which God is declared to be " absent."

---

[1]This theme of " alienation " is treated, for example, in *Six Existentialist Thinkers* by H. J. Blackham (Routledge and Kegan Paul, 1952, pp. 149 f.) and, much more fully, in *Existentialism and the Modern Predicament* by F. H. Heinemann (Adam and Charles Black, 1953).

It may be said, of course, that all this is too highly coloured and dramatic. In practice most people take things as they come, act more or less according to common standards, are absorbed in everyday concerns, and do not occupy themselves with tormenting existential problems. No doubt this is true. The number of people who give any real consideration to the problems which plagued, say, Kierkegaard or Unamuno, is limited. Many tend to accept their opinions more or less passively from their social milieu, and most at least of their actions follow the pattern of habit and convention. But this type of existence, characterized by absorption in " the one " (" one thinks," " one feels," " one does ") is just the type of existence which the existentialists tend to depreciate. To do the latter justice, they do not demand that everyone should lead a strikingly heroic life; nor do they identify authentic existence with eccentricity in the ordinary sense. Kierkegaard's " knight of faith," for example, was described as a man who lives outwardly like others and who is singular only in his inner attitude. But in order to facilitate authentic existence, deliberate self-commitment in the light of realization of man's existential situation, they try to break through the crust of social consciousness and crowd-mentality and awaken the individual to a vision of his existential situation and of his responsibility and potentialities as a free individual. And this, I think, is one of the reasons why some of them use or seem to use such dramatic and highly coloured language. For in many cases they use this language to draw attention to a real or supposed truth which is in some sense already known though it has not been realized by the individual as a truth affecting and deeply involving himself. For instance, everyone is aware in a vague way that " one eventually dies." But it is one thing to be aware that " one dies," and it is another thing to realize that I personally am advancing towards my death from the first moment of my existence, to see this as a sign of my finitude and to realize vividly the problems concerning the significance and value of human hopes and ideals which arise out of finitude and its consequences. And if a writer wishes to encourage a man to live *sub specie mortis* instead of, as Spinoza wished, *sub specie aeternitatis,* he will probably use dramatic and perhaps emotively coloured language in order to facilitate a man's changing his point of view, language which may well appear to the "disinterested" onlooker to be over-shrill and even to betray a making of much ado about nothing or at least about a familiar empirical truth, the presentation of which does not call for such dramatic effects.

Perhaps at this point it may be as well to remark that preoccupation with the drama of human existence is not all that is to be found in the existentialists. It is, indeed, the feature which most strikes the reader; and it is the feature which most obviously qualifies these philosophers for the title "existentialists." For if one meant by "existentialist" no more than a philosopher whose chief object of consideration is existence as such, one might be inclined to follow Maritain and Gilson in saying that Aquinas is the existentialist *par excellence.* But the so-called "existentialists" are, as we have seen, primarily concerned with human existence, considered in a dramatic light; and the term "existence" has for them a special meaning, referring first and foremost to man as free, self-transcending subject. Yet this dramatic preoccupation by no means exhausts all that is to be found, as a matter of fact, in the writings of these philosophers. For one can find in their writings phenomenological analyses of considerable interest and value. The phenomenological method, associated with Husserl, may be said to consist, in part at least, in the objective analytic description of phenomena of any given type. Husserl himself insisted on the *epoche* or suspension of judgment about the existence or mode of existence of the object selected for contemplation, analysis and description; and he regarded the application of the method as a necessary propaedeutic to ontology, which it should precede. For instance, the phenomenologist will consider the essence of "being conscious of" without presupposing any ontology or metaphysic but letting the psychic phenomenon "speak for itself." He applied the method to the invariable structures of psychic experience, such as "intention," being conscious of and perceiving. But it can be applied, and has been applied by some of his followers, in other fields, to religious or aesthetic experience, for example, or to the perception of values. Now among Husserl's pupils was Heidegger. But the latter disregarded the *epoche* and used the phenomenological method, not as a propaedeutic to ontology, but as an instrument in ontology. And Sartre, who gives to his work *L'Être et le Néant* the subtitle *Essai d'ontologie phénoménologique*, has done the same. We find him giving long descriptive analyses of themes such as time or temporality, " bad faith," *le regard* and love. And Marcel too can be said to make use of the phenomenological method, provided, however, that this statement is not taken to imply that he was ever a pupil of Husserl. Marcel discovers and analyzes basic attitudes and relations, such as hope, love and availability (*disponibilité*), which reveal the response of the human person to " the other "; and he considers them as manifesting the nature of being and of participation in being. Husserl himself rejected Heidegger's use of the phenomenological method in the service of ontology and existentialism; but it is questionable whether the former's rule about the observance of the *epoche* can be successfully obeyed, and, even if it can, whether this rule is anything more than the expression of a personal decision. In any case the point which I wish to make is that the phenomenological analyses carried out by existentialists such as Heidegger, Sartre, Merleau-Ponty and Marcel constitute one, if not the principal, of their philosophical achievements. I do not mean that their analyses are all acceptable. One could not simultaneously regard as adequate the analyses of love, for example, performed by Marcel and by Sartre. But their analyses are careful pieces of work which merit attention for their own sake, whatever one may think of some of the more dramatic aspects of existentialism.

As a conclusion to this lecture I should like to come back to the existentialists' use of the term " existence." I have alluded to the distinction between authentic and unauthentic existence. And this suggests that the existentialists who make this distinction understand by existence the specific mode of being of man whereby authentic and unauthentic existence are both open to him as potentialities, as possible determinations of his original mode of being. Thus for Jaspers the position from which the individual starts is potential existence (*mögliche Existenz*); and in a sense " existence " is always potential existence. For Heidegger too one of the component elements of the meaning of " existence " is potential being (*Seinkönnen*), the possibility of being oneself (authentic existence) or of not being oneself (unauthentic existence, absorption in " the one "). Marcel's use of the term " existence " is different. At first he described existence in terms of the relation between object and consciousness. Further, he tended to define the existent as the spatially given, with the result that, not being a materialist, he had to distinguish between reality and existence. Later, however, he subordinated the idea of existence to the idea of participation in being. The level of pre-conscious or pre-reflective participation is the existential level, while that of conscious and free appropriation of one's participation in being is the level of " being." The meaning of such statements is hardly self-evident; but they indicate at least a use of the term " existence " which is different from the use to which the term is put by Jaspers and by Heidegger, and which we think of as the characteristic existentialist use of the term.

If one speaks of man as " possible " or " potential " existence, faced with the choice between authentic and unauthentic existence, the terms " authentic " and " unauthentic " seem, at first sight at least, to imply valuational judgments. And, whatever may be the case with Heidegger, who professes to be concerned simply with analysis and not with passing valuational judgments or with moralizing, it is difficult to believe that the terms, as used by a writer like Sartre, have not in fact a valuational connotation. But even if the term " authentic " is not used in a valuational sense, it must, I think, if it is used meaningfully, indicate a mode of existence which bears a special relation to what man already is. Man is the sort of being who, if he exists authentically, exists in this particular way. Whether this fits in with Sartre's interpretation of the proposition " existence precedes essence " is another question; but if it is proper to make the distinction between authentic and unauthentic existence, it must, it seems to me, be proper to speak of man as willing or as not willing to become what in some sense he already is. And in fact Kierkegaard does speak in this way. The question then arises, what is man, and what is the precise content of the specific mode of existence which is called " authentic existence." Here, I think, we come to the parting of the ways. Does authentic existence involve, for example, the free affirmation by man of his relation to the Transcendent, to God, so that, to use Marcel's way of talking, man freely and consciously appropriates and affirms on the plane of " being " a relationship which already holds good on the level of " existence " ? Or is there no God, and is authentic existence to be interpreted without the affirmation either of God or of any given set of absolute values or of any universally obligatory moral law? Looked at in the light of these questions, existentialism can be divided into theistic and atheistic existentialism. And I shall speak in the next lecture of theistic existentialism. I place it first, not simply because I myself believe in God, but because, as far as the modern existentialist movement is concerned, it is historically prior. Kierkegaard's philosophy was a deeply religious philosophy; and both Jaspers and Marcel are older men than Sartre.

CHAPTER X

THEISTIC EXISTENTIALISM

I

TO represent the modern existentialists as so many disciples of Kierkegaard would be extremely misleading. At the same time he has exercised a profound influence on the existentialist movement, particularly perhaps on the philosophy of Jaspers; and there is, I think, a sense in which it is true to say that he is the existentialist thinker *par excellence*. While, therefore, it would be out of place in a series of four general lectures to attempt to investigate in detail the historical antecedents of existentialism, it is necessary to include a treatment of Kierkegaard, even if it amounts only to a brief and inadequate sketch of his thought. Schelling's doctrine of human freedom may be relevant to a consideration of the genesis and development of existentialism; but he could hardly be called an existentialist. Kierkegaard, however, was an existentialist: his philosophy is part of the movement and not simply a factor contributing to the rise of the movement.

Kierkegaard's attitude towards Hegel has already been mentioned. It may, of course, be said that he did scant justice to Hegel. For the latter had no intention of advocating the suppression of individuality: what he maintained was that the human being attains the fulfilment of his true nature, not as an atomic individual, but by accepting his moral responsibilities as a member of society. Furthermore, the state was not for Hegel the highest good. The state belongs to the sphere of " objective spirit "; and above this sphere stands the sphere of " absolute spirit," in which the human spirit reveals itself in the activities of art, religion and philosophy. Moreover, it is a mistake to think that Hegel attached no value to freedom. He believed that, whereas in the oriental despotisms only one was free, the despot, and whereas in Greece and Rome only some were free, the idea of the freedom of every man entered the world with Christianity and is not an idea which can be set aside as false or worthless. At the same time, it may be claimed, he had a rational conception of human freedom, looking on it as expressed in obedience to the law which is itself the expression of spirit rather than as capricious and purely arbitrary choice.

But though Kierkegaard may not have done full justice to Hegel, he was certainly well acquainted with the contents of the latter's system; and the notion of a higher synthesis whereby individuality and personal freedom are lifted dialectically on to a higher plane was repugnant to him. The individual expresses or finds his true self, not by being caught up, as it were, in a higher synthesis, but by becoming more and more of an individual. Kierkegaard's point of view was different from that of Hegel, and it remains different even when we have made allowances for what may constitute misinterpretations of the Hegelian system. In any case, however, the question whether Kierkegaard did or did not misinterpret Hegel is irrelevant for our present purpose. For Kierkegaard's Hegel is not simply the historic Hegel; he is also a concrete symbol standing for all those beliefs and tendencies which Kierkegaard hated and attacked. The important point is not his interpretation of the Hegelian system but rather his doctrine of the existent individual.

What does it mean to become more and more the individual? We can approach the matter in this way. Kierkegaard, who was born in 1815, was brought up by his father, a deeply religious man but one afflicted by melancholy and tormented by a sense of guilt. And it is not surprising that as a student Kierkegaard should have revolted against his upbringing and should have become detached from Christianity, the atmosphere of which he regarded as stifling. For a time he adopted the attitude of a cynical observer of life, ready to enjoy the experiences which might offer themselves but remaining the ironical spectator, fundamentally detached and uncommitted. In 1836, however, after having apparently contemplated the possibility of suicide, he underwent a moral conversion. And this was followed in 1838 by a religious conversion, when he turned once more to Christianity. But these stages in his life had a wider significance for a reflective thinker like Kierkegaard than that of merely personal events; and he universalized these stages as distinguishable phases or possibilities or levels of human existence. We thus at once see the close relation between personal experience and philosophical reflection. He says himself that all his work revolves round himself; that the whole of his production is the process of his education; and that he sought from the first a truth by which he could live. In this sense he was a personal thinker and the existentialist *par excellence*. True, he turned everything into reflection; and as we have just seen he universalized his experiences and struggles. But he was deeply conscious that, as he put it, an existential system cannot be formulated. His aim was not to create a philosophical system, but rather, by speaking, as it were, to himself, to speak to others with a view to drawing attention to the concrete possibilities of human existence. As we shall see in a moment, the movement from one " stage " to another is accomplished by choice, in the instant, not by learning and understanding a philosophical system. The existential thinker can draw attention to possibilities and illuminate the scene; but if truth means *my* truth, the truth by which I live and to which I commit myself, I alone can appropriate it and make it my truth, by my personal choice and self-commitment. I cannot achieve this end by sitting at the feet of a professor and imbibing his words of wisdom. I can attend Hegel's lectures and marvel at his ingenuity, learning and speculative ability. But when I leave the classroom I am the same as I was before. And what I have learned or think I have learned is not a truth by which I can live.

Kierkegaard's personal phase of cynical observation, of absence of self-commitment, was universalized by him as the aesthetic stage. But by this term Kierkegaard does not mean merely the life of the artist or art-lover. He means rather the attitude of those who have no continuity in their lives, a continuity due to fixed and observed moral standards and principles. He called it the Don Juan stage, but it includes much more than the life of mere sensuality. It includes the attitude of those who hate fixed lines and definite contours, who wish to taste all experiences, to put on all characters, who strive after a " false infinity." The aesthetic man refuses to recognize and to choose himself, to commit himself; anything which binds him down and gives shape and definiteness to his life, such as morality and religion, he rejects. He may be a sensualist or he may be an ironic observer of life; but if he refuses to commit himself, he belongs to the aesthetic stage.

Above the aesthetic stage is the moral or ethical stage. The shapeless " individualism " of the first stage is renounced in favour of subordination to the universal, that is, the universal moral law, with its claims on all. In this stage, typified by Socrates, we have the reign of the universal. But though the law is affirmed absolutely, and though the individual gives shape and determination to his life, thus becoming more of an individual than the aesthetic man, ethics by itself looks to happiness, to something temporal, without the relation to the Transcendent being affirmed.

Thirdly, we have the religious stage, the standpoint of faith. The specific character of this stage is that the individual does not subordinate himself simply to an impersonal universal law but stands in an immediate relation, affirmed by faith, to the supreme Subject, the personal Absolute, God. He realizes what he is, a finite individual, a creature, and affirms this self before God. He can thus be said to choose himself in the deepest sense. And Kierkegaard speaks as though in the affirmation of his relationship to God man transcends the universal. He liked to use the Scriptural account of Abraham's willingness to sacrifice his son Isaac as an illustration. The action which Abraham was willing to perform was against the universal, that is, it was contrary to the moral law; but in faith he recognized that the absolute relationship of individual to God transcends the universal. It is through the affirmation, in faith, of his relationship to God that the human being becomes the individual in the highest possible degree; for the relationship of finite person to infinite and personal Absolute transcends the universal and is appropriated in pure inwardness with passionate interest.

In the theory of these stages we have, indeed, a dialectic. But it is an existentialist dialectic. That is to say, the stages are not continuous in the sense that the mind can pass smoothly from one to the other just by thinking. Thinking is involved, of course; but it is a thinking in which the whole man is engaged, and the passage from one stage to the other is effected by choice. The stages are thus discontinuous. To say this is not to say that there is no connection at all between them. On the aesthetic level a man never comes to the integration of his personality; he does not give form and definiteness to his existence, and in this sense he has no self. This dispersion of the personality produces melancholy, one form of despair; and the way out is achieved by making the leap to the ethical level on which a man overcomes the formless dispersion of the personality characteristic of the aesthetic level by subordinating himself to the universal. But the ethical man as such knows nothing of sin. For Socrates moral evil was a result of ignorance; it was an intellectual defect rather than sin. And it is the rising of the consciousness of sin, with its accompanying form of "despair," that prepares the way for the transition to the third stage, the standpoint of faith. The stages cannot, therefore, be said to have no connection at all with one another. At the same time to pass from one stage to the other one has to commit oneself, to venture all; and one cannot do this without choice, which is in indivisible act and is accomplished, not by a temporal process of discursive thought, but "in the instant." And so Kierkegaard, disliking anything which seemed to him to minimize the element of self-commitment and of venture in the passage from one stage to another and to constitute an attempt to reduce the existential dialectic to a purely intellectual dialectic, emphasized the discontinuity between the different stages. This is especially apparent in the case of transition to the third stage. Kierkegaard speaks not only as though proofs of God's existence could not be found but also as though they would be irrelevant, and indeed undesirable, even if they could be found. We are left with the leap of faith, the passionate appropriation by the individual of an " objective uncertainty." The truth which matters is *my* truth (truth is " subjectivity "), the truth which I have chosen, to which I have committed myself, for which I venture all and by which I choose to live, rather than public-property truth, achieved as the conclusion of logical argument.

Kierkegaard asserts that the tonality of existential choice is " dread," though sometimes the term " anxiety " is preferred as a translation. In any case we have to distinguish it from " fear," which is fear of something definite and can be got rid of by appropriate action. Dread is described as a " sympathetic antipathy and antipathetic sympathy." And its nature may be seen most clearly in the case of the man faced with the choice for or against God. God is transcendent, invisible and unprovable. To choose oneself before God, to commit oneself to faith, appears to be equivalent to losing oneself, to throwing oneself into the abyss; and man recoils from it. On the other hand, if a man risks all and leaps, he finds himself; he chooses his true self, which is both finite and infinite. a finite being, that is to say, related to the infinite. He who has no God is alienated from himself: he is " in despair." He who makes the leap of faith " recovers " himself, his true self, after the dispersion of the aesthetic level. Faced with the leap, therefore, man is simultaneously attracted and repelled. He is like a man standing on the edge of a precipice and simultaneously attracted and repelled by the yawning chasm below him. He experiences a " sympathetic antipathy and an antipathetic sympathy."

We can now understand what Kierkegaard means by " existence." It does not mean simply being there, in the world, nor even simply living. Kierkegaard uses the illustration of a drunken peasant who is asleep in his cart and lets the horses proceed on their accustomed way. Inasmuch as he is there with the reins in his hands he is in some sense a driver. But we can also say that he does not drive. So there are many who exist but who at the same time do not " exist." That is to say, they drift along, following custom and convention and

without ever becoming individuals in anything but an ontological sense. To " exist " means choosing one's true self;
" existence " is something to be won by choice. Kierkegaard
can therefore speak of it as a " process of becoming " and as
a " striving." And because man's true self is the finite self as
related to the infinite Subject, " existence " can also be
described as " the child that is born of the infinite and the
finite, the eternal and the temporal." True, these descriptions
may not seem to be very clear; but Kierkegaard insisted that
existence, like movement, is very difficult to define. " If I
think it, I abrogate it, and then I do not think it." The meaning
of existence is recognized by the engaged or self-committed
individual. All that the philosopher can do is to draw attention
to its concrete forms and thus facilitate its understanding.

I have entitled this lecture " Theistic Existentialism." But it
would be a great mistake to think of Kierkegaard as concerned
simply with " theism." One of the great problems which beset
him was, What is authentic Christianity and what does it
mean to be a true Christian? In the first place he rejected
altogether the process of rationalization which he found in
Hegel, the substitution of mediation for faith. According to
Hegel, Christianity is indeed the absolute religion, and the
doctrines of Christianity are true; but it is philosophy which
apprehends the rational essence of the truths which Christian
theology presents to the religious consciousness in pictorial
form. For example, the Christian doctrine of the Incarnation,
considered as the doctrine of the unique historic incarnation
of the Son of God, is true; but the mind of the philosopher
pierces through the pictorial forms in which this truth is
presented to the religious consciousness and sees its rational
essence, namely the fact that the human spirit is in essence
divine, a moment in the life of the cosmic reason or mind.
And some Christian thinkers thought that they had found in
Hegel a means of making Christianity acceptable to sceptically
minded humanists who could not stomach the Christian
doctrines if they were represented as the final truth in their
traditional forms. For Kierkegaard, however, this procedure
was simply a dishonest betrayal of Christianity. The Hegelian

dialectic is an enemy within the gates; and it is not the business of any Christian writer or preacher to dilute Christianity to suit the general educated public. The doctrine of the Incarnation was to the Jews a stumbling-block and to the Greeks foolishness, and so it will always be. For the doctrine not only transcends reason but is repugnant to reason; it is the Paradox *par excellence*, and it can be affirmed only by faith, with passionate inwardness and interest. The substitution of reason for faith means the death of Christianity. Similarly, the reduction of Christianity to a polite and moralistic humanism, with theism thrown in, which was represented, in Kierkegaard's opinion, by the Danish State Church, was declared to be only a caricature of genuine Christianity. He felt it to be his duty to bear witness to the nature of true Christianity and to disabuse the majority of " Christians " of the notion that they were in fact Christians. Hence the polemics against the Lutheran State Church and one of its leading representatives which reached their culminating phase towards the end of his short life.

Kierkegaard's influence has been widespread and profound. But he has influenced different people in very different ways, as, indeed, might be expected if one considers the ambiguities of his thought. On the religious level his plea for " common honesty " led some who classed themselves as Christians to recognize that they were not and did not wish to be Christians. Others turned towards Catholicism, since, whatever the shortcomings of many Catholics, even of ecclesiastics in high places, may have been, the Church had never surrendered to rationalism and had always upheld the ideals of Christian sanctity and renunciation. Others again came to the conclusion that what was needed was a renewal of Protestantism, a recapture of the spirit of the reformers. After all, was not Kierkegaard himself a Lutheran, and does not his teaching re-echo in many ways the teaching of Luther? We have only to think of the latter's doctrine of justification by faith and his dislike of philosophy. And in point of fact Kierkegaard's writings have been a contributory factor in the formation of the neo-Protestant theology of Karl Barth and others.

If we turn to the purely philosophical level, making a distinction between Kierkegaard's philosophy and his specific affirmation of Christianity, we see that two main lines of development are possible. One can retain the idea of the Transcendent as an essential element in the philosophy of " existence," while discarding the affirmation of Christianity as the absolute truth. And then we have a system like that of Jaspers. Or one can interpret Kierkegaard's doctrine of truth as " subjectivity " and of the affirmation of God as the affirmation of an " objective uncertainty " as meaning that his theism was a personal idiosyncrasy which is not essential to existentialism as such. I am not trying to make out that Sartre, for example, was a disciple of Kierkegaard. This would be a gross historical inaccuracy. I mean rather that precisely because of the highly personal character of his thought it is possible for the latter to act as a source of inspiration and stimulus in the mind of a philosopher who is by no means prepared to go the whole way with Kierkegaard. Thus the latter has exercised an influence on the mind of Heidegger; but though Heidegger makes use of Kierkegaardian concepts and distinctions, he does not affirm God, even if he does not deny Him.

2

Turning to Karl Jaspers, who was born in 1883, I think that he may be described, so far as such descriptions have any value, as a Kantian who underwent a profound shock through meditation on the lives and thought of Kierkegaard and Nietzsche, two men whom he regards as " exceptions," as men who reveal in themselves to an exceptional degree the diverse possibilities of human existence. At the same time it is essential for an understanding of his conception of philosophy and its function to realize the serious attention which he has paid to the problem of the relation between science and philosophy. And it is useful to remember that he has some first-hand knowledge of scientific method, having studied in his earlier days both medicine and psychology.

In the preface to the first volume of his *Philosophie* Jaspers asserts that " the philosophy of the present day is, like that of former times, concerned with Being." He thus stresses the continuity between his thought and the European metaphysical tradition. Indeed, in his view there is one eternal philosophy which pursues its course through the centuries. But this does not mean that our understanding of the nature and scope of philosophy has not changed. There was a time when philosophy was regarded as a kind of universal science, the time, that is to say, when the particular sciences as we know them had not yet arisen and developed. Once this development had taken place, however, the problem of the nature and scope of philosophy became acute. Some thought that the advance of the sciences had rendered philosophy superfluous. Others reduced philosophy to the history of philosophy. Others made philosophy the handmaiden of the sciences. Its function is, for instance, to analyze and clarify the fundamental concepts of the sciences. Others tried to turn philosophy into a special science alongside the other sciences, reducing it to logic or to phenomenology or to epistemology. But all these lines of thought are, according to Jaspers, misguided. Philosophy is still concerned with Being. But the rise of the sciences has made it impossible any more to regard philosophy as the " science " of Being. It is neither a universal science nor a special science alongside the other sciences. Kant saw clearly that metaphysics is not a science, though it does not follow that we can profitably assign to philosophy a specialized epistemological subject-matter and so retain the claim that it is a science. Metaphysical philosophy is still concerned with Being; but it is not a theoretical science of Being. Its function and approach are different. We can see now that philosophy raises the problem of Being and awakens man's mind to the Being which transcends beings by illuminating " existence," man considered as free, self-transcending subject, something which cannot be objectified in the way that would be required for him to fall within the scope of any particular science. Kant has shown us that there is no theoretical science of Being. But we should not conclude that philosophy is not concerned with Being. What follows from the truth contained in the Kantian criticism is that we have to change our conception of philosophy's approach to the problem of Being and of its scope and aim in its consideration of this problem.

The first task of philosophy is to justify itself, to show that there really is room for philosophy. And this is done by breaking through the idea of an all-comprehensive scientific system of reality, that is, by breaking down, not only the positivist conception of an all-inclusive scientific conception of reality, but also any idealist notion, of the type defended by Hegel, of a comprehensive system.

Now, it is obvious that any particular science has its limits. Botany, for example, is limited in the sense that it is not the same as atomic physics or as psychology. It has its own particular subject-matter and method. We must admit, therefore, that, though one cannot set limits *a priori* to the advance of any particular science, it is limited *in itself*, so that it can never become a universal science. For instance, when we say that psychology is limited or has limits, we do not mean that psychology cannot advance beyond a certain determinable point *within its own field*: we mean that the field is itself limited, so that psychology can never become a universal science, however much it may advance as psychology. But, it might be asked, can there not be a universal science which takes the whole of reality as its province and which employs a universal method? Jaspers' answer, I think, is that an examination of the nature of scientific inquiry and method shows that there cannot be a universal science or a universal method. Every science deals with a determinate type of object or with objects regarded from a determinate point of view. Science necessarily takes the form of the particular sciences. And the idea of a universal science is contradictory. A universal science would deal with Being; but there cannot be a science of Being. In order for there to be one, Being would have to be objectified, to be turned into a determinate object. And then it would not be Being; it would be a being. If it is said that a universal science would have the whole world as its province instead of particular types of beings or beings considered under particular aspects, Jaspers answers that the phrase "the whole world," if used to signify the whole of reality considered as an object capable of being scientifically investigated, is nonsensical. There is no complete world which could be so investigated. The world is not a finished complete totality; it consists of particular things, related to one another, no doubt, but still particular things.

A kind of negative indication of the limits of science is seen by Jaspers in, for instance, the way in which atomic analysis comes up against the unpredictable. Another, and much more important, indication is seen in the impossibility of a complete scientific understanding of the human being in terms of universal concepts and causal laws. The positivist spirit endeavours to understand man scientifically. It is right to make this attempt; and it succeeds up to a point which cannot be determined in advance. But, however far the scientific understanding of man may progress, the very process of understanding implies that man is more than that which he understands. In order to understand the world scientifically, myself included, I must, as it were, stand back from the world; I must turn myself into an object. But though I can do this up to a certain point, it is absurd to think that I can objectify myself completely. To do so would be to cancel out the significance of understanding. I cannot be simply an object of my mind. But if positivism falls short, so does idealism. The idealist tries to subordinate all things to mind, or even to reduce all things to mind, in a way which neglects both the individual, in favour of consciousness in general, and the being which presents itself as "the other" and as irreducible to mind or consciousness.

For a true understanding of the nature and function of philosophy, therefore, it is necessary to grasp the fact of the limitations of science. But these limits cannot be well understood by the philosopher unless he has an acquaintance with science and its methods. And as science takes the form of the particular sciences, Jaspers regards it as desirable, if not essential, that a philosopher should possess some first-hand knowledge of a particular science. Although for him philosophy lies in a sense beyond science, his position cannot be called that of an "anti-scientific" philosopher. It does, however, follow from his position that what lies beyond the grasp of the particular sciences and falls within the province of philosophy cannot be known scientifically, cannot be turned into a clearly definable object. If it could, it would not lie beyond science. Thus any idea of philosophy as possessing a subject-matter of its own which is definable in the sense in which the subject-matters of the particular sciences are definable is quite alien to Jaspers' thought.

The being which stands over against the world of objects, in the sense that it cannot be properly said of it that "it is," is that being which is essentially the potentiality of its own being. This is what Jaspers calls *Existenz*. As an empirical being which is "there," which can be objectified and analyzed scientifically, I am *Dasein*, object. But I am something more than something "there." I am, in a sense, not there at all: I am the possibility of my own being, in the sense that I am never something already made, something finished and classifiable: I am constantly creating myself, as it were, or freely realizing my being through my own choices. Existence in the sense of *Existenz* is always possible existence (*mögliche Existenz*). It is true that one can talk about this in general terms; but my possibilities are not yours and my relationship to myself is not yours. *Existenz* is "something" individual and personal. Philosophy, therefore, while it can draw attention to and clarify the meaning of *Existenz*, cannot treat it as a scientifically investigable object. One cannot properly use the categories of Kant in the description of *Existenz*: one has to use categories such as freedom. But the function of the categories suitable for the clarification of existence (*Existenzerhellung*) is rather to draw attention to realities which can be known only through personal experience than to permit scientific knowledge and classification.

The influence of Kant on Jaspers is, I think, clear. The Kantian categories apply to objects of scientific knowledge; the notion of freedom is applicable to the self which transcends scientific treatment. Freedom cannot be proved or disproved; it is not something given which enters the sphere of phenomena.

Freedom is, however, experienced in actual choice when I am aware of my responsibility for what I make of myself. In fact, admission of freedom is the act of one who has the courage to recognize that what he makes of himself is his own creation. This does not mean that there are no empirically ascertainable factors which can be interpreted as " causes " of my conduct and choices; but these are part of the general situation which I assume in order to come to my true liberty. Nor is the moral law denied. But the moral law is freely adopted by the self as a law which enables it to become itself in actuality and not simply in potentiality.

It may be asked, of course, how it is that if *Existenz* cannot be described in universal terms Jaspers devotes the whole of the second volume of his three-volume *Philosophie* to the clarification of it, when any such clarification is bound to be given in universal terms. This is certainly a pertinent question. But one has to bear in mind the fact that the purpose of this clarification is not to give a scientific analysis of *Existenz* but rather to appeal to the individual to recognize his peculiar character as potential existence. It is a means of reminding or of awakening rather than of instructing. This is partly the reason why Jaspers lays such stress on the " exceptions." Consideration of the lives of men like Kierkegaard and Nietzsche shows us the potentialities of human existence. This does not mean that we are given a model or told what to choose: it means that the possibilities of choice are clarified. Again, Jaspers thinks that it is largely in and through what he calls " communication " that one comes to realize one's own possibilities. If we imagine Kierkegaard and Nietzsche revealing each to the other his inmost soul and ideals and strivings, without any attempt to " convert " the other, we can see each man growing in the understanding of the meaning and direction of his own existence. So we, by meditation on Kierkegaard or Nietzsche, can grow in knowledge of our own several concrete possibilities.

Now, I began by saying that for Jaspers philosophy is concerned with Being. And it may appear that we have lost sight of this theme. But this is not really the case. For we have been approaching the position in which the problem of Being becomes real, that is, in which it becomes an existential problem. On the purely scientific level the problem of Being has no meaning. For science deals with the world of objects, and Being is not objectifiable. If it were, it would not be Being. To ask what Being is, is not a scientific question, and it can receive no scientific answer. But the philosopher can show, as we have seen, that science is limited, not in the sense that we can set limits *a priori* to the possible advance of science, but in the sense that it necessarily takes the form of the particular sciences, no one of which can become a substitute for metaphysics. I have already remarked that Jaspers is not an enemy of science. He does not wish to take anything away from science. By pointing out the " limitations " of science he simply leaves the door ajar for metaphysics, a door which is closed by positivism.

It may be said that modern positivism closes the door on metaphysics, not because of some *a priori* dogmatism, but because metaphysical questions are not meaningful questions. But Jaspers could agree with this at the level at which the remark is made by the positivist. The central problem of metaphysics is not a meaningful question if by " meaningful question " we mean a scientifically formulable and answerable question. But the problem of Being does not arise in a positive way on the scientific level; it arises on the plane of *Existenz*. It arises in the context of man's forward-movement towards the discovery of himself in liberty. And this is why it is proper to treat of the clarification of existence (*Existenzerhellung*) before going on to treat of Being considered as the Transcendent. Man does not and cannot discover the Transcendent by science. He discovers the Transcendent only because he is himself a " transcending " being. It is, as it were, in the flight towards his true self that man discovers the Transcendent. But even then he cannot discover it as an object. For the world of objects and of the objectifiable is the sphere of the sciences. Philosophy is, fundamentally, an opening-up of the mind to the Transcendent; and it passes through the stages of considering first the world of science and secondly man as

Existenz. But this does not mean that in the third stage it can achieve a system of the Transcendent, definite and systematic knowledge of the Transcendent. Kant was right in saying that such knowledge is not possible.

In man's forward movement towards the achievement of his true self in liberty he becomes conscious of his finitude. He is conscious of his limits and at the same time of his movement towards the transcending of limits. This is specially clear in the so-called " limiting situations " (*Grenzsituationen*). In the realization of death, for example—not of death in general but of my death as the seal of my finitude—I become conscious at the same time of my limiting situation and of the movement of my liberty to transcend the limiting situation. I thus become aware of myself and of my situation as grounded in Being. I become conscious of the enveloping presence of Being as the ground of all beings. But this does not mean that I apprehend Being as an object or thing alongside or in addition to myself and other things. It is rather that in the awareness of limits I am aware of the Transcendent as the negatively apprehended complement of limits. This awareness is a purely personal act. It cannot be reduced to any universally-valid proof of the Transcendent. Nor have I any private proof of the existence of the Transcendent. I apprehend the Transcendent, not by mystical experience of a positive nature, but only in the authentic exercise of my liberty. And I do not then apprehend it as an object. Rather do I become aware of myself and of all objects as grounded in unobjectifiable Being.

It follows that I cannot attain any scientific assurance of the existence of the Transcendent. I can affirm my relationship to the Transcendent by " philosophic faith," as *my* truth, affirmed in the exercise of my liberty. Or I can deny the Transcendent and my relationship to it. True, a man can remain immersed in " unauthentic " existence, immersed purely in the world of objects; and then he will remain blind to the Transcendent. But even if a man rises above unauthentic existence, the so-called bourgeois mentality, he can still deny the Transcendent. For the Transcendent is not something the existence of which can be proved. Its affirmation or denial is a matter of liberty. I can affirm it and come to my true self, grounded in Being, or I can deny it: the two possibilities, represented by Kierkegaard and Nietzsche, remain open. All that philosophy can do is to clarify and facilitate choice. It cannot make a man's choice for him; nor can it provide proofs as a substitute for choice.

It follows also, of course, that philosophy can give no universally-valid description of the Transcendent. Indeed, every metaphysical system, every religion, is a subjectively-grounded deciphering of unobjectifiable Being. They certainly have their value; but no one of them can be considered as final. This is one of the reasons why Jaspers has spoken of a tension between philosophy and religion and why he distinguishes sharply between theological faith, that is, faith in definite doctrines accepted on authority, and " philosophical faith," the latter being the leap involved in the affirmation of what can neither be proved nor disproved nor described.

At the same time we can see, I think, a definite movement in Jaspers' later philosophy towards a more clearly theistic position. He has always spoken of " God "; but the word seems to have meant for a time simply enveloping and comprehensive Being, which is not, indeed, identifiable with the world of objects but which is not a Being apart from the world. He has more and more tended, however, to emphasize the symbolic character of the world and of all events. For philosophic faith they are all signs of God. Even historical disaster and ruin can be for faith a sign of or pointer to God. For the shipwreck of man's ideals and hopes reveals the finitude and contingency and passing character of all objects and is a sign for faith of the fact that though all the finite perishes God remains. Moreover, Jaspers seems to attach more value than he formerly did to the traditional proofs of God's existence. He does not regard them as logically cogent arguments, it is true. But he is more ready to recognize their perennial value as signs or pointers to God or as expressions, in a formalized way, of man's awareness of the relation of things to God.

I have already remarked that we can see in Jaspers a

Kantian who has undergone the shock of prolonged meditation on the significance of Kierkegaard and Nietzsche and other " exceptions." Probably we can also see in his philosophy echoes of his Lutheran upbringing. But the main point which I wish to make is that we find in him a man who, while fully conscious of the advance and scope of the sciences, really does believe in the value and peculiar function of philosophy and who, in the modern world, bears witness to man's need of and orientation to the Transcendent. At the same time it is easy to understand that though his philosophy is capable of providing stimulus and inspiration his influence is comparatively limited in the academic philosophical world. For his philosophy has really one aim, to illuminate and facilitate man's act of transcending all that can be clearly conceived. And though, for my own part, I have considerable sympathy with Jaspers I can appreciate the fact that in his own country university professors and their students find something more tangible to bite on in Heidegger's phenomenological analyses. One can understand the attitude of those who say that Heidegger does at least take us somewhere whereas Jaspers' concern is to take us into the realm of the unthinkable. I do not say that it is a fair or adequate judgment. I merely say that it is an understandable judgment.

3

I have left myself very little time to speak of Gabriel Marcel. And all that I can do is to make some general remarks about his philosophy which may make it easier to understand what he is about. He is a peculiarly elusive thinker, a philosopher whom it is extremely difficult to summarize. This difficulty arises partly from the fact that his philosophy is dispersed in journals, plays, articles, lectures and books and that he has never worked out any systematic presentation of his thought. But the difficulty which confronts the would-be summarizer arises much more, I think, from the nature of his reflections than from the fact that they are dispersed in a variety of writings. Marcel is a personal thinker in the sense that he reflects on experiences which have for him in his own life a special importance and which seem to him to possess metaphysical significance and implications. His reflections are thus part and parcel of his own spiritual itinerary. I do not mean by this that his thought centres round privileged experiences in the sense in which a mystic's experiences are privileged. On the contrary, Marcel reflects on experiences such as hope, love and fidelity, which can in principle be shared by anyone. In his meditations he does not inhabit a shut-off world of his own. By reflection he advances on to the level of communication and universalization. But his reflections do not take the form of exposing " results "; they are rather a series of explorations of various themes. In reading them, therefore, we are following out the actual process of reflecting rather than learning the conclusions arrived at. Marcel doubtless does arrive at " conclusions "; but these are often not properly intelligible apart from the highly personal process of reflection by which he arrives at them. Hence no systematized summary of his thought can really convey the spirit of his philosophy.

However, one must begin somewhere. And I begin with the distinction which is mentioned by every writer on Marcel, namely the distinction between problem and mystery. A " problem " is a question which can be considered purely objectively, a question in which the being of the questioner is not involved. A mathematical problem is a case in point. I can, of course, be extremely interested in a mathematical problem; and it is obvious that it is I who raise and consider the problem. But when I consider it I abstract altogether from myself; I objectify the problem, hold it over against myself, leave myself out of the picture. There may, of course, be accidental reasons why it is important for me in particular to solve the problem (I may be sitting for a vital examination, for instance); but I do not enter into the problem as such. As far as the problem itself is concerned, I am simply the epistemological subject, and my place might be taken by anyone else, perhaps even by a machine. A " mystery " on the other hand is a question which involves the being of the questioner, so that in considering the question or theme the questioner cannot disregard himself. Suppose that I ask

" What am I ? " I can reflect on this question from the outside, as it were, from the point of view of a physiologist, for instance. I then make of the question a " problem." But by doing so I leave out of account the questioner to the extent that the questioner cannot be objectified as the object of the physiologist. There is something which escapes analysis. If, however, I really mean to ask about the totality of myself, I must consider the self that asks and considers the question. And I cannot objectify myself as questioner. In order, therefroe, to consider the totality of my existence, I must make use of another method of reflection than the method of objectification. The method of reflection which is appropriate for " problems " is not appropriate for " mysteries."

Before going any further I had better make it clear that the word " mystery " must not be here understood in the theological sense of a truth revealed by God which cannot be proved by the human reason alone. Nor does " mystery " mean that which is mysterious in the sense of that which we do not now know because we lack the means at present of answering the relevant problem. " Mystery " is neither revealed truth nor the unknown. The word is used to refer to that which is given in experience but which cannot be objectified in such a way that the subject can be simply disregarded.

The matter may be made clearer by introducing Marcel's distinction between " first reflection " and " second reflection." And to explain this distinction I take the concrete illustration of love. First of all there is the level of immediate experience, the existential level. John and Mary love one another. Here we have a concrete unity. Each doubtless thinks about the other; but, we will suppose, neither reflects about love in general. Loving and reflecting about love are distinguishable activities.

But let us suppose that John, who loves Mary, does begin to reflect explicitly about the nature of love. One way of doing it would be this. John stands back from the activity of loving in order to look at it and analyze it from outside; he objectifies love, holds it over against himself as a kind of public-property object " out there," apart from himself. His attitude becomes not that of the lover but that of the scientist. Perhaps he then proceeds to analyze and describe the activity of loving in physiological terms. Or he may frame hypotheses, say on the Freudian model, to account for the genesis and nature of the activity of loving. John is no longer John-loving-Mary. He is an instance of scientific mind impersonally regarding its object and analyzing it into its component factors. For his present purposes Mary is no longer the unique beloved: she is simply one possible object of an activity which is itself turned into an object and subjected to scientific analysis and description. The magic of love fades away in the sharp cold light of impersonal objective science.

This kind of reflection is called by Marcel " first reflection." And it is clear that in the example which I have taken the question, What is love? is treated as a " problem " in Marcel's technical use of the term. First reflection, objectification and the notion of " problem " go together.

On the level of first reflection the concrete unity of pre-reflective immediate experience is broken up. But it is possible to envisage another type of reflection, called by Marcel " second reflection," which endeavours to combine, so far as this is possible, the immediacy of experience with reflection. To carry on with the example chosen, it is possible to envisage a reflection which holds together all the time the concrete unity established by the personal communion of love. John reflects; but he reflects, so far as this is possible, from within the experience itself, not from outside. He reflects on the metaphysical significance of love as a communion or together-ness of persons, as a participation in Being. He asks not, What is love seen purely from the outside? but, What does this experience reveal to me of myself as a human person in communion with another and of Being in general? He is concerned, not with a " problem," but with a " mystery." Second reflection and the notion of " mystery " go together.

All this is obviously very difficult. As long as one keeps to very general ideas, one may think that one understands. I mean, one can understand the dream of recapturing at a higher level the immediacy of the existential level, which is lost on the level of first reflection or scientific analysis. But once one begins to make the attempt to state in precise terms the nature of second reflection one very soon gets into difficulties. However, one thing at least is clear. Just as Marcel is resolutely opposed to all those social and political forces which tend to " objectify " completely the human person, turning him into an " it," a mere member of a collectivity, or reducing him simply to his social function, so in philosophy he is opposed, not only to positivism, but also to absolute idealism (to which, in its Anglo-Saxon form, he was once attracted) and to all forms of philosophy which appear to him to surrender to the spirit of " objectification " and, in particular, to slur over, disregard or mutilate the concrete experience of the human person as person. Indeed, the idea of the person is so important in his philosophy that I propose to centre my concluding remarks round the question " What am I? " or " What does it mean to be a person? "

The fundamental human condition is to be in a situation, not in this or that particular situation, but in the world. I am from the start in the world, participating in Being and open to Being. The subject-object. relation arises on the level of reflection; but the primary datum is not myself as a self-enclosed ego but myself in the world, present in a situation.

My insertion into the spatio-temporal synthesis, the cosmos, is through my body. I am present in the world as " incarnated." This does not mean that my body is simply an instrument whereby I receive messages (sensations) from a world which is alien to me. My body is not an instrument which I possess in the same sense in which I possess and use a fountain-pen or a pair of binoculars. True, I can say " I have a body," but my relation to my body is not adequately expressed by the word " having." Nor is it adequately expressed by saying that " I am " my body. Neither expression is adequate. My relation to my body is " mysterious." The relation is irreducible, *sui generis*: it does not lend itself to description in terms like " having " which are taken from the world of objects. But in any case through " incarnation " I participate in Being, primarily in the spatio-temporal world.

169

Yet I do not participate in Being simply in the sense of the physical material cosmos. As a human person I am essentially open to " the other." But my relation to other human beings can be of two main types. First, the other person can be for me an " object," an " it." This can be illustrated in various ways. For instance, in that kind of " love " where one human being is for another simply an instrument for his self-satisfaction the former is an " object " for the latter. Again, to take a less dramatic example, as long as someone is for me no more than an anonymous tram-conductor, he is for me an " object." We are caught, as it were, in the grip of the subject-object relation which is characteristic of the level of first reflection. Secondly, a human being can be for me, not simply an " object," an " it," or a " he " or " she," but a " thou " (*tu*, *Du*). We are here on the plane of intersubjectivity. And on this plane, where I transcend the narrowness of egoism and the subject-object relation, there arise personal relationships like love and fidelity and " disponibility " (being available, as a person, for another) which can be explored by second reflection. On the plane of intersubjectivity I consciously realize and appropriate my participation in Being at the level of personal communion and communication.

On this plane of intersubjectivity my exigency or demand for Being is partially satisfied. In communion with another and in fidelity towards another I transcend the relation of " having " (an object) and am in the sphere of Being. The other is present to me, not necessarily in the local or spatial sense, and we both participate in Being, this participation being appropriated in an activity like loving. But my exigency for Being is set towards the absolute and unconditioned, though not to the exclusion of the finite and conditioned. I aspire to an absolute self-commitment and to an absolute fidelity and loyalty. I may first aspire towards this within the sphere of human relationships. But reflection shows me that this involves the invocation of the absolute Thou who is the ground of all being and value and who alone makes eternal fidelity possible. Thus in the exploration of the relationships which arise on the plane of intersubjectivity I " discover "

God as the personal transcendent Absolute, and I become conscious of the orientation of my personality towards the absolute Thou, God. I am open to Being from the start; and the conscious appropriation of this openness leads from the transcending of egoism in communion with others to a personal self-relating, in adoration and prayer, to God. Through second reflection on the relationships which arise on the plane of intersubjectivity I come to see their metaphysical significance within the context of my existence as a person. And I see that I become effectively a human person only through self-transcendence, only through actual and conscious communion with other human beings and with God.

Marcel thus endeavours to reawaken the sense of depth and the awareness of metaphysical significance in the familiar and common. He often starts with a familiar term, such as " have " or " presence," and proceeds to analyze its meaning. For a moment we may think that we are listening to a linguistic analyst. But very soon we find him opening up for us the metaphysical significance which lies hidden behind the apparently ordinary and trivial term. We can say perhaps that he is concerned with revealing the implications of personal experience. But he does not do this by presupposing a set of principles and concepts which imply a whole system and then forcing experience into this preconceived mould. Rather does he attempt to unfold the metaphysical significance of an experience from within that experience itself. He endeavours to make us look, see and appropriate rather than to prove to us propositions in a deductive sense of " prove."

The absence of " proof " in Marcel's writings is, indeed, apt to give rise to dissatisfaction in the reader. True, it is unlikely that anyone will complain that he does not prove the existence of the external world and of other persons. For it is sufficiently obvious that any attempt to do this would be quite inconsistent with his point of view. If the fundamental datum is a self in the world, and if consciousness of the self as subject arises only *pari passu* with consciousness of the object, and if knowledge of oneself grows concomitantly with knowledge of others, it would be clearly inappropriate to attempt to prove the falsity of solipsism, as though the primary datum were in fact a self-enclosed and isolated ego. And Marcel's point of view here fits in with the common-sense point of view. For nobody really believes seriously in solipsism. At the same time it is natural to ask how Marcel shows that God exists. For whereas the external world and other people fall within the ambit of common experience, God is transcendent. But we have to remember that Marcel is concerned with leading a man to the point at which God is " encountered " as the absolute Thou, and that arguments for the existence of a " First Cause," for example, appear to him to have little relevance with respect to the attainment of this end. If a man persists in remaining on the level of " first reflection," he could at best be brought only to recognizing God as what He in fact is not, an " object," the conclusion of a syllogism or an astronomical hypothesis. If, however, a man places himself on the level of " second reflection," he can discover God as the personal Absolute who gives significance and value to those personal relationships which arise on the plane of intersubjectivity. It will be seen that we have here a version of the old distinction between the God of the philosophers and the God of Abraham, Isaac and Jacob. I certainly do not say that I consider Marcel's point of view adequate. I simply wish to draw attention to what it is. In his eyes the discovery of God on the level of second reflection is " wishful thinking " only for the man who remains obstinately on the level of first reflection and shuts his eyes to the metaphysical significance of personal experience.

In view of the fact that Marcel is a convinced Catholic it may occur to some of you to think that his philosophy is the outcome of his Catholicism and that his reflections have been deliberately arranged so as to lead on to the idea of the divine response, in terms of Christian revelation, to man's invocation and appeal. But this would be a mistaken view. Apart from the fact that he does not have recourse to Catholic dogmas in his philosophical reflections, the foundations of his philosophical approach were laid long before he was received into the Church in 1929, when he was already thirty-nine years old.

His own spiritual itinerary, of which, as I have said, his philosophical reflections form an integral part, led him to Christianity; and he philosophizes, of course, in the light of his Christian faith, for the simple reason that he thinks and reflects as a definite human person, as Gabriel Marcel. But he is not a disguised Catholic theologian: he is and remains a philosopher, and a philosopher of a highly original stamp. True, in some important respects his thought is akin to that of both Kierkegaard and Jaspers; but this affinity is a matter of fact, not the result of borrowing or of historical influence. Marcel pursued his own independent path.

4

These sketches of Kierkegaard, Jaspers and Marcel should have made it clear that the theistic existentialist philosophies (so far as it is legitimate to call Marcel an " existentialist ") have certain traits in common. For example, none of them arrive at the affirmation of God as the result of cosmological speculation: for each of them God is discovered or encountered by the individual in the movement towards the free realization and appropriation of his true self rather than as the term of impersonal objective argument. To say this is not to say that the act of self-relating to God as " my truth " is for them an irrational act, a purely capricious act of choice. Kierkegaard, indeed, may tend to give this impression on occasion. But Jaspers emphasizes the insecurity and evanescent character of finite existence and what may be called the " experience " or " apprehension " of the Comprehensive, of enveloping Being, provided that one does not understand " experience " here as meaning privileged mystical experience or anything approaching direct contact with God. As for Marcel, he certainly would not admit that cosmological proof and an irrational leap are alternatives which exhaust the possibilities of a positive approach to God. In his eyes exploration of the significance of those forms of experience which involve one as a person leads us to God. We are already in the sphere of Being, and, according to him, we cannot here legitimately dissociate idea from reality or idea from the certainty which attaches to it. If a man maintains that the world and human existence are " absurd," we can only invite him to reconsider personal experience and its significance. And even if we cannot compel him to change his point of view by irrefutable demonstrations, we can at least help him to see a metaphysical significance which is there to be found by anyone who approaches it with an open mind.

The theistic existentialists thus strive to overcome human alienation by the rediscovery of the world of personal communion with other persons and with God. They try to reawaken modern man to a sense of depth and mystery in the familiar and to show how he can find his true self only in the conscious appropriation of his relation both to the finite and to the infinite " thou."[1] Modern man, alienated from his true self, strives to find it. Philosophy can illuminate his way. But the last word rests with man's liberty. Philosophy can illuminate choice: it cannot perform a man's act of choice for him.

---

[1]Perhaps this sentence does not fit Jaspers very well, since the personality of God is for him a subjectively-grounded deciphering of the Transcendent; but general statements are apt to fall short somewhere.

CHAPTER XI

ATHEISTIC EXISTENTIALISM

I

THE atheistic existentialist starts from the position of the man for whom, in Nietzsche's phrase, " God is dead "; that is to say, from the position of the man for whom the idea of God, at least of God as revealed in the Judaeo-Christian tradition, no longer possesses any validity. For such a man belief in God is more or less on a footing with belief in elves or fairies. It has never been proved that there are no elves or fairies. If someone persists in saying that there is an elf behind the tree and that when we look at the tree the elf always slips with incredible rapidity to the other side, so that he remains invisible, we cannot prove to him that what he says is false, even though he may be unable to produce any evidence to show that what he says is true. None the less most people, at least in our technical civilization, do not believe in elves and fairies. Similarly, some would claim, it cannot, in the nature of the case, be proved that God does not exist; but there is no good evidence that He does exist, and many people have simply ceased to believe that there is a God.

Now, Nietzsche argued that once belief in the Christian God is dead belief in the Christian moral code, as a universally valid moral code, must also eventually perish. To put the matter more generally, if there is no God, there is no universally-obligatory moral law and no absolute objective values. If there is no God, " everything is permitted," as Dostoevsky's character said. The free human being is thus thrown back on himself and made totally responsible. In a godless world he has to choose his own set of values, and if any meaning is to be found in human life it can only be the meaning which man himself has given it. We have, therefore,

175

the man who has to act in this world in which he finds himself and who at the same time cannot look for help or guidance either to God or to an autonomous and universally valid moral law or to a realm of absolute values. It is to man in this state of alienation and loneliness that the message of atheistic existentialism is primarily addressed.

What I have been saying will fit pretty well the philosophy of M. Sartre. But I have also included in this lecture some remarks about Heidegger. And this fact prompts both an apology and an admission. I must apologize to Professor Heidegger for including him in a lecture entitled "Atheistic Existentialism" when he has rejected the atheistic interpretation of his philosophy. And I must admit that my reason for including him here is that I do not know where else to put him, once given the division of lecture-themes which I have adopted. For even though he does not state that there is no God, he does not affirm God's existence. Hence his philosophy could not have been treated in the previous lecture. And if I am not to omit him altogether (which he would probably prefer, but which you might reasonably resent), I have to say something about his thought in the present lecture. If I am brief in my remarks on the subject, this is not because I do not consider his philosophy to be of importance, but rather because of its complicated character and because it is at any rate disputable to what extent it is legitimate to introduce him at all in the present context.

2

Martin Heidegger was born in 1889 and was brought up as a Catholic. Although he later came under the influence of the Neo-Kantian tradition and subsequently under that of Husserl, before developing his own line of thought, it is worthy of note that he has an extensive knowledge of Greek and mediaeval philosophy and that his first published work was on the British mediaeval philosopher, John Duns Scotus. He makes no secret of the fact that his own philosophy stands in a close relationship with past European speculation and that it is, or was, his ambition to be the Aristotle of our time, so far as the problem of Being is concerned.

At the beginning of *Sein und Zeit* Heidegger speaks of renewing this problem, the problem of the meaning of Being (*das Sein*). We all have some preliminary understanding of the meaning of Being, since we are constantly using words which imply such an understanding. On the other hand, it is improbable that we can give any clear account of what is meant by the term. But though the problem of the meaning of Being is a classical problem, it does not follow that the approach which was adopted by Aristotle, for example, is a suitable approach. The problem needs to be taken up afresh, and, in particular, the way of approaching the problem needs to be reconsidered. To ask for the meaning of Being is not to ask a grammatical question: it is to ask what the Being (*das Sein*) of beings (*die Seienden*) is. We have to settle, therefore, what particular kind of being is to be selected for philosophical analysis as the first step in the search for the meaning of Being. And, according to Heidegger, we must start with the being of the questioner himself. Man stands in a peculiar position with regard to the problem of Being. It is he who raises the problem; and he is able to do this because he has a special relation to Being. The raising of the problem is itself a mode of being. Aristotle drew attention to this when he said that philosophy begins with wonder; for the capacity for this contemplative wonder is a mark of man. But it does not follow that we should begin, as Aristotle did, by investigating the different objects of human knowledge and endeavouring in this way to discover the categories of Being. We should start rather with man considered as the being who is capable of raising the problem of Being.

A natural question to ask at this point is, what precisely is Heidegger looking for; what is this problem of Being? It is not the problem of ultimate reality, of transcendent being in the sense of God. For according to Heidegger God would be a being rather than Being. And it is Being, not beings or a being, with which we are concerned. The problem is that of the being of beings. What is Being in itself? One might be inclined to comment that apart from beings there is no Being. For if there were, it would be a being. But Heidegger knows this, of course. And we might therefore expect of him an analysis of what it means to say of anything that " it is." And then, some would say, we are concerned with a problem of linguistic analysis. And I suppose that the problem is for Heidegger a linguistic or logical problem up to a certain point. Yet at times he appears to speak about Being as though he were talking about the Absolute or about the Transcendent. And it seems to me, though I have very probably misunderstood him, that he oscillates between the point of view of a logical analyst and that of a metaphysician without making it really clear with what precise problem he is engaged. Professedly, however, he is concerned with a problem in ontology, which is prior to any problem about God. Before we can even raise the problem of God we must answer the question, What is the Being of beings? And as it is man who raises this problem and who thus has a preliminary idea of Being and stands in a special relation to Being, we should start with an analysis of man as the being who is open to Being. And it is this analysis of man which has attracted most attention from Heidegger's readers.

Man, *Dasein*, is " existence," *Existenz*. But human existence cannot really be defined; for it is potential being or a potentiality of being. Man is continually in advance of himself, so to speak, reaching out into the future, transcending himself. At the same time we can analyze the ontological structure and mode of existence of man. And the first thing to notice is that man is being-in-the-world. Now, that man is *de facto* in the world, in the sense that he stands in relation with other things and persons, is obvious enough. But Heidegger does not mean merely that man finds himself standing, as a matter of fact, in relations with other things and persons. He means that man exists as a being which is necessarily preoccupied or concerned with " the other." He is not, of course, necessarily concerned with this or that particular thing which one can mention. But the relationship of being preoccupied or concerned with is a constitutive mode of his existence: he exists as being preoccupied or concerned with " the other." He is concerned with " the other " in his forward movement towards the realization of his own possibilities; and through his preoccupation or concern he constitutes the world as a meaningful system of objects standing in intelligible relations to one another and to man himself. The world of things is for Heidegger the world of tools (*Zeuge*) or instruments. Their mode of being is to exist for. . . . The earth *is* for the farmer that which he ploughs in order to grow corn. It means, however, something else for the geologist, and something else for the general or the military strategist. What it means for each is determined by the particular form taken by that fundamental preoccupation or concern which constitutes him as a human being. In his forward movement towards the realization of his own possibilities as being-in-the-world, preoccupied with " the other," man constitutes the intelligible or meaningful system of objects which is at the same time the result of his forward movement and the field in which his particular projects can be realized. Man is being-in-the-world as concerned with things as tools in the realization of his own possibilities. But to say that man is concerned with things as tools or instruments must not be understood as excluding a variety of perspectives or points of view. It may appear at first hearing that to say that a razor-blade, for instance, receives its meaning or intelligible function through man is to place all the emphasis on " practical " concern (the point of view of the man for whom a razor-blade is an instrument for shaving) to the exclusion of the scientific point of view, the point of view, say, of the man who is interested simply in " objective " study of the physical constitution of the thing which we call a razor-blade. But the scientist also has a purpose, though it is not the same as the purpose of the man who wishes to shave, and his perspective or view of the object is determined by his purpose. The practical point of view does not enjoy an exclusive privilege. But neither does the point of view of the scientist. Preoccupation can take different forms and can give rise to different, though complementary, meaningful systems.

Perhaps it may be as well to point out that Heidegger is

not saying that the human ego is responsible for the being of everything other than itself. That which is created by my preoccupation is the meaningful system or systems which form my world, not the brute " thereness " of the other. Again, the individual comes to discover himself as an individual subject only as a being within the world and as a being in relation with other persons. Social interdependence, being-with, is also (that is, in addition to preoccupation with things as tools) constitutive of my mode of existence as a human being. The human being is in the world as a member of " the one " (*das Man*); and this fundamental social interdependence shows itself in his participation in established ways of thinking (" one thinks ") and feeling (" one feels "). Being-in-the-world is being-with (*Mitsein*); and private perspectives arise only on the basis of a common world constituted by the concern or preoccupation which is a fundamental characteristic of man considered as a member of " the one." " My " world pre-supposes " one's " world. Man is a being who is set towards the realization of his possibilities, not as an isolated ego, but as a being who is necessarily interrelated with the world of things and the world of persons.

It follows that man can never wholly escape from the impersonal anonymous form of existence which is rooted in membership of " the one." At the same time man, as potential being, is not condemned to one way of realizing himself, of existing. Two main paths lie open to him. He can acquiesce in his membership of " the one " to the extent of becoming absorbed or immersed in the crowd-consciousness, thus gaining assurance at the expense of personal responsibility and resolute self-direction. This is " unauthentic " existence. Or he can, within limits at least, assume personal responsibility for his destiny, freely choosing his own possibilities, above all his destiny to death. This is " authentic " existence.

But how is it that these two paths lie open to man? In order to understand this we must realize that man is in the world as " thrown " into the world. It is as a being which is " thrown " into the world, finite and abandoned, that he reaches out towards the realization of his possibilities and, in doing so, interprets the world and forms his particular projects. And his final " possibility," which itself annihilates all other possibilities, is death. Man is the being who transcends himself in his movement towards the future, as a being who is " thrown " into the world and who is destined to death. And the effective tonality of the obscure consciousness of contingency and finiteness and dereliction and destiny to death, the obscure consciousness, that is to say, of his fundamental situation or condition, is " dread." But he can attempt to flee from the dread which accompanies the obscure consciousness of what it means to be in the world by immersing himself in " the one " and absorbing himself in his preoccupations. Death then becomes for him something which happens to " one." Or he can resist the temptation to distract himself from the consciousness of his radical contingency and freely assume his situation as a being in the world. To do this is to choose authentic existence, living *sub specie mortis*, provided that he at the same time commits himself to the fulfilment of the possibilities which are here and now open to him and which only he can fulfil. For authentic existence does not mean withdrawal from all self-commitment within the world. As we have seen, a pure authentic existence is not possible, since a man always retains his membership of " the one." But authentic existence is possible within limits.

I must now introduce a further idea. According to Heidegger, the fundamental structure of man is Care (*Sorge*). And this comprises three moments or elements. First, there is man's concern with what he is to be. *Existenz* means being-in-front-of-oneself or self-projection. And as man is *Existenz*, we must say that futurity characterizes man. Or, rather, man, self-projection, grounds futurity. And his concern with what he is to be is the first moment of Care. Secondly, man also finds himself in the world as " thrown." And man's concern with himself as thrown into the world (the second constitutive moment of Care) grounds the past. Thirdly, man's being-with (the things in the world) and his entanglement with particular preoccupations in the world grounds the present. Care, therefore, has three temporal moments, the primary moment being futurity. And as Care is the fundamental structure of man (of him who exists as self-projection in a world in which he finds himself as thrown and in which he is entangled through his preoccupations), it follows that man is temporal in structure. My being is a flight from nothingness to nothingness in which, as accepting and willing my throwness into the world and my relations in the world, I constitute past and present as I reach out to the future.

Now, if the general problem of Being has to be approached through an analysis of the being of man, and if the being of man reveals itself as essentially temporal, may it not be that time forms the horizon for an interpretation of Being? With this question the first volume of *Sein und Zeit* closes. And we still await the second volume. It is understandable, therefore, that attention has been devoted to Heidegger's analysis of man rather than to his examination of the general ontological problem of Being; for the latter has been withheld from us.

Now, those who, on the basis of the first volume of *Sein und Zeit*, have interpreted Heidegger's philosophy in an atheistic sense cannot, in my opinion, be blamed for doing so. True, he does not deny the existence of God in so many words. But he seems, at first sight, to suggest that apart from man himself and the brute impenetrable existence of things there is Nothing. And the way in which he handles the problem of Being seems to suggest that for him Being is necessarily finite and temporal. And, if this were the case, the existence of an infinite Being, transcending the temporal order, would be ruled out. Indeed, we could not significantly raise the problem of God.

Heidegger, however, has protested in energetic terms against the atheistic interpretation of his philosophy. He does so, for example, in his *Letter on Humanism (Brief über den Humanismus)*. The existential analysis of man, we are told, neither affirms nor denies God (a statement also made in *Vom Wesen des Grundes*). Yet this is not indifferentism. The problem of the existence of God cannot be raised on the level of thought to which the existential analysis of man belongs; it can be raised only on the plane of " the holy." Modern man is so absorbed in his preoccupations in the world that he is not open to the plane of " the holy," and the idea of God, as traditionally interpreted, has retreated from his consciousness. But the " death of God," in the sense that the Christian idea of God has lost its hold on men's minds, does not mean that there is no God. Heidegger tells us that his philosophy is a waiting for God, for a new manifestation of the divine, and that here lies the problem of the world. Meanwhile poets like Hölderlin bear witness, in an obscure and prophetic way, to the divine; and in his *Hölderlinstudien* Heidegger depicts the poet as discerning the presence of the Transcendent in " the nothingness of beings." As for the question whether time forms the horizon for the interpretation of Being, this does not mean that Being is necessarily temporal and finite. It is, rather, equivalent to asking whether the new method of approach to the problem of Being is the right one. And the answer to this question can be given only after the attempt has been made to solve the problem of Being in this way.

Heidegger is also careful to insist that when he said that man is being-in-the-world he did not mean to affirm that man is a this-worldly being in the metaphysical and theological senses. And the term " the world " (*die Welt*) should not be taken to mean " this world " in contrast with " the other world " or the material world as contrasted with the spiritual world; to say that man is a being in the world means, according to Heidegger's interpretation of his philosophy, that man is open to Being. And in later writings he has depicted man as the " shepherd " or guardian of Being. It is man who can raise the problem of Being; and he can do so because he ex-sists or stands out from the background of Nature as open to Being. This openness can be obscured, and has been obscured; but this does not alter the fact that man, as man, is potentially open to the mystery of Being. And it is only when he is effectively open to this mystery that he can profitably raise the problem of God.

Whether Heidegger's interpretation of his earlier statements is simply a case of clearing up misunderstandings or whether it constitutes a re-interpretation and a transition to a different point of view is not a question which matters very much.

More important from the point of view of the student of Heidegger's philosophy is the difficulty experienced in deciphering his meaning, especially perhaps when he speaks about Being and Nothingness. In his later writings at least man appears as ex-sisting or as ek-sisting as guardian of Being. But is Being to be interpreted as a general concept contained by emptying out all determinations, so that in its vacuity it seems to glide into Nothingness, or is Being to be taken in the sense of the Transcendent? Or is it a mixture of both? The answer does not appear to me to be at all clear. And the ambiguities in Heidegger's philosophy are, of course, the reason why it is always possible for him to insist that nobody has understood him. Some of his ardent disciples, indeed, go so far as to suggest that any criticism of the Master manifests an incapacity to understand him. But if they themselves understand him clearly, it is a great pity that they do not have compassion on the weakness of the rest of us and reveal the secret in unambiguous terms. Or does ambiguity belong to the essence of Heidegger's philosophy?

3

When we turn to M. Sartre, who was born in 1905, we are not left in such perplexity. It is true that Sartre uses strange and obscure terms and phrases, borrowed in part from German forms of expression; but at the same time there is no very great difficulty in making out the general plan of his philosophy. In spite of his determination to be " profound " the clarity of the Frenchman makes itself apparent. And Sartre has, of course, given a very clear popular account of his thought in his lecture on *Existentialism and Humanism* for those who feel unable to cope with the mysteries of *L'Être et le Néant*, his chief philosophical work.

Sartre appears to be a man for whom " God is dead," a man, that is to say, for whom God has passed away into the realm of mythology together with elves and fairies. The remark made by Matthieu Delarue in *Le Sursis* when he reads part of Daniel Sereno's long letter narrating his conversion (a conversion which, to judge by the next instalment of *Les Chemins de la Liberté*, seems to have been of short duration) and then throws it out of the window with the exclamation, *Quelles vieilleries!* illustrates, I imagine, M. Sartre's own attitude. In his case there is no ambiguity, as there is in the case of Heidegger; there is no doubt about his atheism. Sometimes, indeed, he says that, even if God existed, this would make no difference (in the sense at least that man would still be free and so responsible); but in his lecture on humanism he declares explicitly that " existentialism is nothing else but an attempt to draw all the consequences from a consistent atheist position." And, as we will see, the conclusions which he draws from atheism are important conclusions.

I do not, however, wish to give the impression that Sartre simply assumes atheism without more ado. For he argues that the idea of God is self-contradictory; there cannot be a God. And I wish to illustrate this point of view in a way which at the same time will throw light on Sartre's general philosophical position. I can, however, mention only a few points. Anyone who desires to acquaint himself with the details of Sartre's analysis of Being and of consciousness must consult *L'Être et le Néant*.

The shadow of Descartes lies over French philosophy. And it is no matter for surprise that Sartre starts with " subjectivity," with the idea of consciousness. Consciousness is always consciousness of something. True, implicit in consciousness and accompanying it is awareness of my consciousness. But awareness of my consciousness is awareness of my being conscious of something. And this something, the object of consciousness, is other than the subject. To say that consciousness is always consciousness of something is not to say that consciousness creates the being of the object: it is to say that consciousness by its very nature implies an object which cannot be reduced to consciousness. And if consciousness always implies an object which is itself irreducible to consciousness, there is no sense in starting with consciousness and attempting to prove the existence of an object which is other than consciousness. For this is already given in the starting-point. To follow Descartes in starting with consciousness does not commit one to following him in his attempt to prove the existence of the external world.

We have, therefore, the conscious subject, *le pour-soi*. Now, all objects of consciousness are phenomenal in the sense that they appear to or for consciousness. And we cannot, according to Sartre, properly inquire what lies " behind " appearance. But we can investigate the being of appearance or the being of the phenomenon. And if we do so, transphenomenal being turns out to be opaque, self-identical being. Strip away all determinate characteristics and all those meanings which are due to human interpretation in function of human purposes, and you are left with being-in-itself, of which we can only say that it is. This is *l'en-soi*.

There are, therefore, two fundamental modes of being, *le pour-soi* and *l'en-soi*. But let us examine the former a little more closely. Consciousness, as we have seen, is consciousness of something. It is therefore distance from or negation of. And this idea gives us the key to the nature of consciousness. Consciousness is a separation from; and yet what separates the *pour-soi* from the *en-soi* is nothing. Consciousness comes into being through the secretion of nothing. A rift or fissure, as it were, appears in being; and this rift or fissure cannot be described because it is nothing. Nothingness lies at the heart of consciousness. The latter is said by Sartre to secrete the nothingness which separates it from opaque, self-identical being; and man can thus be described as the being by which nothingness comes into the world. This does not mean that consciousness achieves a separation from the *en-soi* and a constitution of itself once and for all: it is constantly reconstituting itself as separation-from in regard to every particular object. Consciousness is always contingent; it always depends on the *en-soi*. At the same time it is separated from the *en-soi*, though that which separates it is nothing.

I must confess that as consciousness is said to be separated from the *en-soi* by nothing, and as it is said to secrete this nothing, it is not at all clear to me how consciousness is supposed to arise in the first place. However, let us take it that consciousness means separation from the *en-soi* to which it is present. We must add that *le pour-soi* does not separate itself only from the *en-soi* in the sense of the " external " object in the ordinary sense; it also separates itself from itself, constituting its own past as *en-soi*. By doing this I project myself into the future. By my self-transcendence and flight into the future I constitute past and present. Man's mode of being is thus temporal or historical. Temporality is in fact created by consciousness. This does not mean that there is no sense in talking, for example, about the history of the world. But the world as phenomenon comes into being through the act by which the *pour-soi* separates itself from the *en-soi*; and it is the world as phenomenon which has a history. Transphenomenal being is opaque, self-identical, non-temporal.

Further, the act by which *le pour-soi* separates itself from its past constitutes man's liberty. I am not simply my past: on the contrary, I separate myself from it, though the interval is nothing. I am thus not determined by my past; for I am separated from it. I am free. And I remain free, freely constituting my future, until death supervenes and extinguishes all my possibilities. (Sartre does not accept Heidegger's notion that my death is itself one of my possibilities. It is rather that which annihilates all possibilities.) Death reduces me finally to the condition of *l'en-soi*; so that I become identical with my past and remain an object for others. Liberty can thus be described as the human being separating himself from his past " by secreting his own nothing." My essence is what I have made of myself, it is myself considered historically. In this sense existence precedes essence; and the enunciation of this proposition is bound up with the affirmation of liberty.

Consciousness thus means being present to oneself as distant from oneself; and this distance is nothing. Nothingness is present at the heart of consciousness, haunting it; and consciousness is inherently and perpetually unstable and contingent. *Le pour-soi*, however, always aspires to overcome this instability and lack, this constant flight from itself as *en-soi*, by achieving self-identity without ceasing to be consciousness. The fundamental drive in self-transcendence, in the flight into the future, is the drive towards the unification of *pour-soi* with *en-soi*, towards consciousness' self-grounding as conscious being-in-itself, and so towards the overcoming of its contingency. But this ideal project is doomed to frustration. And in this sense man is *une passion inutile*. For consciousness means presence to oneself as distant from oneself, whereas being-in-itself means the absence of that fissure or rift which is essential to consciousness. It is thus impossible for *pour-soi* and *en-soi* to be united in one self-identical being.

Now, this idea of the *pour-soi-en-soi* is, when raised, as it were, to infinity, the idea of God. The idea of God is the idea of an infinite, personal Absolute, the infinite *pour-soi-en-soi*, the idea of an infinite, conscious self-identity. But this idea is self-contradictory. Consciousness excludes self-identity, and self-identity excludes consciousness. It is not simply that God does not exist as a matter of fact: there can be no God. For to affirm the existence of God is to enunciate a self-contradictory proposition. There can be no God. And man's striving after divinity is doomed to frustration. (The problem here seems to be whether consciousness necessarily means the finite human consciousness which we experience in ourselves. But I do not wish to interrupt the course of my exposition of Sartre's thought by pausing to discuss this matter.)

On the one hand, therefore, there is being-in-itself. This is neither created nor necessary: it is simply there, gratuitous, *de trop*. On the other hand there is being-for-itself, consciousness, which is necessarily finite and contingent. But perhaps I had better make it clear at once that for Sartre there is no question of its being necessary to prove the existence of a plurality of consciousnesses. In consciousness I am conscious of " being regarded," of being object for others, not for Peter or James in particular, but for " men " in an indefinite sense. And this fact of my " objectivity " shows the existence of other consciousnesses. I cannot be self-conscious without being conscious of the other in an indefinite sense; and the problem of the existence of other selves is a false problem. If, however, one asks why there is a plurality of consciousnesses, no answer can be given. I and others are alike gratuitous, *de trop*.

Now, I said earlier that Sartre draws important conclusions from atheism. And the most important conclusion which he draws seems to be this. If there is no God, there are no universally-obligatory moral law and no set of absolute fixed values. In his lecture on humanism he can say, therefore: " Dostoevsky has written that if God did not exist, all would be permitted. That is existentialism's starting-point." Man is the sole source of values, and it rests with the individual to create or choose his own scale of values, his own ideal. But " rests with " is not a happy phrase. The fact is that man cannot help being free, and he cannot help acting in the world. Even if he chooses to commit suicide, he chooses and so acts. And these acts are performed with motives. But it is man himself who makes the motive a motive, who gives it value. And the choice of particular values depends on an initial project, an initial choice of an ideal. The individual, simply because he is a free, self-transcending subject, cannot help projecting an initial, freely-chosen ideal, in the light of which he determines particular values. The individual, as I have said, is for Sartre the sole source of values, his liberty being their foundation.

Man's liberty is thus unrestricted. There is no given universally-obligatory moral law, according to which he ought to act. He is the source of his own moral law. There are no absolute values which it is his task to realize in the world in concrete acts. He is the source of the values which he recognizes. It may be said that man's liberty is in fact restricted, even if there is no universally-obligatory moral law. For it is restricted by his own character, by his physico-psychological make-up, and by the historical situation in which he finds himself. But Sartre tries to make the individual responsible even for his physico-psychological make-up and for the historical situation in which he finds himself and in which he has to act. For by constituting his own past man assumes and makes himself responsible for himself as *en-soi*. And it is man who creates his own situation by projecting his ends. Whether this mountain is " too steep " or not depends, for instance, on whether I am out to obtain a good view with the minimum of trouble or to scale a difficult height. Similarly, my historical situation is what it is *for me*; and what it is for me depends on the end which I have set before myself. And since I choose my ideal or end freely, it also depends on me what my historical situation is. By choosing my ideal or end I choose and assume my historical situation. My liberty is thus unrestricted. It can hardly be said to be " restricted " by death; for death simply extinguishes the *pour-soi*.

One great difficulty about this interpretation of liberty is that the word " free " seems to be used in such a wide sense that it tends to become vacuous. If, for example, we are going to call both reflex acts and deliberate acts free, the word " free " tends to lose all clear meaning. Sartre does, indeed, allow for some distinctions. For instance, in the process of composing these lectures I perform a multitude of acts, such as the various movements of my fingers on the typewriter. These acts are free acts in the sense that I am not bound to perform them and that I could *not* perform them. But they are performed with a view to an end, and, though I could perform them at other moments than the moments at which I actually perform them, without any change in this end being involved, I could not *not* perform them at all without choosing another end than the one which I actually chose. This seems to allow for some distinction between acts at any rate from a psychological point of view. Let us suppose that the decision to give this lecture was the result of deliberation. It does not follow that all the particular acts involved in composing the lecture are the result of any conscious deliberation. Yet they are free acts in the sense that I am not determined to perform them. I am not even determined to perform them by the motive of composing and giving this lecture. For it is I who make this possible motive an actual and effective motive, and I could change my end. In this case I should cease to perform the particular acts involved in composing the lecture. Of course, the end of composing and giving this lecture is constituted by me as an end within a general pre-supposed frame of values. And Sartre speaks as though there were an original or initial free projection of an ideal or end by which I create my " world " and my values and in the light of which all my particular choices can be interpreted. And we may therefore be tempted to think that in his eyes there is an initial free choice of a very general kind which settles once and for all all particular choices. But this seems to me to be a misinterpretation. For just as I can change a particular end, so I can change the general end or ideal, through the projection of which I constitute my past and my historical situation and my scale of values. True, a change of this kind would mean a " total conversion "; it would mean becoming " another man." But though such a fundamental exercise of liberty may be rare, it is at least possible. Hence, according to Sartre, I am never determined. He says explicitly that man cannot be sometimes free and sometimes determined: he is either entirely and always free or he is never free. In the case of some acts I am conscious of the " nothing " which separates my choice from my " essence," while in the case of other acts I am not conscious of this " nothing." And these are what we call unreflective or indeliberate acts. But they are none the less free acts. It remains true, therefore, that for Sartre liberty is unrestricted.

The affective tonality of this unrestricted liberty, or rather of the apprehension or consciousness of this liberty, is dread. (Sartre uses the word *angoisse*. Some writers translate this by " anxiety," others by " anguish." But while the use of the word " anxiety " has much to recommend it, it seems to me rather weak. And " anguish " rather suggests the wringing of hands.) This dread is to be distinguished from " fear." Fear is directed towards something other than oneself. For instance, a man on a narrow path above a precipice may be afraid of the path giving way or of a rock falling. But if he is afraid of himself, that is, of the possibility of his throwing himself over the precipice, this is dread. The man is aware that what he resolves now, at this moment, does not determine the future; for between present and future there intervenes " nothing," *le néant*. It is in dread that man becomes conscious of his freedom. In unreflective acts, as we have seen, a man is not conscious of the " nothing " which characterizes liberty, and these acts are therefore performed without dread. But dread accompanies the perception of this " nothing " which separates my essence from my choice; and it is thus in dread that I become consciously aware of my liberty.

I can attempt to flee from this dread, which bears some analogy to the vertigo which seizes the man on the precipice, by trying to mask my liberty from myself. That is to say, I can attempt to hide from myself the " nothing " which separates my essence from my choice. I can, for instance, refer my choice to my essence, to my physico-psychological make-up or to the influence of the social environment or to divine predetermination. I am then in " bad faith " (mauvaise foi). Bad faith is to be distinguished from lying. To lie is to say what one knows or believes to be false; one attempts to deceive others rather than oneself. But in bad faith one attempts to mask the truth from oneself. And the possibility of bad faith is always present; its possibility is part of the structure of consciousness. And determinism in all its forms is one example of surrender to this ever-present temptation.

It follows from what has been said that the philosopher cannot tell a man how he ought to act, if by telling him how he ought to act means relating a possible particular act to a universally-obligatory moral law or to a set of absolute values. For there is no universally-obligatory moral law and there is no set of absolute values. The individual cannot evade the total responsibility for choice which rests on his shoulders. He may, indeed, attempt to evade this responsibility by surrendering to bad faith; but then he has himself chosen this bad faith. All that the philosopher can do, and, indeed, all that one man can do for another, is to illuminate the possibilities of action and the meaning of liberty, with a view to promoting authentic choice or self-commitment as contrasted with drifting into decisions under the influence of the pressure of social conformity.

Ultimately, therefore, every individual human being creates his own values and his own moral law. He is totally responsible, and he can find no justification for his choice from without. For there are no God, no transcendent values, and no universally-obligatory moral law. A man may, of course, make his particular choices as a member of " the one " and try to throw the responsibility on society. But he is merely masking from himself the fact that he has chosen this way of acting. The individual as free subject is essentially isolated and alone. And it is in this isolation and loneliness that he creates his world and his values. Indeed, Sartre accentuates the individual's loneliness and isolation by his existential analysis of the phenomenon of love. When two people love one another, each desires to possess the liberty of the other, to possess the other not simply as object but as *pour-soi*. For it is precisely the liberty of the other which separates him or her from the lover. But it turns out in the end that all that is possessed is the body of the other, the other as object. And physical possession of the other as object is not possession of the other as liberty, as subjectivity, a goal which remains always beyond reach. The process by which the lover strives to gain his or her end is self-frustrating. Hence the analysis of love serves to emphasize the loneliness of the individual. And the question arises whether the philosophy of Sartre does not present us with an atomic, and indeed chaotic, individualism. It is not very difficult to understand Marxist criticism to the effect that Sartre's philosophy represents, as it were, a last convulsive effort of the alienated individual in a dying bourgeois world.

In order to avoid any possible misunderstanding I had better make it clear perhaps that I have no intention of suggesting that M. Sartre himself, as a man, is devoid of a sense of social responsibility or that he can be justly accused of withdrawing into self-centred isolation. As is well known, he took part in the Resistance movement, and he has decided social and political ideas. It is not the behaviour of M. Sartre which is in question, but the character of his philosophy as set forth in his writings in " academic " terms.

The question, however, whether the philosophy of Sartre is a philosophy of atomic individualism is not an easy question to answer as it stands. An analysis of the term " atomic individualism " would be required. And the effect of such analysis would be perhaps to render any further question unnecessary. I remember once reading a paper at Oxford with the title, " Is existentialism a philosophy of decadence? " After the paper one member of the audience remarked in the discussion that he had been disappointed by what he had heard. He had expected a trenchant attack on existentialism from the point of view of a " mediaeval philosopher." Instead he had heard analyses of the terms " existentialism " and " decadence." It seemed, however, to have escaped his attention that the question could not be profitably discussed without analysis of the meanings of the terms involved and that the very process of analysis might result in the question being answered.

If by " atomic individualism " we mean the proposition that a man's free acts are his free acts and nobody else's, then Sartre is, of course, an " atomic individualist." But so is anyone else who affirms human liberty. And there may very well come a time in the life of any individual when he or she experiences in an exceptional degree solitude and isolation in the exercise of choice. M. Sartre in *The Republic of Silence* has drawn a memorable picture of such a case, namely the situation of the member of the Resistance movement who has been captured and who is alone with the torturers.

If, however, by asking whether Sartre presents us with a philosophy of atomic individualism we mean to ask whether he recommends withdrawal from all self-commitment in the world, the answer is that he does not. He recommends the contrary. Moreover, he does not recommend choosing values without any reference to society. Rather does he attempt to show that a tremendous responsibility rests upon a man's shoulders in the exercise of choice of values. If a man chooses, for example, the values represented by Communism and commits himself to the Communist creed, he ideally legislates for other men as well. For by adhering to Communism he declares that all should be on the Communist side.

But if by " atomic individualism " we mean the doctrine that there is no universally-obligatory moral law and no values which are not created by the individual's choice, Sartre's philosophy is obviously a philosophy of atomic individualism. Furthermore, it appears to me that the notion of choosing and legislating ideally for all men simply masks, and in no way really diminishes, the individualism latent in the system. For if to choose with a sense of social responsibility is a value, it is the individual who creates this value, on Sartre's premisses that is to say. If someone does not regard it as a value and exalts capricious choice without any sense of social responsibility, I can, indeed, disapprove of his attitude from within the set of values which I have chosen; but, if I am a follower of Sartre, I must admit that in the long run the other man's set of values is as good as mine. It may be objected that I not only need not admit this but also cannot admit it. For I have already chosen my set of values, and I cannot help judging other people's values by reference to my own. But it is either possible or impossible to adopt the point of view taken in M. Sartre's philosophy. And if it is possible to adopt his meta-ethical point of view, it is possible for me to admit that in the long run no one set of values is intrinsically superior to any other set of values. And if I do in fact adopt Sartre's meta-ethical point of view, it seems to me that I must admit it. And if I admit it, no amount of reference to legislating ideally for all men will alter the fundamental individualism of the theory. Someone may perhaps be inclined to say that Sartre's point of view is the right one. But this observation would be irrelevant. For I am not now discussing whether Sartre's meta-ethics is true or false; I am discussing the question what it is. And though I am, of course, very far removed from being a Marxist, I consider that the Marxist description of it in terms of atomic individualism is very much to the point.

In conclusion I should like to add that M. Sartre's philosophical writings contain long phenomenological analyses which show great virtuosity and intelligence. His ability as a novelist and dramatist should certainly not lead one to underestimate him as a philosopher or to think that he is a mere dilettante. He is by no means a mere dilettante. We cannot judge him in terms of existentialist cafés. But a man may, of course, possess great ability and yet at the same time give a most inadequate picture of human existence and human experience.

4

I have already had occasion to mention M. Sartre's description of man as *une passion inutile*. And I have also mentioned his view that Being is gratuitous, *de trop*. Roquentin's experience of this character of Being in the municipal gardens of Bouville in *La nausée* is well enough known. One can say, therefore, that for Sartre the world and human existence are " absurd." But he does not dwell much on this theme. The " philosopher of the absurd " is rather Albert Camus, who, like Sartre, is a gifted novelist and dramatist. True, Camus disclaims the label " existentialist," and he thinks that a philosopher such as Jaspers is an escapist. But he seems to me to belong to the same general movement of thought to which Sartre belongs and to speak to men who are in a similar spiritual situation to that of the men to whom Sartre's message is primarily addressed.

In his play *Le malentendu* Camus puts into the mouth of the mother these words: " But the world itself is not reasonable and I am entitled to say so, I who have tasted of the world, from creation to destruction." The world is unreasonable and it is impossible to find any significance in it. The human reason is naturally impelled to seek for clarity about the meaning of the world and of human life and history in particular; but it can find no given meaning either in the world apart from man or in human life itself. And it is through the perception of this fact that there arises the feeling of the absurd (*le sentiment de l'absurde*). " I said that the world was absurd, but I was going too fast. This world in itself is not reasonable, one can say that of it. But the absurd is the confrontation of this irrational world with the desperate desire for clarity, the appeal of which resounds in the depths of man. . . . The absurdity arises from this confrontation of the human appeal with the irrational silence of the world. . . . The irrational, the human nostalgia and the absurd which arises from their *tête-à-tête*, these are the three personages of the drama " (*Le mythe de Sisyphe*).

The feeling of the absurd can arise in many ways, from the

perception of the "inhumanity" or indifference of nature, from the realization of man's temporality or of death which reveals the uselessness of human life or from the shock occasioned by perceiving the ultimate pointlessness of daily life and its routine. "Get up, tramway, four hours at the office or in the factory, a meal, tramway, four hours' work, a meal, sleep, and Monday, Tuesday, Wednesday, Thursday, Friday and Saturday in the same rhythm . . . one follows this path without difficulty most of the time. One day, however, arises the question ' Why? ' . . ." (*Le mythe de Sisyphe.*) But the feeling of the absurd is not the same thing as the notion or conviction of the absurd, though it is its foundation: the conviction of the absurd belongs to the sphere of clear consciousness. Moreover, this consciousness is essential to the very existence of the absurd. For the absurd does not exist in the human mind alone nor in the extramental world alone, but in their presence to one another: destroy one of the terms and the absurd is destroyed. Thus the absurd, like all things, ends with death. It is only through man that the absurd originates and it cannot exist apart from him: the world in itself is not absurd but simply irrational. However, technical expressions apart, one can say that for Camus the world and human life are absurd, or at least that they appear as absurd, once their irrational and meaningless character is clearly perceived.

Such a view of the world is admittedly repugnant to man. In Camus' play *Caligula* Cherea asserts that he rejects the world as Caligula sees it and that the emperor must "disappear" "because I want to live and to be happy. I believe that one can neither live nor be happy if one pushes the absurd to all its conclusions." Again, "to lose one's life is a little thing and I shall have the courage to do so if necessary; but to see the meaning of this life dissipated, to see our reason for existing disappear, that is what is unbearable. One cannot live without meaning." The thinkers whom Camus calls the existential philosophers (*les philosophes existentiels*) try to escape by means of a "leap." Kierkegaard, for instance, makes the leap of faith, his thought leaping beyond the world and human life, as they are given in perception, to the affirmation of God, to whom reason does not lead. Jaspers makes a leap from experience to the Transcendent, a somewhat vague Transcendent, it is true, but still the Transcendent. Chestov makes the leap to a God who is beyond reason. In fine, for the existential philosophers " reason " is simply an instrument of " thought," and the thought (*pensée*) of a man is before all things his nostalgia, his heart's desire. Reason denies itself when it makes the leap; it gives place to wishful thinking. Desire for escape from the absurd carries these thinkers beyond the confines of reason, whereas in reality there is nothing beyond reason.

The world of *l'esprit absurde* is thus a godless world and a world in which there are no absolute objective values. Yet it is in such a world that Camus would have men live, those at least who have the courage to do so. And man's belief in the absurdity of existence should direct his conduct. This is, of course, the reason why Camus raises the question of suicide. But he raises the question only to reject suicide as a solution. He rejects it, not because it is immoral, but because it involves a surrender to absurdity, resignation to the absurdity of the world and of human life. But the absurd has no meaning unless man holds himself apart from it, and revolts against it: if one fully consents to it, as in suicide, it ceases to be the absurd. The proper conduct for the man who is conscious of the absurd is to make the absurd live by living in the consciousness of the absurd, in revolt against it, without committing suicide or, on the other hand, making the irrational leap of escape. This revolt gives its worth to life. And when maintained over a lifetime, it gives it its greatness: " the spectacle of human pride cannot be equalled." " This world is without importance," says Caligula, " and he who recognizes the fact wins his freedom." *L'homme absurde* (that is, the man who is clearly conscious of the absurd and lives in a manner compatible with this consciousness) refuses all specious consolations and hopes; his reason is enlightened and his will his own.

But what sort of a life will the " man of the absurd " live? Obviously one cannot lay down what he ought to do, in the sense of what he is morally obliged to do. For in a meaningless world all is permitted. But this does not mean that crime is recommended. " All is permitted does not signify that nothing is forbidden. The absurd simply makes the consequences of these acts equivalent. It does not recommend crime; that would be childish; but it restores to remorse its uselessness. In the same way, if all experiences are indifferent, that of duty is as legitimate as any other. One can be virtuous by caprice " (*Le mythe de Sisyphe*). And in his novel *La peste* Camus raises the question whether there can be an atheist saint. Some actions will indeed be illogical for *l'esprit absurde*, and in this sense they are " forbidden," but there is no moral obligation. The man of the absurd is, therefore, free of moral obligation; but he has his own ethic, which is one of quantity rather than of quality. What counts is to live in the fullest manner. The Don Juan who realizes to the full, as long as he is able, his capacity for experiences of a certain type, while recognizing that none of these experiences is of ultimate significance; the combatant who, while recognizing the meaninglessness of history, chooses integration into and commitment in his historical situation and setting (by fighting, for example, for the Resistance); the creative artist who sees clearly that the work of art, like the artist himself, is inevitably doomed to death, but who yet gives expression to his intuitions of the world; these are all types of the man of the absurd. The man, for instance, who joins in some movement of resistance against a tyrant, knowing or believing that his cause is a lost cause and that in any case history will one day reduce both causes to an equivalence, to nothing, lives the absurd but at the same time revolts against it and against his destiny, proclaims his freedom and adds greatness to life. True conquest is not a geographical matter; it consists in revolt and sacrifice without a future; it is man's protest against his destiny. Camus' ethic is thus not simply a recommendation to fulfil the Horatian *Carpe diem*. There is no reason why one should give any decided preference to a refined Epicureanism of the Horatian type, though Epicureanism is not, of course, excluded as a possibility. The absurd is made to live rather by self-commitment in one's historical situation, provided that one recognizes the ultimate equivalence of all actions, rather than by withdrawing, so far as this is possible, from all self-commitment.

5

It seems clear to me that both Sartre and Camus speak for and to the man who has lost, or who has never had, faith in God and who at the same time is unable to rest content with the comfortable notion that atheism makes no difference to human existence and its problems. They both try to show the consequences of atheism as they see them and to make clear to the solitary and alienated individual the situation in which he finds himself. What, then, is to be done? How should a man live in a world in which there is no given meaning? How can he give some meaning to his life? Both Sartre and Camus preach an ethic of self-commitment, of *engagement*.

But though both writers express a very real mentality and outlook, a mentality, that is to say, which is undoubtedly one feature of our time, it does not follow that either of them gives an adequate theoretical justification of this mentality and outlook. Sartre, it is true, attempts to do this. But Camus seems to me to start with the assumption that the world is " irrational." And behind even Sartre's theoretical arguments in favour of atheism one can discern, I think, a preliminary choice. It may be said, of course, that the theism of writers like Kierkegaard and Jaspers also rests ultimately upon a choice. It may even be said that in such a matter the decision must rest ultimately with choice. But it may also be the case that the extreme emphasis placed on choice is one of the main weaknesses of existentialist philosophy. But this is a question which belongs rather to the next, and final, lecture.

CHAPTER XII

A CRITICAL DISCUSSION OF EXISTENTIALISM

I

EXISTENTIALISM, as we have seen, lays emphasis on the human situation or condition. We are told, for example, that man finds himself in the world, that he is a being in the world. We are told that he is a finite, unstable being, menaced by death from the start. We are told that he is free, that he transcends his past and inevitably shapes himself by his free choices in such a way that he is never a mere " object " until death has extinguished his possibilities. As a conscious free being, man stands out from the background of nature. He is not immersed in the stream of life in the same sense that a cat or a dog is immersed in the stream of life; and his intellect is not bound exclusively to the service of his biological and economic needs. He can, indeed, by his own choice endeavour to identify himself with society, with the group-consciousness, and thus try to evade the responsibility of freedom. But he can also acknowledge in " dread " his own freedom and responsibility, which set him apart in lonely isolation. He can raise the problem of the meaning of his own existence and that of human history in general. He can seek for clarity about the goal of human life and about values.

But, it may be objected, is not most of this stale news? The truth of the proposition that man is free is, indeed, a matter of dispute. And if the existentialist says that man is free, he is not uttering a triviality in the sense of a proposition, the truth of which is admitted by all. But we are surely all well aware that man is a being in the world. Whatever some philosophers may have done, no ordinary man questions this fact; he simply takes it for granted. Why, then, do the existentialists make such a fuss about it? There is not much point in adding that the proposition that man is a being in the world does not mean that I just happen to be in the world when I might possibly be somewhere else. For nobody in his senses thinks that he " just happens " to be in the world. The thesis that man is essentially orientated towards other things and persons is not new. After all, Aristotle observed centuries ago that man is by nature a social being. Again, are we not all well aware that we are menaced by death? Do we not already know that we are doomed to death from the start, in some sense at least of the word " know "? Again, we are all well aware that man differs from cats and dogs and that man can torment himself with problems with which cats and dogs, so far as available evidence goes, cannot torment themselves. And we are not ignorant of the fact that while some human beings do torment themselves with problems of human destiny others do not, either because they already firmly believe in certain answers to these problems or because they are too preoccupied with the cares of daily life or with scientific preoccupations. We do not require philosophers to tell us such truths. And if we wish to receive further information about, for example, man's particular relations to other things or about the causes of death and the nature of the process which is known as " dying," the scientist is a better source of information than the philosopher. What the existentialist does is to enunciate trivialities, in the sense of propositions which tell us what we all know already. And the fact that these familiar truths are dressed up in solemn and often rather obscure language does not alter the fact that they are familiar truths. We are given no new information.

At the same time, it may be said, the existentialist obviously has a special purpose when he enunciates these trivialities. And this purpose is betrayed by his use of the word " dread." He himself obviously experiences certain emotions when he considers these familiar truths, and he wishes to communicate the same emotions to others, or rather to evoke similar emotional attitudes and dispositions in others. And in order to be able to do this more effectively he states his trivialities in particularly solemn language and talks in dramatic and tragic tones about one's presence in the world, about man's finiteness, about death and about dread. His language is part of a technique for the communication or evocation of affective attitudes and of emotions. We can say, therefore, that existentialism mingles triviality with theatricality and that it specializes in the emotive use of language. The existentialist's activity is doubtless psychologically understandable in terms of the social and political upheavals of the twentieth century and, in cases such as that of Kierkegaard, in terms of his own peculiar character and history. But this does not alter the nature of the existentialist's activity.

I have mentioned this line of objection against existentialism at some length because it seems to me to be a line of criticism which ought in any case to be faced. Further, I think that it contains truth, though at the same time it seems to me to fail to do justice to existentialism. I should like, therefore, to make a necessarily brief attempt to sift what is just from what is unjust. This will help to show my own attitude towards the existentialist philosophies.

In the first place it seems to me undoubtedly true that many of the assertions made by the existentialists do not convey fresh information in the sense in which a physicist or an astronomer or an explorer may give us fresh information. The news that we are beings in the world and that death is the common lot of men is stale news. Again, no sane person thinks that he or she is anything else but finite. And the ordinary man, if left to himself, believes that some of his acts are free in the sense that it is possible for him to will otherwise than he does will.

Yet at the same time it must be added that precisely because human finiteness and dependence and instability are so obvious we do not normally advert to these facts. Nor does the normal man think much about his own death, although he does not doubt that eventually he will die. In normal circumstances death is not a pleasant or congenial subject for meditation; and it may very well appear to the ordinary man that there is nothing to be gained by dwelling on the thought. In any case a man's natural impulses tend to divert his attention from the blankness and emptiness of death and to absorb him in day-by-day concerns and cares or in scientific and professional pre-occupations. Nor, again, does the ordinary man, unless he has the special interests of a theologian, a philosopher, a psychologist or perhaps a student of criminal law, think much about freedom. He is implicitly aware of a distinction between acts for which he feels himself responsible and acts for which he does not feel himself responsible; but his interest is in acting rather than in reflecting about acting. And we can say in general that there is much of which we are in varying degrees aware and which we in some real sense " know " but to which we do not normally advert or which we do not normally " notice."

The relevance of these remarks is this. The fact that the truths to which our attention is drawn by a philosopher do not convey fresh information in the sense of telling us what we did not know already or what we could not have discovered for ourselves without the aid of a professional philosopher does not constitute a fatal objection to the propriety of drawing attention to these truths, provided, of course, that there is sufficient reason for doing so. Perhaps I may take an example from another sphere, even though the example is by now a little hackneyed. I may have seen a picture many times and yet have failed, as we say, to appreciate it. I see and yet I do not see. Then one day a friend " shows " me the picture. In one sense he does not show me what I have not seen before; yet he may very well show me what I have not noticed before or what I have not previously adverted to. He does not show me lines or colours which my eyes have not previously seen; but he may draw my attention to form or pattern or " significance " which I have not previously noticed. He thus enables me to see the picture in a new light. It is the same picture which I have seen many times, and yet it is not the same picture which I have seen before. Here we have paradox, it is true; but the paradox serves to draw attention to what is after all no very uncommon experience. And I suggest that the philosopher may fulfil, at least in some cases, a function analogous to that of the friend who shows me the already familiar picture. He may enable us to see in a fresh light what we had seen before but had not " noticed."

Now, it seems to me to be true that we all share in member-ship of what existentialists call " the one." Although there is, indeed, no such thing as a group mind or a group consciousness in the same sense in which there are individual minds and individual consciousnesses, there are certainly ways of reacting to events, ways of thinking and ways of feeling which are characteristic of individuals as members of the group. For each individual is integrated into society from the start, and many of his opinions and ways of acting are formed under the pressure of environment and of social education. Language, which is itself a social construction, is one very important means of communicating and perpetuating these shared opinions and reactions and standards of action, though it is not, of course, the only means. And if we bear in mind the fact that we cannot point to any thing or substance which is connoted by the terms group mind or group consciousness, we can, I think, make significant use of such expressions. The pressure of society is with us always, and, normally speaking, it is not felt as a burden, as a pressure from outside, because each individual is from the start integrated into society and orientated to society. The group mind or consciousness is, as it were, prefigured in the structure of the individual.

It is only natural, therefore, that I should be normally absorbed in the discharge of my social function and taken up with my cares and preoccupations within the framework of society. It is only natural that the world should be looked on as the field in which these functions are discharged and that meaning should be given it in terms of one's cares and pre-occupations as a member of society. It is only natural that an event such as death should be regarded as something which happens " to one," to each member of society because he or she is an organism which in the natural course of events inevitably undergoes the process which is known as " dying." The death of someone who is dear to me may obviously affect me deeply; but preoccupation with my own death naturally tends to appear to me as something disordered, something

" morbid," as a dereliction of duty, a withdrawal from society and a retreat from the proper discharge of my social function. As a member of society I am, indeed, aware that I am finite and that I shall die. If we ask anyone whether he or she is finite or infinite, for example, the person will, given the requisite understanding of the terms, undoubtedly answer " finite." And this shows that he is aware in some sense of his finitude. But, as a member of society, I look on finitude and death in a social perspective. I have my social function and my particular preoccupations within the framework of society; and although I know that my capacity is limited and that the time in which I can discharge my function is limited, I do not dwell on the thought of these limits. They form the background, as it were, for the positive interests which absorb my daily attention.

The existentialist, it seems to me, changes or tries to change the perspective in which we see certain facts of which we are already aware. He directs my attention to limits which are normally marginal to my consciousness and focuses my gaze on my finitude, on my limitations, on my death as the extinction of my possibilities. Instead of my seeing my existence in the world from the point of view of a member of " the one," absorbed in my social functions, he tries to make me see my existence in the world from the point of view of the individual subject who finds himself as a pilgrim in the world, who strives after the realization of ideals and values and who is from the start menaced by death which extinguishes himself and his ideals. The existentialist tries to make me stand back, as it were, from my absorption in " the one," from my absorption in my social cares and preoccupations, and to make me take stock of my position as an individual. It is as though he pointed his finger at certain features of the picture of human existence and said " Look ! " He thus tries to make me focus my attention on the fundamental existential situation of the human individual as such, a free finite being, condemned, as it were, to act in the world and to commit himself in the world and to shape himself in the world, and then to perish. That he is able to undertake the task of directing my attention and that I am able to follow and appreciate his direction is possible only because the human being, as conscious and free subject, is not so immersed in " the one " and in the stream of life, in, that is to say, the pursuit of biological and economic ends that he cannot stand back and take stock of his existential situation. At the same time, owing to the natural tendency to absorption in " the one " and in the stream of life, the existentialist has, as it were, to administer a shock in order to bring about the change of attention which he desires. And this may be one explanation of the solemn and dramatic language which he tends to employ.

The question immediately arises, however, why the existentialist acts in this way. Has he any good reason for so acting? Or can we, on his behalf, find any good reason? The friend who shows me aspects of a picture which I had not previously adverted to and who thus enables me to appreciate a work of art which previously meant little or nothing to me is a benefactor in the sense that he enriches my aesthetic experience. But in what way, if any, is the existentialist a benefactor when he focuses our attention on features of human existence of which we are in a sense already aware but on which we do not normally dwell? Does he simply seek to evoke a certain emotion or range of emotions? And, if so, are these emotions worth experiencing? Do they not tend towards morbidity, concentration on self, withdrawal from social duty and responsibility? It may be said, and with truth, that thinkers like Sartre and Camus insist strongly on self-commitment and that they by no means strive to withdraw us from social responsibility and activity. But at the same time they seem to think it desirable that we should commit ourselves in the world with an awareness of the ultimate futility of committing ourselves. And is there the slightest advantage to be gained by experiencing this feeling of futility? If it is aroused, does it not tend to prevent the very self-commitment which these writers advocate?

I think myself that it is a mistake to interpret the existentialists as though they were primarily concerned with evoking emotions, however much they may refer to " dread."

It seems to me that the chief function of drawing attention to the features of man's existential situation to which these thinkers draw attention is to make us aware of problems. For example, if I become acutely conscious of my existence in the world as a passage to death, I am naturally led to ask whether my existence has any meaning or purpose. If I become reflectively conscious of man's constant striving after the realization of values and ideals in a cosmos which seems to be indifferent to man's strivings and ideals, so much so that the history of the human race appears to be a transitory episode in the cosmic process, I am driven to ask whether human history has any goal or purpose. Again, if I am conscious of myself as free and as choosing with a view to ends, I can ask whether there is any ultimate end in the light of which my striving after subordinate particular ends becomes intelligible. As long as I am absorbed in my social function and in practical concerns and preoccupations I shall hardly raise such questions. But once I stand back from these concerns and preoccupations and direct my attention to those features of man's fundamental situation to which the existentialists point, these problems naturally arise in my mind.

It seems evident to me that problems of this kind are " real " problems in the sense that they arise spontaneously in the mind of anyone who focuses his attention on certain aspects of man's existential situation. If we are immersed in a definite task within history with a definite end in view we are unlikely to raise questions about the end or purpose of history in general. But if we stand back and contemplate the history of man against the background of the silent and indifferent cosmos, it seems to me perfectly natural to ask whether man's strivings and hopes have any point, whether there is any meaning or purpose in the whole thing.

And I think that these problems can be called " perennial " problems in the sense that they arise through concentration of attention, not on some temporary circumstance of man's life or on some situation in which man is temporarily involved (that is to say, in which a certain group of men are involved at a certain historical period owing to circumstances peculiar to that period), but on man's abiding situation and on the conditions of human existence as such. Yesterday, for example, I may have been involved in some situation which gave rise to a problem. Today the situation has changed, and the problem no longer arises. But my radical instability and mortality as a human being are not factors which change from day to day; they are with me always. The problems to which they give rise are not always in my mind (they are not perennial in this sense); but the situation which gives rise to them lasts as long as I exist in the world.

It may be objected, however, that to say that these problems are real problems because they arise through concentration of attention on certain features of man's existential situation is to offer an explanation, perhaps a valid one, of the psychological origin of the problems; but it is not the same thing as showing that they are real problems when regarded from the point of view of the philosophical analyst. And I think that I ought to say a few words on this point, though I must necessarily be brief if I am to say anything further about existentialism in this lecture.

Nobody would wish to define a real problem as one which we here and now have the means of answering. For to do this would involve excluding scientific problems which we are now unable to solve in a definite manner. But perhaps some would wish to define a pseudo-problem as a question which we are unable to answer, not simply because we here and now lack the means of answering it, means which may be available in the future, but because no way of answering it is conceivable. But one of the difficulties attaching to this way of speaking is that it may conceal a tacit identification of " answer " with " scientific answer." And though metaphysical problems of the type of which I am speaking cannot be answered by any particular science, since they are not the sort of questions which any scientist as scientist raises, it is open to anyone to claim that metaphysical answers are conceivable and even possible. In other words, a problem which is a " pseudo-problem " for a scientist within the ambit of his particular science is not by any means necessarily a pseudo-problem for a metaphysician. If I am a positivist, I may wish to call metaphysical problems " pseudo-problems "; but if I am not a positivist, I shall probably not wish to do this. In any case it is by no means immediately evident that an unanswerable problem is *ipso facto* a pseudo-problem; unless, of course, we define a pseudo-problem as an unanswerable problem, in which case it becomes a matter of definition. The only way to show conclusively that a problem is a pseudo-problem is to show that no intelligible question is asked; to show, that is to say, that to one or more words in the question no sufficiently clear meaning can be attached and that this is the reason why the question cannot be answered, or that there is a defect in syntax or logical structure such that the question is unintelligible, even though each term, taken separately, has an assignable meaning. There is, of course, considerable room for difference of opinion about what constitutes sufficiently clear meaning in any given case; and I very much doubt whether any unanimous agreement is likely to be reached. However, as far as I can see, a linguistic analysis of individual metaphysical questions would be the only way of showing that these questions are not real questions, though it would be obviously necessary also to show that the standard of meaningfulness adopted was not arbitrary and did not involve disputable presuppositions. And this is perhaps not quite such an easy task as some people seem to suppose.

Now, to ask whether human existence has a " meaning " is presumably to ask whether it fits into any finalistic pattern; and to ask this is much the same thing as to ask whether it has any purpose or end. Is such a question a " scientific " question, capable of receiving an empirical, non-metaphysical answer? It can be turned into a scientific question; but then it is no longer the original question. What I mean is this. I might interpret the question as meaning, " What ends or purposes have different individuals or cultural groups assigned to human existence? " In this case I have a question to which the historian and the sociologist can in principle provide a definite, even if necessarily incomplete, answer. But the question is then not the original question which was asked.

For the questioner did not intend to ask, What have people thought to be the end or purpose of human existence? or what ends they have as a matter of historical fact assigned to human life and activity: he intended to ask what is the " real " purpose of human existence, irrespective of what individuals and groups may have thought about it. And this question may appear to involve an illegitimate use of terms uch as " purpose " and " end." And so it does if " purpose " and " end " necessarily mean purposes and ends determined by man. For in this case it would be absurd to ask what is the ultimate purpose or end of human existence, apart from and independent of the purposes and ends which human beings have set before themselves. Human existence and human history cannot have a purpose or end in the sense intended unless it is given or fixed " from outside," as it were. And it cannot be given or fixed from outside unless there is a Being capable of determining it. Thus to ask whether human existence has a purpose is to ask whether there is a Being capable of determining such a purpose. It seems to me, therefore, that the question whether human existence has a purpose necessarily implies a reference to the Transcendent. And a question about the Transcendent is not a scientific question. But it does not necessarily follow that it is a pseudo-question, unless one from the start identifies " real " questions with scientific questions. And though it is open to anyone to recommend this identification, it is also open to anyone to say that he sees no adequate reason for this identification.

Let me apply what I have been saying a little more clearly to the existentialists. It seems to me that Sartre would agree that to raise the question of the meaning or purpose of human existence is to raise the question of God. For in his opinion, as in that of Camus, human existence can have no purpose or end other than that given it by man himself, if there is no God. And as he denies the existence of God he denies also that human existence has any end or purpose other than that given it by man himself.

But Sartre would go further. As we have seen, he maintains that the notion of God is a contradictory notion. It is not merely that there happens to be no God, or rather that there is not sufficient evidence for affirming that God exists: there cannot possibly be a God. To affirm that there is a Being possessing the attributes predicated of God is to affirm a proposition, the self-contradictory character of which is revealed by analysis. The problem of the existence of God cannot, therefore, be a real problem. It follows that the problem of the end or purpose of human existence, when this means an end or purpose determined " from outside," cannot be a real problem either. Human existence has not and cannot have an end or purpose in this sense. Furthermore, Sartre maintains, though by no means everybody would agree with this opinion, that if there is no God there is not and cannot be a universally-obligatory moral law or a set of absolute objective values. And it is at this point that Sartre's problematic begins. Given man's presence in a godless world, with all that this implies, what is man to do? What attitude is he to adopt?

We are left in a rather curious position. On the one hand the problem of God's existence is not a real problem; for it is impossible that there should be a God. On the other hand Sartre says, and rightly, that his existentialism is an attempt to draw the logical conclusions from a consistently held atheism. And some of these conclusions are of great importance. If, therefore, they depend on atheism, this inevitably suggests that the problem of God's existence is itself a problem of great importance. And this suggests that it is a real problem. It may be objected that to say that existentialism is an attempt to draw the conclusions from a consistent atheism is simply to say that existentialism is an attempt to draw the logical conclusions from the exposure of the proposition " God exists " as a nonsensical proposition and that it does not make the problem of God's existence a real problem. But if the problem of God's existence is no real problem and if the proposition " God exists " is nonsensical, can one draw any logical conclusions from the proposition " there is no God "? It may be said, of course, that one can draw logical conclusions from it in the sense that one is logically justified in throwing out all the other nonsensical propositions which are bound up with the nonsensical proposition " God exists." One then gets rid of a bundle of nonsense; and the fact that what remains is important does not show that the nonsense is important. But will this answer pass muster? If someone says that there is a pak-chak and can give no indication whatsoever of what this strange term means, neither his affirmation that there is a pak-chak nor his adversary's denial that there is a pak-chak is of any significance or importance. But if the denial that there is any universally-obligatory moral law is significant and important, it seems to me that the affirmation that there is a universally-obligatory moral law must also be significant and important. And if the denial that there is a universally-obligatory moral law follows from the denial that there is a God, it seems to me that this denial must be of significance and importance. And in this case the affirmation of God is of significance and importance. And consequently the problem of the existence of God must be a real problem. Indeed, if Sartrian existentialism is, as he claims, a deduction from atheism, the problem of God's existence must be of supreme importance. Hence I should say that the philosophizing of M. Sartre, by drawing attention to man's situation in a godless world, serves to emphasize the importance of the problem of God. For he clearly links up this problem with the problem of man's conduct and of man's destiny.

Let me turn for a moment to Professor Jaspers. For him we cannot know what is the meaning or purpose of human history; but it can have a meaning or purpose only if the Transcendent or God exists. The secret of human history is hidden in the Transcendent. Our belief that human existence and human history have an ultimate purpose or significance is bound up, therefore, with our belief in God. And to ask whether human existence and human history have meaning and purpose is to ask whether God exists. But this is not a scientific question, and it cannot receive a scientific answer. To raise the problem of the Transcendent as a real problem is, indeed, to possess the answer, in the sense that it involves some awareness of the Transcendent. For the problem is raised above all in the presence of certain " limiting situations," such as death, and the raising of the problem implies an awareness of the Transcendent as a kind of background or negatively-conceived complement of limits. But we do not have, and cannot have, any clear apprehension of the Transcendent, as though it were an object or thing. For God is precisely the being that transcends all objects and things. The Transcendent cannot be objectified without ceasing to be the Transcendent. The mind cannot, therefore, apprehend the Transcendent once and for all, as it were, and put away in the appropriate pigeon-hole a note to the effect that the Transcendent exists. God is apprehended by " philosophic faith "; and this philosophic faith has always to be renewed. To raise the problem may be to possess the answer; but the problem, which comprises the answer, has always to be renewed. We cannot pack away the problem and retain the answer. The problem thus remains; and there is a constant objective uncertainty which can never be turned into objective certainty. We can say, then, perhaps that the effect of Jaspers' philosophizing is to renew and intensify the problem of God as a problem arising out of man's awareness of his existential situation.

Perhaps I should apologize for having talked at such length about what I may call the " problematic " aspect of existentialism. But I have not done so without reason. In the first place, by emphasizing the fact that the existentialists raise problems of importance I have tried to show that existentialism is a serious type of philosophy in the sense that it deals with questions which cannot be dismissed as trivial. The fact that Sartre publishes plays and stories and the fact that he not infrequently presents us with scenes and themes which we are not accustomed to find treated by philosophers may give the impression that he is, even in his philosophical works, a storyteller, out to create a stir and to win the attention of the public. With the German existentialists on the other hand one may easily form the impression that they deal in portentous terms and solemn phrases designed to conceal the enunciation of trivialities. I should not care to say that either of these impressions is entirely lacking in objective foundation; but at the same time I think that they are both inadequate. For they do not allow for the fact that the existentialists raise and consider serious and important problems.

In the second place I have argued that at least some of the main problems with which the existentialists deal arise out of concentration of attention on certain features of man's abiding existential situation. And if this is true, we cannot properly dismiss existentialism as being no more than a product of transitory historical circumstances. No doubt, conditions in Germany after the First World War helped to create the state of mind which was receptive to the message of Heidegger as popularly interpreted. And it is reasonable to think that the defeat of France in 1940, together with experience of the Occupation and of the accompanying and subsequent divisions and mutual suspicions within the nation, helped to prepare in the minds of young Frenchmen a soil well adapted for the seed sown by Sartre. In a certain sense one may perhaps say that the latter exploited the conditions of France at the close of the war. But all this does not seem to me to alter the fact that the existentialist philosophies deal with themes which are not intrinsically bound up with any particular set of historical circumstances. It is doubtless true that the relevant problems may remain in the background at certain periods, either because most people, as in the Middle Ages, already believe in definite answers or because people are too absorbed in other matters to consider them seriously. But this does not change the relation between these problems and man's perennial existential situation.

It may be said that well-adjusted persons do not raise such problems. They attend to their concrete tasks within the framework of society. It is only people who suffer from social maladjustment that raise such problems; and though abnormality may be psychologically interesting, the ideal is that it should disappear. Further, when people not only raise these questions themselves but also try to force them on the attention of others, they become a social menace. The theistic existentialists are escapists; and escapism is a socially undesirable phenomenon. The atheistic existentialists do, indeed, insist on self-commitment in the world; but by questioning the ultimate value and purpose of human activity and strivings they tend to impair social cohesion and devotion to social tasks.

This is to some extent a matter of definition. If " properly-adjusted " is defined in such a way that it means resembling a human ant as closely as possible, it follows that those who fail to achieve this resemblance to a human ant are mal-adjusted. But the ideal of the human antheap is by no means everybody's ideal; and it is by no means evident that man is no more than an intelligent ant. Indeed, the fact that he can raise the problems which are raised by the existentialists tends to show that he is not. And if philosophers such as Jaspers and Heidegger are right in seeing in man's ability to raise metaphysical problems an indication of the fact that he is not simply a member of " the one," it follows that those who would reduce him to the condition of a human ant are anti-humanists. Social adjustment should be understood with reference to the whole nature of man and not simply with reference to his biological and economic interests. I have no intention of suggesting that the raising of problems is or should be considered a desirable end in itself. And there is doubtless something disagreeable in the notion of an individual torment-ing himself with problems simply for the sake of tormenting himself. If questions are asked, the purpose of asking them is presumably to obtain answers. But answers can hardly be sought until the questions have been asked. And to my mind existentialism has fulfilled a useful rôle to the extent that it has drawn attention to questions which, if they can be answered, are of great importance but which may be evaded by absorption in daily cares and concerns and in scientific preoccupations. In other words, I think that existentialism can serve as a stimulus to metaphysical reflection and that, owing to the character of the problems raised and the context in which they are raised, this metaphysical reflection can more easily be seen as " actual " and as important for man than if it were simply an academic continuation of a past tradition. The problems are not in fact novel; but they present themselves in a fresh light. And this can contribute to a reawakening of appreciation for metaphysics.

2

I hope that I have made it clear that my attitude towards existentialism is not merely negative. And there are a number of individual points on which I find myself in agreement with the existentialists. For instance, for various reasons I am inclined to agree that the Cartesian problem of the existence of the external world is a pseudo-problem. At the same time I think that each one of the existentialist philosophies is open to serious objections of one kind or another. For example, though I agree that if we once admit the foundations of Sartre's philosophy the ensuing problems about human conduct, as he raises them, become real problems, I do not think that these foundations are sound. Again, though I find the philosophy of Jaspers stimulating and suggestive, it seems to me to be lacking on the side of positive rational construction and of theoretical support for the positions asserted. But I cannot be expected to enumerate all my objections to this or that existentialist system, still less to discuss them. I shall therefore confine my attention to Sartre and Jaspers.

Let me recall to your attention the fact that for Sartre consciousness is always consciousness of something. This means that consciousness is other than the object, that it is not the object. But what is the object of consciousness? It is not consciousness itself, *le pour-soi*. I never catch my undiluted consciousness, so to speak: in self-consciousness I am conscious of myself being conscious of something other than my consciousness. And the self which is present to my consciousness as being conscious of something other than myself is my past self: I am always ahead of myself. What I grasp in self-consciousness is my past self, the self which has become *en-soi* and is no longer *pour-soi*. Hence I can say quite generally that the object of consciousness is always *l'en-soi* and never *le pour-soi*. But the *en-soi*, the in-itself, is being. It follows, therefore, that consciousness is always consciousness of being.

217

But we have seen that consciousness is that which is not the object. It follows, therefore, that consciousness is not being, and that it is consequently not-being. It is the negation of being. It is, as Sartre puts it, a " hole " in being, a lack of being. I am not the external object which I know; nor am I the self which I know as *en-soi*. Consciousness is thus characterized by negativity, by not-being. It is that through which nothingness (*le néant*) enters the world *L'en-soi* on the other hand is self-identical without gaps. Hence it cannot be conscious. Indeed, if consciousness is the negation of being, it necessarily follows that being cannot be conscious. And from this it follows that the idea of God contains a contradiction. For the idea of God is the idea of infinite conscious Being, of an infinite *en-soi-pour-soi*. And in forming such an idea we try to synthesize two incompatible and mutually exclusive notions.

Now, Sartre makes a distinction between his phenomenological ontology and metaphysics. The question of origins does not really pertain to the former; it is a matter for metaphysics to consider. None the less, certain conclusions about origins follow necessarily from the propositions which I have just mentioned. In the first place, if God is impossible, there can be no question of consciousness and being-in-itself having a common creative source. If we are able to solve the problem of origins at all, we have to derive either *le pour-soi* from *l'en-soi* or the latter from the former. And, quite apart from scientific difficulties which we would encounter if we tried to derive the object from the subject, the very notions of *le pour-soi* and of *l'en-soi* show that the latter must be prior. For we have seen that consciousness is a negation of being, a " hole " which arises in being. Yet if we ask why or how the emergence of consciousness from opaque, impenetrable, self-identical being took place, no answer is forthcoming. Sartre says, indeed, that everything happens *as though l'en-soi* wanted to project itself and take the modification of consciousness. But he recognizes explicitly that this is in fact impossible: *l'en-soi* cannot wish or intend to do anything at all. We cannot explain, therefore, the origin of consciousness. As for *l'en-soi*, this is simply there, gratuitous, *de trop*. The exclusion of God does not imply that being-in-itself created itself. Neither was it created, nor did it create itself. It is simply there; and that is all that we can say.

That this piece of reasoning is extremely ingenious can hardly be denied. But a little analysis shows up a number of important fallacies. In the first place, though I have no wish to quarrel with Sartre's adoption of the Hegelian distinction between being-for-itself and being-in-itself, I think that his account of the former is open to the charge that he constantly speaks as though the word " nothing " signified a peculiar kind of something. If consciousness exists, it is certainly something; and if we then go on to describe consciousness as not-being, we inevitably imply that not-being is a peculiar kind of being. Again, on being told that nothing separated them from their pasts most people, I imagine, would understand this as meaning that they were not separated from their pasts. But Sartre gives the impression that nothing is a very special kind of thing which separates me from myself as *en-soi*. Furthermore, I apparently secrete this nothing. Consciousness constitutes itself, or at least tries to do so, by secreting a nothing. This ought to mean that it does not do any secreting at all. But let us take it that consciousness does perform the act of secreting, even if it is only nothing which is secreted. Most of us, I think, would be inclined to think that consciousness could do no secreting unless it were something. This may be a banal remark; but perhaps it is just the trivial and the banal that is here required. And if consciousness is something, it cannot be not-being. And if it is not not-being but being, it cannot truthfully be said that being is necessarily not-conscious. And in this case any argument for the impossibility of God which is based on the impossibility of a synthesis between being and consciousness is fallacious.

It might be objected that Sartre's play with the word " nothing " should not be taken too seriously. In experience we find being-in-itself and being-for-itself. And since being-for-itself is by definition conscious being, it follows that being-in-itself is non-conscious being. And it is obviously true that the two cannot exist in one. Quite so; but then who said that they could? When Sartre talks about God, he is talking about the personal God of Christianity and Judaism. But I have yet to learn that either Jews or Christians conceive God as a synthesis of consciousness and material being, which is what *l'en-soi* really is for Sartre.

I am not concerned here with arguing in favour of God's existence or with offering any rival philosophical theories in place of those put forward by M. Sartre: I am concerned simply with pointing out some very questionable propositions in the foundations of his philosophy. As I have said, the problem of human conduct in the form in which it is raised by Sartre follows the assertion of the free individual's existence in a godless world. And it is my contention that this fundamental atheism is not backed up by any compelling cogent argument. Indeed, it shows distinct signs of being a postulate. And it is open to anyone to lay down another postulate.

If Sartre's use of the word " nothing " is open to serious objections, so also is his use of the words " free " and " freedom." For, as I have already had occasion to remark, he gives these terms such a wide field of application that their meaning tends to be evacuated. If all human actions without exception are to be called " free," it is difficult to know what the word " free " adds, as it were, to the word " action " in the term " free action." Nor, of course, does it square with what anyone normally thinks if one says that all human actions are free or that a man freely chooses his historical situation, his parents, and so on. In other words, I have considerable sympathy with the criticism which has already been levelled against Sartre by logical analysts. And I should like to add to this criticism the expression of my belief that Sartre sometimes tends to universalize in an over-hasty manner subjective impressions or " experiences." For example, it is quite possible to have an impression or " experience " of the strange, inexplicable, gratuitous presence of things; and Sartre has given an admirable description of this impression in *La nausée*. But one is not entitled to conclude without more ado that this impression gives us the truth about the existence of things. It may be said that Sartre does not conclude this " without more ado." For he gives reasons for saying that being is gratuitous, *de trop*. But are these reasons cogent reasons? I do not think that they are. And even if Sartre's conclusion were correct, this would not validate the arguments offered in its defence. I may be wrong, but it looks to me as though the arguments followed, rather than preceded, a fundamental atheistic postulate and impressions which are turned into ontological assertions because they are in accordance with this postulate.

I have spoken about Sartre's atheism, and I have used the word " postulate " in this connection. But it was certainly not my intention to deny what I said in the last lecture about the importance of the problem of God in the philosophy of Sartre. Not only does he assert that his philosophy follows from an atheistic position, but he also interprets man as a striving towards deity, although this striving is doomed to inevitable frustration. In a sense, therefore, he recognizes not only the importance of the problem of God but also a human urge towards God. This is why certain writers have been able to maintain that in a certain sense Sartre's philosophy is religious. To say this is, indeed, to utter a paradox; but it draws attention to the fact that the philosophy of Sartre, by its very character, emphasizes and throws into a clear light the importance of the problem of God. So for the matter of that does Camus' philosophy of the absurd. I am inclined to think that with Camus too atheism tends to be a postulate, and that he tends to pass over-hastily from subjective impression to ontological or metaphysical assertion. But it can hardly be denied that his philosophy accentuates rather than minimizes the importance of the problem of God.

3

I turn now to theistic existentialism, especially as represented by Professor Karl Jaspers. And I had better say at once that I have a profound sympathy with a great deal that these writers say. No doubt, many of Kierkegaard's assertions are exaggerated; but his polemics against the Hegelian reduction of the divine transcendence and the Hegelian notion of a knowledge which is attainable by the philosopher and which is superior to faith seem to me to possess considerable value. And I should say the same of, for instance, his attack on the reduction of Christianity to a polite humanism and on the reduction of the individual to a member of the crowd, as well as of some of his positive remarks about freedom, " the instant," and so on. Again, Jaspers, in my opinion, has given us valuable and stimulating discussions about the relation between science and philosophy, for example; and his view of philosophical reflection as proceeding towards the Transcendent as its goal is one with which I have profound sympathy. As for Marcel, I think that he explores a field which badly needs to be explored and that his analyses of hope, fidelity and other human experiences draw attention to many truths which we may already know in some sense but which we often tend to overlook. Moreover, I think that his distinction between, say, being and having is a valuable one. And, in general, I am convinced that the theistic existentialists have performed the valuable task of opening up in a fresh and striking manner a world of experience and reflection which our technical civilization has tended to obscure. Their very exaggerations have been of some service in that they have helped to draw attention to experiences to which the existentialists wished to draw our attention and so to enable us to see for ourselves.

But in spite of my very real appreciation of many features of theistic existentialism I think that it suffers from some grave defects. And the one which I especially wish to mention is the (to my mind) exaggerated opposition to " objectivity." This is, I think, a particularly appropriate defect on which to dwell briefly since it appears to be, not a mere accidental defect, but one bound up with the " existentialism " in theistic existentialism. I mean that without this defect, or what seems to me to be a defect, it is questionable whether theistic existentialism would be " existentialism."

Kierkegaard's insistence that truth is " subjectivity " and his incessant warfare against " objectivity " are understandable in the case of a man who was more concerned with " existing " and choosing than with theorizing about existence and choice. He was convinced, and rightly, of course, that to relate oneself to God in faith and adoration is more important than to speculate about God and that to be a Christian, to appropriate Christian truth " subjectively," in one's own life, is of more importance than to talk about Christianity, to treat Christianity from outside, " objectively," and to forget that one does not become a Christian in this way. Kierkegaard doubtless neglected complementary truths; and I have no intention of denying this. My point is, however, that his exaggerations and one-sidedness are understandable and that they do not become so apparent in the case of a man who made no pretence of offering to the world a systematic philosophy as they would in the case of a systematic philosopher. After all, Kierkegaard never occupied a chair of philosophy; and he constantly attacked systematic speculative philosophy, which he identified to all intents and purposes with the philosophy of Hegel.

The situation is rather different, however, when we turn to Karl Jaspers, who is a professor of philosophy and who has published large tomes in which he systematically sets forth his own philosophy of existence.

On the one hand Jaspers recognizes and accepts the validity of Kierkegaard's assertion that an existential system is impossible. If existence (*Existenz*) is possible being, man's possibility of becoming himself through transcendence or transcending, and if existence in this sense is so bound up with individuality that it eludes universal categories, it is scarcely possible to construct an " objective " philosophy of existence, because in such a philosophy existence would be viewed as an object capable of being described in universal terms rather than as the unique individual subject. Again, the *Transcendent*, God, is apprehended by me, not as an object capable of being described in universally valid terms, but solely in relation to my personal act of transcending. God is known, so far as He can be known, subjectively and not objectively. This does not mean that God is known by mystical experience, by some form of contact, as it were; it means that I apprehend the Transcendent from my unique standpoint, through signs or symbols which are *my* signs or symbols. The truth that God exists is *my* truth, appropriated in *my* act of transcending. There can be, therefore, no natural theology in the traditional sense, in which it is proved by universally valid arguments that the Transcendent exists and that it possesses certain attributes. That God exists is not an objective truth which can be learned and passed on as a piece of objective information: it is the subjective truth of each individual who performs the act of transcending, not in the sense that it is simply a fiction of the individual mind or imagination, but in the sense that the truth is known only in the personal approach and so far as this approach is maintained and constantly renewed.

On the other hand Jaspers has constructed a philosophy, a philosophy of existence. It is true that he insists that the function of the philosopher of existence is to illuminate existence, to draw attention to it, not to treat it as though it were an object of scientific investigation and analysis. And it is true that he insists that all descriptions of the Transcendent are relative to the individual describers, so that the utter transcendence of God is maintained. But at the same time it seems clear to me that any philosophy must involve analysis and description and that this description cannot help being expressed in universal terms. Jaspers distinguishes between categories which are applicable in the sciences and categories which are applicable to existence or terms which serve as signs to indicate existence. And this is doubtless a distinction of value. None the less, the categories or terms applicable to existence are universal categories or terms, in the sense that they are applicable to every existence. And to this extent existence is inevitably turned into an object if we wish to philosophize about it at all. Again, if we are going to talk about the Transcendent at all, we cannot avoid " objectifying " the Transcendent to some extent. We can insist, of course, that the Transcendent is unique, that it is not a member of a class, either actually or potentially, and so on; but by the very fact that we do this, we " objectify " it. I hope that you will understand that I am not criticizing Jaspers simply on the basis of a philosophical system which is not his. I have been doing my best to avoid this sort of criticism. What I am maintaining, whether rightly or wrongly, is that all philosophy inevitably involves universalization and objectification and that Jaspers' philosophy is no exception. And if this is true, it follows that the pronounced hostility of the theistic existentialists towards objectification is exaggerated. I am well aware that it is founded on the perception of certain truths; for example, on the truth that human beings differ from other beings in the world. But this does not alter the exaggerated character of the hostility towards objectification. If we wish, we can hold fast to immediate experience and renounce philosophy. Anyone is free to do this. But if we philosophize, we cannot remain in the sphere of immediate experience. We can talk against Hegel as much as we wish; but philosophy is and must always be " mediation." It may be suggested that Marcel's idea of " second reflection " shows the possibility of a third way. But valuable as Marcel's second reflection may be, it is still reflection and mediation.

Perhaps I ought to emphasize the fact that what I am criticizing in Jaspers is the combination of an exaggerated and initial hostility towards objectivity with the systematic construction of a philosophy of existence. For the two seem to me to be incompatible. I am not now concerned to find fault with him because, for example, he does not recognize any of the traditional arguments in favour of God's existence as a cogent and universally valid proof. The point of my criticism, so far as it affects the existence of God, would be that while showing how the idea of the Transcendent can arise he seems determined from the start to leave assertion and denial of God's existence as two subjective possibilities without any adequate examination of the objective grounds for the alternative which he himself certainly adopts. To leave the issue of a problem in suspense because one sees no valid argument which favours this rather than that solution is one thing: to choose deliberately to leave the issue in suspense is another thing altogether. It may be said that Jaspers does as a matter of fact offer reasons for believing in God, for adopting the standpoint of " philosophic faith." For he shows how the idea of the Transcendent arises. My point is, however, that as a philosopher Jaspers is committed to endeavouring at least to investigate the objective and universal validity of the relation between the impressions or " experiences " which give rise to the idea of the Transcendent and the actual assertion of the Transcendent. Yet his dislike of " objectivity " tends to hold him back from doing this and encourages him to leave the issue in suspense for the sake of leaving it in suspense, in order that " subjectivity " should have the last word.

The objection can be raised against what I have been saying that it takes no account of the tendency in Jaspers' later writings to attach more importance to " mediation " and to abandon the determination to leave things in suspense. I think that this objection would be valid. But this simply shows, I think, that existentialist philosophy, in order to be philosophy, has to overcome the hostility to objectivity which has been associated with modern existentialism since its first clear beginning with Kierkegaard. The fact is, I am inclined to think, that the primary function of the existentialist movement is to awaken and stimulate a fresh approach to philosophical problems. At various periods in the history of philosophy thinkers have arisen who appear, as we look back on them, to have been primarily stimulators and fertilizers and to have directed subsequent philosophical thought towards fresh paths. Socrates was, I think, one of these. Perhaps the existentialists will be seen to have performed a like function. I should not care to put the matter more strongly than this. I am not a prophet. In any case I think that the initial hostility towards objectivity which Jaspers inherited from Kierkegaard and which is present independently in Marcel's thought, though to a much less extent, is out of place in a philosopher, however suitable it may be in a man who rejects philosophy altogether. It is doubtless understandable and explicable. But this suggests that what is needed is an analysis of the idea of " objectivity," in order that it may be made clear precisely what it is to which the existentialists legitimately take exception when they write against objectivity. There is, one hopes, some medium between the idea of a fixed and final system which only needs to be handed on and learned and which dispenses us from any further original philosophizing and the idea of a philosophical reflection which is directed towards the raising of problems, the solution being left to a personal decision or choice without objective and communicable justification.

I do not, however, wish to end on this critical note. In spite of its defects existentialism seems to me to have been of value in drawing attention in a modern context to the human person as a free and responsible subject. Atheistic existentialism, by its attempt to draw the logical consequences from the postulate of atheism, underlines the importance of the problem of God. In this respect it can perhaps be described as a long footnote to the writings of Nietzsche. The theistic existentialism of Jaspers and the reflections of Marcel open up in a fresh way the approach to the Transcendent. And if these final remarks give the impression that for me the problem of God is *the* metaphysical problem, this is a correct impression.

INDEX